Never Put a Ten-Dollar Tree in a Ten-Cent Hole

Never Put a Ten-Dollar Tree in a Ten-Cent Hole

...and Other Stories

Ed Grisamore

Mercer University Press
Macon, Georgia

MERCER
UNIVERSITY PRESS

Endowed by
TOM WATSON BROWN
and
THE WATSON-BROWN FOUNDATION, INC.

MUP/H822 | ISBN 978-0-88146-233-3

© 2011 Mercer University Press
1400 Coleman Avenue
Macon, Georgia 31207
All rights reserved

First Edition.

All stories and columns are copyright of *The Macon (Ga.) Telegraph.* Used by permission.

Books published by Mercer University Press are printed on acid free paper that meets
the requirements of American National Standard for Information Sciences—
Permanence of Paper for Printed Library Materials.

Mercer University Press is a member of Green Press initiative (greenpressinitiative.org),
a nonprofit organization working to help publishers and printers increase their use of recycled paper
and decrease their use of fiber derived from endangered forests.
This book is printed on recycled paper.

Library of Congress Cataloging-in-Publication Data

Grisamore, Ed.
Never put a ten-dollar tree in a ten-cent hole / Ed Grisamore. — 1st ed.
p. cm.
Collection of previously published Macon Telegraph newspaper columns and essays.
ISBN 978-0-88146-233-3 (hardcover : alk. paper)
I. Title.
PN4874.G755A25 2011
814'.6—dc22
2011002063

(J. M. Grisamore, 1924-2006)

To the memory of my father, the greatest man I've ever known.
I still hear his voice.
I try to do something to honor him every day.

Contents

Fatherhood

Life's lessons with a shovel

June 20, 1999

When I was 14 years old, I was convinced I was spending too many Saturday afternoons with my father.

I didn't know it at the time, but I was being taught valuable lessons. I was fortunate to have such a great teacher. I probably didn't appreciate that at the time, either.

To a 14-year-old boy who had discovered music, mini-bikes and girls, spending a Saturday afternoon with Dad was pure misery. To add insult to injury, the old man compounded my pain and suffering by making me work.

These weren't just menial chores around the house. This was back-breaking, blister-bringing, sweatshop-quality labor. I used to think it bordered on child slavery. I believed it was a conspiracy to keep me unhappy.

My friends would ride by the house and shout across the yard. When would I be finished? My dad would ignore them and tell me to grab the shovel and wheelbarrow. We needed to move another tree from the back yard to the front yard.

Deep in that muddy hole in my heart, I believed my father would never achieve true happiness until I had helped him move every tree and shrub on our property at least twice.

So I was a son who had been ordained to dig. Long before I picked up a pen and began to dig across the journalistic minefield of human experiences, I would turn spades through topsoil, red clay, roots and rocks. Sometimes we would strike water (never oil) and often burrow so deep, I assumed we eventually might be shaking hands with the Chinese.

We dug fence posts. We unearthed so many big rocks I swore Stone Mountain was beneath us. I realize now that was just a capsule of my life. At the time, however, it seemed my toil in the soil would last forever.

I obviously felt sorry for myself. After all, I was the only teenager on the planet being so mistreated on a Saturday. It was my birthright to be indoors watching a football game on TV or rafting on the river with my buddies.

In my haste to finish, I sometimes would try to get by with the least amount of effort.

My holes would be too shallow or not wide enough to accommodate the tree's roots.

And my dad would always say: "Never put a 10-dollar tree in a 10-cent hole."

He insisted that I keep digging. He preached that results don't come without elbow grease. Don't be shoddy. Don't be satisfied with the minimum. If you go through life accepting less than the best, quite often that's exactly what you'll get.

It took a sturdy shovel, but that message eventually was planted in my thick skull. It followed me through school, my career and as the father of three sons, who are now being taught about trees and holes.

My dad still is the most hole-digging man I've ever known. Maybe it comes from those Missouri farm roots. Just a few weeks ago, he produced a hole in his back yard big enough to bury a couple of elephants.

He will be 75 years old in November, a man who lived through the Dust Bowl as a Midwestern child of the 1930s and who later served his country in two wars. As both a small-town doctor and a big-city physician, he healed thousands of broken bodies and saved thousands of lives. He's a tough old fellow himself, having survived a brain tumor and prostate surgery.

Oh, he still dispenses advice, as if we were still out there together digging holes on a Saturday afternoon. His e-mails always encourage me to "keep chugging." Apparently, I'll never be too old to hear his lectures about the virtues of sunscreen or the dangers of saturated fat.

I dig out his lessons every day. No, you shouldn't put 10-dollar trees in 10-cent holes.

Compassion, though, also will teach you to provide 10-dollar holes for the 10-cent trees of the world.

Thanks, Dad, and pass the shovel.

My dad, the real True Gris

November 8, 2006

The room was dark, except for a soft light reaching through the door at the hospice facility.

The only sounds were a clock on the wall and my father's labored breathing from the bed.

It was his 82nd birthday, one week ago today. There were balloons and flowers in the corners of the room. The younger grandchildren had colored some pictures.

Dad was sleeping, so he did not see me crying. He did not hear me praying that he would not die on his birthday.

Earlier, I sat on his bed and held his hand. I read the most difficult words I have ever written to the most remarkable man I have ever known.

Dear Dad:

My gift to you is these words.

Your gift to me has been a lifetime.

You have been the most wonderful father a son could ever have. I will always hold the memories dear.

I will remember the things we did together, the places we traveled, the laughter we shared, the fences and ponds we built, the holes we dug.

Thank you for the love you have shown me, the encouragement you have offered me, the advice you have given me and the lessons you have taught me.

Thank you for your service to our country in World War II and Vietnam and in both the Gemini and Apollo space programs. Thank you for the thousands of lives you saved as a medical doctor over four different decades.

Thank you for the living example of always putting others above yourself.

A part of you will always be with me here on earth. I rejoice in the day I will see you again in heaven.

I love you, Dad.

He died early Friday morning, just minutes after I had witnessed a beautiful sunrise. Clouds gathered low across the horizon, combed and parted as if they were preparing a place for him.

We buried him Sunday. Appropriately, it was a day churches were celebrating All Saints Day. We laid six roses across his grave on the side of a hill. We will hold a memorial service for him Sunday, Nov. 26, at 3 p.m. at First Baptist Church at the top of Poplar Street. It will be less of a funeral and more a celebration of his life.

My dad was full of love.

He loved my mother, his five children and 12 grandchildren. He loved his country and his church. He loved going to the movies and traveling. He had been to all 50 states and all seven continents. (Yes, even Antarctica.)

He loved cameras, computers and comfortable chairs. He loved to piddle in the yard and dig his fingers in the dirt. (The Missouri farm boy in him never left.)

He loved to tell me what to do and how to do it. He was proud of me, but not half as proud as I was to be his son. He was called "Gris" long before I was.

Oh, he had a few faults. He could be as stubborn as a mule. We cringed every time he put sugar on his grits. (He blamed it on his Yankee roots.) He was so cold-natured, he would wrap up in sweaters in the middle of summer. (He always joked the reason he wanted to be cremated was so he could finally get warm.)

He and Mama moved to Macon in 2002. I can honestly say the past four years were among the happiest of his life.

My heart is heavy. I miss him so much.

But I also remember what he told us.

He promised he will be in every sunrise and sunset, in every breeze that blows.

He took a small step, too

July 20, 2009

Some nights, you have to search to find the moon.

It's just a sliver in the sky. Or tucked behind the clouds.

Other times, it's like a giant street lamp, so bright you can read poetry under its glow.

The moon follows us like a shadow through life. We are told there is a man in it. A cow jumped over it. It is made of cheese. It controls the tides.

We howl at the moon. We sing lullabies about it. "Goodnight Moon" is one of the most beloved children's books of all time.

At dusk, the moon sometimes arrives early. It raises its head before the sun slips behind the curtain.

And there are dawns when it lingers until the morning chases it away.

Every time I see the moon, I think of my father.

He never set foot on it, although he probably grabbed a handful of moon dust on his way to heaven three years ago.

I honor my dad today because he had a small part in the Apollo 11 moon mission.

He wasn't on the front lines. It was a minor role. He was a supporting actor in a very large cast.

But the whole is represented by the sum of its parts.

Forty years ago tonight, the world watched Neil Armstrong take "one small step for man" and become the first to walk on the moon.

Dr. J. M. Grisamore took a small step, too.

He was a captain in the Navy and a surgeon for the base hospital at Jacksonville Naval Air Station in Florida.

Five days before the moon walk, he had been given a personal tour of the Apollo 11 spacecraft.

The following day, July 16, he watched the historic launch from the roof of the nearby Air Force hospital.

He had been assigned to a team of military doctors who were on standby. Had there been an accident or explosion during the launch, he would have been part of the medical crew to treat the astronauts for injuries.

It was not his first experience with NASA. On the same July date three years earlier, he had been on board the USS Guadalcanal, where he was the senior medical officer for Gemini 10.

After the capsule splashed down in the Atlantic Ocean 4.5 miles from the aircraft carrier, my father was assigned to perform the post-flight physical on astronaut Michael Collins. It had been Collins' first space flight.

I remember my dad telling stories about how Collins had a small Bible strapped to his left thigh. Of course, Collins later was part of the three-man crew for Apollo 11. As the command module pilot, he orbited while Armstrong and Buzz Aldrin landed on the lunar surface.

I got to see my first space launch a few days before Christmas in 1968. My father drove my sister, my grandfather and me down to Cape Kennedy early that morning, where we watched Apollo 8 rise in a fireball across the Indian River.

Dad was then selected as part of the medical teams for Apollo 9, 10 and 11.

He was always proud of his behind-the-scenes involvement with the space program. He served his country with the same loyalty he did in the military as a veteran of two wars.

I try to honor his memory every day. I still hear his voice of encouragement in my head. Before he died in November 2006, he promised he would be with me in every sunrise and sunset and every breeze that blows.

He didn't mention anything about the moon.

He left that up to me.

To a grad, from his dad

May 25, 2001

I have been trying to prepare myself for this for 17 years, nine months and eight days.

From the day he was born, we were told to enjoy every minute, because he would grow up in a hurry.

We did. He did.

Now that old song, "Turn Around," won't stop playing in my head.

Where are you going my little one, little one?

Where are you going my baby, my own?

Turn around, and you're 2. Turn around, and you're 4.

Turn around and you're a young man going out of my door.

I was there to catch him when he took his first baby steps. I swallowed hard on his first day of school. I clapped when he got his first hit in T-ball, grinned when he caught his first fish, and popped three buttons when he picked up my old guitar and wrote his first song.

I also knew this day would come.

Saturday night, he will graduate from Central High School. He is a pioneer, of sorts. He is the oldest child and the oldest grandchild. He will become the first to make the symbolic leap from the nest.

He is ready for this day.

His mother and I are not.

Central will hold its graduation exercises at the Macon Coliseum. He will receive his high school diploma in the building next door to the hospital where he was born.

He arrived with the sunrise on the morning of Aug. 17, 1983. He has been spreading his own sunshine ever since. When he was 10 days late, we did everything to hasten the delivery. We went for long walks and drove down bumpy roads.

It was a bucket of Popeye's spicy fried chicken on a Tuesday night that finally did the trick. We named him Joel Edward Grisamore. (We laughed and said we should have named him Popeye.)

I was in the delivery room when Dr. Pope handed him to a nurse, who promptly made the handoff to me. So I was the first to actually "hold" him in my arms.

Now he can whip me at arm wrestling. The kid I once chased around the playground can run circles around me in a foot race.

He is almost as tall as I am. We see eye-to-eye on most everything else, too. Oh, there are times when I want to wring his neck. Most of the time, though, I want to hug it.

At first we called him "Eddie." Later, he wanted to be known as Ed. That has been both an honor and a source of confusion. We are forever answering each other's phone calls.

I will refrain from giving him a lecture on his graduation day. I will spare the advice about eating his vegetables, wearing sunscreen and looking out for the little guys.

He has heard all this before.

But I promise never to stop teaching, if he will promise never to stop learning.

His mom and I have tried to do our best. We haven't always hit home runs. He is our first, so there has been plenty of trial and error.

Most importantly, we gave him roots. Now it is time to give him wings.

I have never known him to leave the house or hang up the telephone without telling me that he loves me.

"You must be very proud of your son," someone said the other day.

I got choked up and couldn't answer, because I am.

They grow up in a hurry

May 20, 2005

When your kids are young, those who have been down the road before you always smile. They tell you to enjoy them, because children grow up in a hurry.

You don't really believe it. Or maybe you just don't want to believe it.

And then it happens.

The young boy becomes a young man. The kid who scooted around on the kitchen floor — at eye-level with your kneecaps — is suddenly wearing the same size shoes you do.

The Raffi songs give way to Widespread Panic and Moonshine Still. The Little League games and sand castles disappear in the blur of tail lights at the end of the driveway.

You wish you could slam on the brakes. But you can't stop the wheels of time. You can't even slow them down.

Matthew Grant Grisamore is a special young man approaching the apex of a special week on his calendar. He turned 18 this past Sunday, the symbolic threshold of manhood. He's now old enough to vote. Last week, he registered for the Selective Service.

Saturday night, he will graduate from Central High School and start studying for Life 101.

Delinda and I have always said every family needs a Grant. He keeps us entertained and enlightened. He's smart. He's witty. He's playful. He doesn't need a script, and he probably wouldn't follow one anyway.

We brag on him all the time. Sure, we spend a considerable amount of time trying to correct his faults. At the same time, we have given him plenty of legroom.

Grant has avoided the proverbial "middle child" squeeze. Sandwiched between two gifted and popular brothers, who both enjoy being onstage, Grant is quite content to walk the sidelines. He loves being around people. But he would rather the spotlight fall on someone else.

That's not to say he's meek and mild. Far from it. His volume is always on high. He makes so much noise fixing his midnight snacks, I have threatened to have him arrested for disturbing the peace.

It's sure going to be a lot quieter when he goes off to college in the fall.

He can also delegate authority, which is another way of saying he is constantly telling his little brother, Jake, what to do. Whatever career he decides to pursue, he needs to be in management.

What else can I tell you about Grant? That he hugs all the ladies at church? That he and his friends help keep Ingleside Village Pizza in business? That he is the most organized member of the family?

He has a part-time job at ChiChester's Pharmacy on Vineville, working at the front cash register. I didn't realize so many people know he belongs to me. They compliment him on being polite and friendly.

Trust me. The greatest gift anyone can give you is to love your children.

A few weeks ago, we were watching a baseball game on TV.

"Grant," I said, "it's not going to be the same when you leave for college. I'm going to miss watching these games together."

"Don't worry, Dad," he said. "I'll come home to watch some games with you."

They grow up.

You hold on.

The keys to the car

January 12, 2009

Jake Grisamore is celebrating his birthday today, but I have needed no reminders. This one has been circled in anticipation for so long the ink is starting to fade.

He has been like a kid counting down the days for Santa to arrive, only this sleigh has four wheels.

It has been marked and noted on every mental calendar at our house. We have been hearing about the day he can finally drive a car. There is no tread left on our ears.

Yes, the youngest Gris officially turns 15 years old at 12:43 p.m. today, and we all know what that means. He can check off one more thing on the list of growing up.

He now meets the minimum age requirement to get his learner's permit.

He is eligible to sit behind the wheel — with adult supervision, of course.

Suddenly, everything has changed. I'm sure he is going to want his own set of car keys. He is going to start paying more attention to gas prices and turn signals. He will be begging me to let him drive to school every morning. I'm sure there will be plenty of offers to "chauffeur" his mama to the grocery store.

He has been waiting for this day for so long, it's pure rotten luck that today is Monday and the Macon office of the Georgia Department of Driver Services is closed. He must endure one more day in the waiting room.

Of course, he has had his backseat driver's license since he was about 9, and is often telling me where to turn and how fast to go. (I've almost revoked that license a few times. I hope Jake doesn't drive the way he sometimes tells me how to drive.)

All kidding aside, I want him to understand that driving skills include more than just hands and feet. With privilege comes responsibility.

We've practiced a few times in driveways and vacant parking lots. Still, you might say Jake has been preparing for this day since long before that.

One of the first columns I wrote about Jake ("Fathers need guardian angels") was published on Father's Day in 1997 after my 3-year-old son drove my dad's pickup truck into a tree.

Well, he didn't actually "drive" it.

Carjacked — or maybe "car-jaked" — would be more accurate.

I had borrowed my father's truck for a few weeks. It was parked in our driveway one Sunday afternoon.

I was attending a Little League coaches meeting when I got an urgent phone call to hurry home.

While my wife had gone into the house for a minute, Jake had somehow managed to climb into the cab of the truck and released the parking brake. The truck had rolled into a tree.

I still get chill bumps just thinking about what might have happened to an unrestrained child behind the wheel of a moving truck.

My heart skipped as I stood at the edge of the driveway and followed the tire tracks through the soft dirt. I trembled as I ran my hands across the bark of the tree that stopped his forward progress.

The front of the truck was badly damaged, but Jake somehow escaped without a scratch. There was no airbag, only the soft cushion of a miracle.

I have always believed a guardian angel must have planted that tree. Had it not been there, the truck would have gathered more speed down the embankment and rolled into a ditch.

I told Jake to buckle up after that day. More advice is now on the way.

Be careful. Drive defensively. Look out for the trees.

Overcoming the odds

Life was never beyond her reach

October 2, 2005

They laid Shirley Chambers to rest in the shade of two large oak trees Saturday afternoon. She was buried next to her mother and father at Macon Memorial Park.

Her family and friends gathered to mourn her death but also to celebrate her remarkable life.

Her obituary Friday morning noted she was 65 years old. She was born in Wilkinson County, worked as a cashier in the cafeteria at Warner Robins High School and attended Porterfield Baptist Church in Macon. She is survived by a sister and a number of nieces, nephews and cousins.

But there is much more depth than a 216-word obituary would allow.

Shirley was a 3-foot-9 giant.

She was born without arms. Her right leg was deformed and her left leg was not much more than a thigh with a foot attached.

She had a way of making you not notice all that, though. She was smart and funny. About the only word her vocabulary refused to comprehend was the meaning of "can't."

"She had a spirit that would outshine anything you could see about her or think she couldn't do," said a cousin, Don Ennis.

For 16 years, she used her feet to take money and count change for students in the lunchroom at Warner Robins High. She also kept the books for a credit union and a telephone answering service.

She could brush her teeth, comb her hair and put on lipstick. She sewed and shelled butterbeans. She would fold back the pages of the Sears Roebuck catalog to make door stops.

She could play cards, too, clutching them with her toes. She would laugh and call the cards she was dealt not a "hand" but a "foot."

Growing up, her late father, James Chambers, would tell her: "Now, young lady, don't say you can't. Say you'll try. And, if you can't do it the first time, try again."

About the only thing he wouldn't let her do was drive.

"Too many fools on the road," he said.

A birth defect left her with no real hope. At least that's what the doctors told the family. They said she wouldn't live to be 6 weeks old. Then they adjusted the prognosis and said 6 months.

They never mentioned anything about 65 wonderful years.

"I knew she was different, but it never mattered," said her older sister, Ione Ashley. "When we were young, our mother took us to the dime store down on Third Street. She carried Shirley in her arms, and some women said: 'Poor little girl. Bless her heart.' And Shirley told Mama: 'I am not a poor little girl.'"

She was rich in so many other ways. She learned to accept her body. She grew accustomed to the stares. She got used to the questions.

Her family moved to Warner Robins, where her mother, Annie Mina Chambers, worked in several school cafeterias and eventually became the lunchroom manager at Warner Robins High.

Shirley's first-grade teacher at Thomas Elementary would allow her to stay after school and practice writing on the blackboard. In class, she would sit in a straight-back chair, put her books on top of her desk and use the desk seat to write.

There were no special education classes in those days, so she was mainstreamed with the other students. Her classmates accepted her. In fact, they would sometimes argue over who got to help her put on her socks and shoes.

The only exception made for her was that she would leave class five minutes early at the end of each period. Shirley used to joke that "3-foot-9 is kind of hard to see, and they didn't want me to get run over in the hallway."

She rarely used her prosthetic arms. They were too long and cumbersome.

But she wore them for Warner Robins High School graduation in 1958. There wasn't a dry eye in the house when she went up to get her diploma.

She wanted the arms because they had hands.

She wanted the hands because they had fingers.

She wanted a finger so she could wear her high school ring.

Don Ennis was more than her cousin. He was practically her best friend. In high school, Shirley would go with him when he would cruise Cherry Street with the radio volume up and the windows down. Shirley had a great 45-rpm record collection. She adored Elvis.

"She was my brains," said Don, "and I was her arms."

She never felt sorry for herself. She never lost her sense of humor. She would warn folks not to bite their fingernails. She would hold up her invisible arms and say: "Look what it did to me."

Don's brother, Larry, said Shirley helped make everyone in her family more compassionate and aware of others with disabilities. "She enriched our lives," he said.

He was so inspired by Shirley's story, he interviewed her on videotape last spring. Among those who received a copy of that video was Georgia Gov. Sonny Perdue, who remembered and admired Shirley from his days at Warner Robins High.

This past week, the family gathered at the home of Ione Ashley on Houston Road to be with Shirley in her final days. She had been battling respiratory problems for several years.

When she died late Wednesday night, part of them died with her.

It's amazing how a lady without arms could touch so many people.

Little big man

October 26, 2007

WARNER ROBINS — Kyle Ware got up the morning of March 20 and dressed for school.

Even though it was the last day of winter, it was also a special day.

It was his 18th birthday. He was legal age. He was old enough to vote, join the Army, move out of the house and climb up on the bar stool and order a ... Mountain Dew. (Not that he necessarily wanted to do any of those things.)

His father, David, rode the 9 miles with him to Northside High School that morning. As Kyle was arriving at the parking lot, he saw blue.

Unfortunately, it wasn't a display of Northside's school colors. In his rear-view mirror, he noticed a sheriff's flashing blue lights.

This was not the best way to start his first day of adulthood.

The deputy asked Kyle for his license, looked at it closely and then apologized.

He explained someone had reported a 6-year-old driving a vehicle. Then, that "someone" came forward. The man who had called the sheriff's department walked over and apologized to Kyle, too.

It was a little embarrassing for everybody.

Kyle may have been a bit flustered, but he didn't let it bother him. He is accustomed to having people stare at him when he is driving his bright yellow Ford Ranger truck down Russell Parkway. Or being asked if he needs a child's ticket at the movie theater. Or having to sit at the front of the classroom, so he can see the blackboard.

He lets it roll right off.

Unflappable.

"I forget that I'm different," he said.

In the nine years, four months and 18 days I have been writing local columns for this newspaper, I have interviewed thousands of people.

A few of those, like Kyle, rise to the top.

I don't want to put him on a pedestal. He doesn't need it. He has done plenty of climbing on his own. It's just that I admire this little big man.

Kyle reminds me of that verse about "Attitude" by Charles Swindol. I have often used it to crank my mornings, energize my afternoons and reflect upon it at the end of the day.

Swindol says attitude is more important than what other people think, say or do. It is more important than appearance.

He encourages us to play the one string we have, and that is our attitude. Life is 10 percent what happens to us and 90 percent how we react to it.

That is why Kyle is bigger than most of us. He spends his days at eye level with belt buckles. He'll never be able to play center on the basketball team. Or be tall enough to ride all the rides at Six Flags.

But so what?

Kyle measures up in so many other ways.

He is as long as your yardstick — 36 inches high and 41 pounds on the bathroom scales.

He was born with cartilage-hair hypoplasia, a type of dwarfism. He has endured 33 surgeries in his lifetime. He has no hair.

His condition may have slowed him down at times, but he has never let it stop him from pursuing a normal life. He attended Parkwood Elementary School, Northside Middle School and graduated last year from Northside High School, where he was a popular senior and graduated with a 3.2 grade point average.

He has been watching cooking shows since he was 3 years old. He subscribes to a number of food magazines and is a big fan of Justin Wilson, Alton Brown and Bobby Flay on The Food Network.

He also makes a mean chicken piccata. He grows his own herbs in the backyard and tries out his recipes by cooking supper for his parents, David and Cheryl Ware, several times a week.

He is now a freshman on the Warner Robins campus of Macon State College and drives himself to school every morning. His truck has special adaptive equipment. He is majoring in biology. He aspires to do medical research one day.

There are no pity parties at the Ware house. Kyle has found a way to fit in everywhere he goes and in almost everything he does. He has taken karate lessons, learned to play the trumpet, been involved in theater productions and was elected "prom king" at Northside last year.

David and Cheryl met when they were students at Valdosta State. This past Tuesday marked their 25th wedding anniversary.

They are both normal size. David said they both carried the recessive gene for cartilage-hair hypoplasia, which is more commonly found in the Amish and Finnish communities.

Kyle is their only child. He weighed 6 pounds, 10 ounces when he was born and was 15.25 inches in length. His physical features are more proportionate than those found in people with more common forms of dwarfism.

When he was young, he spent a lot of time in the hospital and underwent numerous surgeries for intestinal disorders.

At school, the only special provision made for him has been a small desk at the front of the classroom. He has also been allowed to have two sets of books so he would not have to carry home a heavy book bag.

"It always amazed me when I would drop him off in high school and watch him walk in the door," said David. "He is only 3 feet tall, and all the other kids were so big. But he never hesitated. He was always so courageous. We are both very proud of him. He's got such a great personality. He's like a magnet."

His parents took him to the National Little People of America convention in Seattle last July.

"It was really weird to be able to look people in the eye," said Kyle.

But it also made him uncomfortable.

"I'm used to tall people," he said. "I like being around them."

Kyle Ware is extra special.

I told you big things come in small packages.

Words that have a happy ending

September 7, 2008

If a picture paints a thousand words, Horace Holmes Jr. should be considered a master storyteller.

He has trained his eye and pointed his camera at life. His shutter speeds have captured Kodak moments. He has photographed babies and brides, fire hydrants and firefighters. His lens has helped preserve mountains, athletes, sunsets and smiles for posterity.

These images have stood on their own — without consonants and vowels, adjectives and verbs to support them.

They have had no choice.

Horace earned his high school diploma more than 40 years ago. He spent two years at a Bible college and was called into the ministry. He preached sermons from the pulpit, pulling words from scriptures and the depths of his heart.

He is a professional photographer and a well-respected citizen in Macon. He is personable and articulate. He is a member of a local Rotary Club and a longtime ambassador for the chamber of commerce.

He also has been carrying around a secret disability.

That's why Horace Holmes is learning to read.

He is being taught the power of the written word. He is learning to construct sentences and to pronounce the words that shape them.

"The dictionary has become my best friend," he said.

He realizes what he has been missing. He is making up for lost time.

Horace is 58 years old, so he figures he's about a million books behind on his reading list. One day, he will no longer have to have someone read the morning newspaper to him. He won't have to rely on "sight words" and memory to quote Bible verses.

Monday is International Literacy Day. An estimated 774 million adults worldwide lack minimum reading skills. That's about one in five adults, according to the United Nations Educational, Scientific and Cultural Organization (UNESCO).

Even to those who know Horace, the revelation that he could not read may be somewhat of a surprise.

It's a story that, until two years ago, he could not read himself.

He fell through the cracks and slipped through the system. It never stopped him from being a terrific husband and father. It never stopped him from becoming a talented photographer or influencing those around him with his servant's heart.

He even had a library card. He managed to tiptoe almost unnoticed through the minefield of life's instruction manuals.

But he also carried around a measure of regret until he enrolled in the literacy program at the Adult Learning Center at Central Georgia Technical College, where he joins others every morning in a classroom with instructor Phyllis Dorn.

He grew up in a family of migrant workers. They would travel to upstate New York to pick cranberries, cherries, apples and pears. When the first snow covered the ground, they would head south to Florida to work in the orange groves.

Seems like every time he adjusted to a school, it was time to pack up and move on. He lagged in his academics, especially reading and phonetics. It was difficult academically and socially.

"I was always trying to impress people," he said. "It was hard to make friends."

When it came to words, the others left him in a trail of syllables, and he never was able to catch up. When his teachers would ask students to read something aloud in class, he would ask to be excused.

"I would start sweating if I thought they were going to call on me," he said.

He managed to dodge and weave his way through high school, reading on the equivalent of about a fifth-grade level. When his parents divorced, his mother was on welfare. She moved the family to Boston, where he once was interviewed as an academic case study by a group of medical doctors.

Two things ultimately changed his life. He became a Christian. And he became involved with Upward Bound, where he was introduced to photography through an art program.

"I picked up a Yashica 120 and it opened up a whole new world for me," he said.

Some of his teachers recognized his struggles. Others didn't. He managed to never fail a class. He earned his diploma. He even had a scholarship offer to run track in college, but opted to attend Miracle Valley Bible College in Arizona.

It was there he met his wife, Yvonne. Soon, his inability to read caught up with him in a big way.

"What's wrong, Horace?" one professor asked. "You are so bright and full of life in the classroom."

When Horace confessed, the professor began allowing him to take oral exams. He went from making all F's on his report card to making the dean's list.

Reading still eluded him, though.

He received an internship at a church starting up on the south side of Chicago.

"It was in an old theater," Horace said. "There was no heat in there in the dead of winter."

There was no shortage of heat when he moved to Macon in 1970, where he worked on the staff with the Rev. Estelle Good at the Lighthouse of Deliverance (now Covenant Life Cathedral) on Bloomfield Road. At the time, it was the only integrated church in the city.

"I would preach about twice a month, but mostly on what I had memorized from the Bible," he said. "I know people could see I was struggling, but I was determined."

He also took a job at Coca-Cola, where he worked his way up to marketing director before opening his photography studio on Cotton Avenue in 1982.

People would recommend books to him, but he never read them. He couldn't. He loved comic books and books about photography because they were visual.

There was a measure of shame, but he managed to hide it publicly.

Regret, too.

"I couldn't read to my own children," he said. "I would pick up the 'Three Little Pigs' and make up my own version of the story."

His wife would help their children with their homework. (Yvette is now 31 years old and is getting married in March. Andre is 27.)

When he enrolled in the literacy program, he wasn't seeking pity. He wanted someone to pull him out of the hole.

"All my life I've had to work four times harder," he said. "But I never gave up."

He could do the math. Now he can do the English, too. The words are coming into focus, much like the lens of his camera.

It is not his intention to become a poster child for literacy programs. Horace has several goals. He wants to write books, starting with his autobiography.

He also wants to volunteer to teach and encourage others in literacy programs. He knows their plight. He has walked in their moccasins.

"I'm a firm believer that we go through life not to benefit ourselves but to help others," he said.

Every picture tells a story.

This is one where the words are on their way to a happy ending.

A face that can write a sermon

December 9, 2007

A face can launch a thousand ships. A face can paint pictures, inspire poetry and make hearts flutter.

We remember people by their faces. Images in the FaceBook of our lives.

We remember soft eyes, puffy lips, furrowed brows and cute freckles running across noses.

Beth Holland has a face that can write a sermon.

It is a face with cheeks that have dispensed a million tears. Her skin is thick. It has to be. She has endured a lifetime of cruelty.

One of her friends described Beth as being "born without a face." I did not completely understand this until I met this remarkable woman.

She did not preach. I still saw a sermon on her face.

She arrived in the world 65 years ago with congenital multiple deformities. The technical term for the genetic disorder is Treacher-Collins syndrome.

Beth's birth defects included having no cheek bones, which caused her eyes to sink into her head. She had a low palate, no chin bone and tiny lobes for ears. Since she had no ear canals, she was deaf and had to wear a bone-conducted hearing aid. There were no air passages in her nostrils.

Her parents fed her with an eyedropper until she was 2 years old. She has endured more than 40 surgeries in her lifetime.

And still, there is a sermon carved on her face.

"I am not ashamed of the way I am," she said. "I just thank God I can do what I can do."

Eighteen months ago, she moved to Macon from her hometown of Jesup to be close to her sister and brother-in-law, Joan and Bill Ivey. She has become active at Forest Hills United Methodist Church. She has joined the North Macon Kiwanis Club and the Red Hat Society ladies group at the Gables at Wolf Creek, where she lives.

Sometimes, at the grocery store, people will notice her face and stare.

"I just ignore them," she said.

If children ask, she will tell them: "This is the way God made me."

And it is.

"God's strength gives Beth an authentic approach to life on good days and bad, inspiring those around her to be themselves," said her sister, Joan. "We see an angel with whom we are fortunate to share our life's journey."

She was born the second of four daughters to Aaron and Dorris Holland. Florence was the oldest girl, followed by Beth and twins Jean and Joan.

Early in life, Beth was told many times: "Somebody sinned. Was it you or your parents?"

In the Bible-thumping South of the 1940s, there could be no other explanation. A child with a face like that was the result of witchcraft. Beth recalls an incident when her father foiled a plan by a group to burn a cross in their yard.

"Everybody wanted to put her in an institution because of the way she looked," said Joan. "In those days, you never saw someone with a mental disability or (physical) deformity outside the home."

But the family learned to develop thick skin right along with Beth.

Aaron and Dorris Holland did not shelter their girls or try to hide Beth. They took their daughters to restaurants, movies and concerts. They gave them a front-row seat of the world.

"Before we would go out, we would always say a prayer together as a family," Joan said. "We would pray for the strength to combat whatever we would face. We knew we were going to have some fun times together. We also knew we were going to have some bad times."

When people would make rude comments or call Beth names, family members would reach across tables and squeeze hands for support.

Why were people so cruel? Aaron Holland would sometimes get so angry his face would turn red. Still, his daughters can count on one hand the number of times he lost his temper.

It just hurt him when people hurt Beth.

She expected name-calling by some of her classmates. But even the teachers sometimes said mean things to her.

Because she was deaf when she started school, she learned to talk and read at the same time. She rehearsed the names of students ahead of her on the class roster so she would know when to answer the roll. When she wore hearing aids, they were as large and cumbersome as giant ear muffs.

Her parents took her all over the South seeking medical treatment. None of it was covered by insurance. Dr. John Lewis, a noted plastic surgeon in

Atlanta, used her as a "guinea pig" in many of his experimental surgeries, and some of her cases were cited in medical books.

Doctors took skin grafts from her hips, borrowed cartilage from her legs and moved the flesh around on her face. Because she had no ears to hold up her glasses, a lady in Jesup crocheted a stocking cap with small loops to hold the frames against her head.

Her parents wanted her to develop independence. They did not want to overprotect her. Still, it was difficult to gently nudge such a fragile young lady into a hard-hearted world.

They would drop her off by herself at a church or school function, then drive around the block and cry.

She wanted to play in the band at Jesup High School, but could not blow air into an instrument because of her restricted windpipe. So she learned to play the xylophone. And the piano.

She graduated on schedule with her high school class, despite missing many weeks because of the surgeries. She went to college and became a successful businesswoman.

Yes, there is a sermon stamped on Beth Holland's face.

When she gives her testimony at churches and schools, she acknowledges her parents, who loved her, challenged her and never stopped believing in her.

She is grateful for her sisters. She believes they suffered unnecessarily because of the way people treated her.

"We had to stand on our feet," she said. "We had to learn to turn the other cheek. The hardest time I had was not all the surgeries but the mental anguish."

Joan said even as a child, she and her sisters knew Beth was special. It wasn't because of Beth's physical traits. It was her unwavering spirit.

"Although I have seen the heartaches, hurt and humiliation she has had to go through, I see what a wonderful person she is," said Joan. "There is not a bitter bone in her body. She's the most forgiving, understanding person I know."

A few years ago, Beth needed new "ears" after the old ones gave out. She qualified as a candidate for an experimental procedure and went to Texas for three corrective surgeries.

Now, she will sometimes ask folks if they can wiggle their ears.

Then she will ask if they can "remove" their ears, like she can.

That is when a smile crosses the face of an angel, an angel who keeps writing a sermon.

Smile and the world smiles with you

March 13, 2005

David Duncan's neighbors at Lake Wildwood never know who will come out of his garage on Sunday mornings.

SpongeBob? Dr. Seuss? Cupid? Looey the Leprechaun?

"Sunday mornings are pretty hilarious with the neighbors peering out their windows," he said.

By now, the neighborhood realizes it's all part of David's ministry as the children's worship leader at Mabel White Memorial Baptist Church. Most everyone has learned to expect the unexpected.

"I remember walking into church one morning and seeing him with a baby bonnet, a diaper and a pacifier, ready to entertain the children," said friend Terri Smith. "Last summer, he showed up for my granddaughter's birthday wearing a multi-colored Shirley Temple wig and a tutu!"

When life gave David Duncan lemons, he didn't just make lemonade. He made chocolate milkshakes.

The past three years have seen David lose both legs (below his knees) to diabetes. Nine years ago, he was at death's door until he had a double organ transplant. He received a kidney and pancreas from a 12-year-old girl who died after being hit by a car.

David spoke to an adult Sunday School class at Forest Hills United Methodist Church a few weeks ago. Afterward, a man approached him.

"You're the most 'unhandicapped' handicapped person I've ever met," the man said.

David is 47 years old, but he tells people he's 74.

"I look pretty good for 74," he said. "I don't look so good for 47."

David is the newest inductee in my Good Attitude Hall of Fame. He could have surrendered long ago. But rather than shake an angry fist at the world, he has embraced it.

"This is my life," he said. "I'm not going to fold up and die. Pain is inevitable. Misery is optional."

David grew up in the three traffic-light town of Pickens, S.C. His childhood revolved around his church, his family and every animal that crossed his path.

When he was 13, he went for a physical before attending a church camp. The doctor discovered David was diabetic.

His wife, Shirley, is from North Carolina. She is an American Indian from the Lumbee tribe. Because of a troubled family situation, she grew up at the Hepzibah Children's Home in Macon.

He met her early one morning in Greek class at Central Wesleyan (S.C.) College, where he was a Bible major. He asked her if she liked Chinese food.

Hmmmm. He asked an American Indian about a Chinese menu in Greek class. Somehow it worked. They married in 1980.

Later, David was working at a church in Wilmington, N.C., when he and Shirley gained custody of the three daughters of a man who had murdered his wife. Jamie is now 28, Aimee is 25 and Halley is 19.

When Shirley accepted a job at Hepzibah in 1989, doctors told her to start preparing for David's funeral. Suffering from neuropathy as a result of his diabetes, he had badly burned his feet and infection had set in. He had a series of 18 surgeries on his feet, and the amputations started with his toes. (He had one leg amputated below the knee in 2002, the other a year later.)

"I don't ever remember feeling good," he said. "Diabetes is like dragging around a dead horse."

His kidney and pancreas transplant in 1996 gave him a new lease on life. It also left him with a heavy heart. The organs came from a 12-year-old girl.

"She took ballet. She was an honor student. She was an only child," he said. "The holidays are always reflective for me. There is a full chair at my table, but I know there is an empty place at the table somewhere else."

A friend, Dianne Clark, said she wished everyone could have the opportunity to meet David and witness his passion for life.

Smith called David and Shirley "remarkable."

"They are extraordinary people," she said. "In a world of takers, they are givers. In a world of complainers, they don't. Despite a multitude of problems that would have put a lot of us under, they not only keep living but they keep doing life with joy."

A great example, she said, are the letters David writes.

"He writes notes of encouragement like nobody I've ever seen, and I'm not the only one who will make that claim," she said. "He has used days and years of being homebound for bolstering the spirits of countless people."

Since becoming the children's worship leader at Mabel White in January, David has dressed in silly costumes as a teaching tool for his ministry. The kids are always curious about his legs. He has one prosthesis that is camouflage. His other is tie-dyed.

"It's a wonderful way to talk to children about people with handicaps," he said. "They love the legs. They are uninhibited. They ask questions. My goal is to make them not afraid to talk to people with handicaps."

There is no better way to illustrate David's spirit than to tell the story of his driving adventure last year. He was in a wheelchair, still recovering from his second leg amputation, when he spied the keys to the van by the back door. No one was home. Although the van didn't have hand controls, he figured at least it had a full tank of gas.

"The more I thought about it, the more determined I became to drive that van to where I needed to go and to do it all by myself!" he said. "So I got out of the house and sat in the driver's seat circumspectly weighing the cost — and possible consequences. Yikes! Sometimes it isn't easy for a man to take the risk of failing. But, without it, then we wouldn't have the light bulb, now would we?"

He cranked the Ford Windstar and felt like he was 15 again, just getting his learner's permit for the first time. He looked to see if anyone was watching, then he prayed a quick prayer.

Lord, please don't let me hurt anyone today, but I need to get back my independence and start living again. Thank you for making my fake foot a size 8 rather than that honker of a size 12 that I originally came with. ... Now, I'm gonna try to back this baby out of the driveway; the rest is up to you!

He mashed the gas, put the van in reverse and tested his artificial foot on the brake.

"I drove all over Lake Wildwood blowing the horn and waving to every dog and cat I saw sitting on the side of the road," he said. "It was a glorious day."

It would be the first of many.

The heart of a champion

September 20, 2009

It took a little time, but I found another winner in Monday's 5K Labor Day Road Race.

Her name is Lawanna Prescott, and I had to search through the tiny type to find her. She finished 1,002nd out of 1,182 runners in the 3.1-mile race. She was a full 24 minutes behind women's division winner Grace Tinkey, who is a ninth-grader at First Presbyterian Day School and one of the city's most accomplished young runners.

By the time Lawanna made it to the finish line at Central City Park, Grace could have done her homework, met her friends for ice cream and run home to change shoelaces.

Still, I'm happy to proclaim Lawanna among the winners. She didn't set any land speed records. Admittedly more of a tortoise than a hare, she broke the 42-minute mark by a scant three seconds.

Inside her, though, beats the heart of a champion.

"At the finish line, everybody was asking me for my time," she said. "I told them I didn't know. All I knew was I started and finished the race ... and I didn't swell."

It's not unusual for runners to shed a few pounds while laboring their legs on the first Monday in September.

The reverse is true with Lawanna. She has been known to gain 5-10 pounds every time she puts on her running shoes. In her first-ever Labor Day race last year, she crossed the finish line with extra baggage.

"I gained almost 20 pounds," she said. "My kidneys had quit working. They were trying to hold on and retain everything. My hands were so swollen, I couldn't move my fingers."

Lawanna is 38 years old and has been battling systemic lupus nearly two-thirds of her life. It's an auto-immune disorder that has played havoc with almost every organ in her body. There is no cure.

Diagnosed at age 13, her doctors told her parents, Bert and Carol White-head, she probably would not live to become a young woman.

She has had almost 100 surgeries, including nearly 20 times on her heart. She is on her third pacemaker. She is awaiting a kidney transplant and a possible eye (cornea) transplant. She has had surgery to reconstruct her stomach and esophagus.

Every day, she has to swallow 52 pills.

With a thick medical chart like that, Lawanna had about 637 reasons to stay in bed Monday morning.

She didn't use a one of them.

Instead, she was pounding the pavement through midtown by the dawn's early light. With her husband, Tracy, at her side, she found enough torque to climb the brutal hill at St. Paul.

"Sometimes it hurts," she said. "But we have to do a lot of things in life that hurt."

Lawanna has participated in about 10 road races over the past three years, including a half-marathon (13.1 miles) for St. Jude Research Hospital in Memphis.

She runs in memory of her mama, who died three years ago. They were as close as a mother and daughter could be.

Lawanna isn't just a patient with a portacath and a long list of ailments. She is a medical professional who is coordinator of the vascular and cardiac lab at The Jones Center in Macon.

She tries to encourage her patients to exercise and be active. She challenges them to strengthen their bodies, heal their wounds and increase their self-esteem.

My guess is she has just inspired plenty of folks.

Now that's a champion.

'Nobody makes my mama cry'

April 30, 2006

GRAY — It's difficult to remember the temperature of the room that day, except that it got cold and dark when the doctor walked in.

"Your son will never walk," he told Charles and Susan Hood.

The tears rolled down Susan's cheek as she looked at her 5-year-old son.

"I will walk," Chris Hood said, breaking the silence. "I will walk."

Chris was born with cerebral palsy. Eight days ago, he celebrated his 19th birthday with a postscript to the doctor's chilly words.

"He had my mother in tears that day," said Chris. "I wanted to prove him wrong. Nobody makes my mama cry."

Oh, but Chris managed to do it himself.

He made his mama cry two weeks ago.

It came on prom night for Jones County High School at Macon's City Auditorium.

Chris pushed himself from the seat of his wheelchair. With his date, Samantha Loth, clutching his left arm, he used his walker to move down the steps and across the dance floor at the lead-out.

"It was unbelievable," said Susan, who was watching from the balcony. "It was almost like he was gliding down those steps. The other students were calling his name. I looked around and everybody was standing."

It's a wonder anyone was able to dance without a mop nearby. The tears were ankle-deep beneath the copper dome. Not a dry eye in the place.

"I told his mother that was the second-most inspiring thing I will ever see in my life," said Kim Hice, a math teacher at Jones County. "The most inspiring will be when he walks across that stage at graduation."

It is a promise Chris has been making for more than a year now. It will add new meaning to the term "graduation exercise."

On Friday, May 19, at the school's football stadium, he plans to walk across the stage to receive his diploma from principal John Trimnell and Superintendent Jim LeBrun.

The other 241 members of the Class of 2006 will cheer so loudly, they're likely to be heard from Haddock clear down to Dames Ferry. Those who plan on being in the audience would be advised to bring an extra box of Kleenex.

"I'm sure it will be that way for me, too," said Chris. "I'll probably fall to pieces when I get off that stage. It will be emotionally and physically exhausting."

If you haven't figured it out by now, Chris Hood is a remarkable young man.

He loves people, pizza and paintball. He already has piled up a stack of college credits in computer classes and has applied to Shorter College in Rome for next fall.

He is learning to drive a car with hand controls. He is a huge Garth Brooks fan and has a date with his mama every Monday night in front of the TV. They watch "Seventh Heaven" religiously at 8 p.m. on the WB network.

He also is a member of the Jones County track team. He throws the shot put and competes in the 200 meters in a special racing wheelchair. He placed second in the shot and was fourth in the 200 at the American Association of Adapted Sports Programs state meet in Jefferson last year.

(He is not the only member of the team with a disability. Sophomore Caleb Poore is blind. He competes in the 100- and 200-meter dashes by holding a tether with teammate Paul Faircloth.)

Chris was born on a sun-splashed April day in 1987. For the first few months of his life, he appeared to be no different than his two older brothers — Steven, now 26 and a Macon police officer, and Douglas, who is 23.

But by his first birthday, his motor skills lagged far behind what would be considered normal development.

And that long-anticipated entry in the baby diary — "Took His First Step Today" — never came.

When he was 5, and the doctors were convinced he never would walk, he had the first of nine surgeries on his legs.

"As he got older, the toughest thing was to see him sit and watch the other children in the neighborhood play baseball," said Susan.

At age 9, while working with a physical therapist at HealthSouth Central Georgia Rehabilitation Hospital in Macon, arrangements were made to purchase a large adaptive tricycle, so he could "ride bikes" with his friends.

That same year, he was selected as a torchbearer by the Macon Paralympic Organizing Committee.

Over time, though, his leg muscles have weakened. He has been limited to the use of a wheelchair since the eighth grade.

Coach Greg Nisbet calls Chris' presence a "triumph of the human spirit."

"I have been coaching for 23 years, and it used to be all about winning," Nisbet said. "I now realize what it's really about is the joy of competition. And you can see that on his face. He loves to compete."

At the Greyhound meets, Chris gets standing ovations from the crowd just for showing up at the track. He does not try to go head-to-head against the others. He competes against himself. His times and distances are recorded by Nisbet, who turns them in to the AAASP to qualify for the state meet.

Nisbet recalls Chris being anxious to get track season started last year. But he had to wait a few weeks until some special gloves could be ordered. The gloves were designed to protect his hands while turning the wheels on his racing wheelchair.

Chris continued to practice while he waited for the gloves. "His hands were covered in blisters," Nisbet said.

At a meet this spring, Nisbet noticed both wheels on Chris' wheelchair were flat. He was intent on racing anyway.

"He refuses to be denied," he said.

Nisbet teaches sociology at the school. He often gives his students an assignment to spend part of the class period in a wheelchair to better "understand what Chris has to experience on any given school day."

Susan Hood has learned never to tell her youngest son NOT to do something. It just makes him that much more determined.

"I don't try to put on a show," Chris said. "I just do what I have to do."

High school proms and graduations are a lot like life.

You don't count the number of steps you take.

You measure them.

The man who knows he can

March 10, 2010

When he was 14 years old, Dick Frame attended the 1954 Indiana state basketball championship game at the Butler Fieldhouse in Indianapolis.

That night, tiny Milan High School, with an enrollment of 161 students, beat Muncie Central to become the smallest school ever to capture the Indiana single-class title. It was David vs. Goliath.

Dick never went to bed that night. His family had followed Milan for much of the season. And he and his twin brother, Steve, were paperboys and had to deliver the *Indianapolis Star* when it hit the streets at 2:30 a.m.

A movie was made about that night and that team. It was called "Hoosiers." The team was known as "Hickory," and it is my all-time favorite sports movie. I always watch it this time of year, the perfect companion to all the basketball tournaments and March Madness.

Naturally, it is one of Dick's favorite movies, too. He also remembers another one. He saw it when he was a teenager. "Pride of the Yankees" was a baseball movie. Gary Cooper was nominated for an Academy Award for best actor in his role as Lou Gehrig.

Gehrig's career was cut short when he was diagnosed with amyotrophic lateral sclerosis, a fatal neurological disease more commonly referred to as Lou Gehrig's disease. Despite his tragic affliction, in his farewell address at Yankee Stadium, Gehrig uttered the famous line: "Today, I consider myself the luckiest man on the face of the Earth."

Dick Frame has Lou Gehrig's Disease. The right side of his body can no longer seem to catch up with the rest of him.

But it has not affected his attitude. Just ask anyone around him. Mr. Sunshine. The luckiest man on the face of the Earth.

He will be 70 years old next month, a guy with boundless energy despite the decline of his mobility. He remains one of Macon's greatest ambassadors for high school sports.

Nobody ever seems to notice he stands only 5-foot-6. The man is a giant.

This marks his 32nd year as a volunteer track coach at First Presbyterian Day School. He has never been paid a dime for it — he spent the other half of his life volunteering at Vine-Ingle Little League — but he is surrounded by the real riches in life.

He has helped coach 23 GISA champions in the hurdles. He has motivated the FPD girls to win six of the last seven state titles and inspired the boys to claim four of the last six.

Since 1982, he has been the official starter at the state track meet — firing the blank pistol at the beginning of almost every heat and race.

It's more of a challenge now. When he reaches to raise the starting gun, he can no longer sustain his arm in the air without using his left arm for support.

He was always a picture of health and fitness. For years, he would run alongside his athletes while they were practicing the hurdles.

Then he had to stop. At first, he told them it was a pulled muscle. He thought it might be his cholesterol. He went to have his heart checked out.

The diagnosis came two years ago, just before the start of track season.

He still shows up to coach every afternoon. He makes good use of the bounce he still has left in his step.

"I've got to do this," he said. "A lot of people go downhill when they're diagnosed. But you can't have a defeatist attitude. You must have something to live for. I'm committed to these kids. They're like my own children."

His doctors shake their heads in amazement.

"They think I'm an anomaly," he said, laughing.

It has been a wonderful ride. As a youngster, he once shot hoops with the great Oscar Robertson. He and his brother came South after earning track scholarships to Georgia Tech.

In the Southeastern Conference championship meet in Baton Rouge in 1959, he won his heat in the 100-yard dash against the legendary Billy Cannon, who won the Heisman Trophy playing football for LSU that same year.

He met his future wife, Marty, three weeks before he graduated from Tech. They married in 1963 and moved to Macon in 1965.

They have four children — Rick, Jacki (Spivey), Jeff and Taylor. Dick is retired after working for 43 years as an area manager for the Trane Co.

It was 10 years ago this spring when Dick received *The Telegraph*'s annual Sam Burke Award for Service to High School Sports. Last fall, he was the recipient of FPD's Alumni Service Award, even though he never attended the school.

Last week, he and Marty took a skiing vacation to Colorado. "I wanted to keep trying to do things," he said. After 10 minutes on the slopes at Vail, the tough reality set in. He realized he could no longer maneuver his legs enough to keep skiing.

The effort is still there. So is the upbeat attitude. His mantra has always been a 114-word poem called "The Man Who Thinks He Can."

The race is not over, he said. Not by a long shot.

Think Hoosiers.

Some of the roads weren't paved

August 29, 2010

When she was 14 years old, her teacher was pushing her in her wheelchair.

Jewell Massey looked down at her hands. She was fussing about her hands. She hated her hands. She did not think they were pretty.

"I've got my daddy's hands," she said.

"But they're such capable hands," said her teacher, Ruth Walker.

When the 14-year-old girl grew up and became a 41-year-old teacher from Macon, those hands were wrapped in glory on the Sunday night of Aug. 28, 1988.

She clutched a dozen roses in her right hand and a microphone in the other. A crown was placed on her head as the winner of the Ms. Wheelchair America Pageant. The smile on her face was almost as wide as the stage itself.

Richard Simmons, the famous exercise guru and television personality, was the master of ceremonies. He gave her a hug and told the audience at the 17th annual pageant in Mobile, Ala., that her mother "must have known something when she named her Jewell."

At the pageant, she gave out T-shirts bearing the message: "Something special will happen today because of a teacher."

Ruth Walker was the teacher who made a difference in her life. Walker taught a special education class in Knoxville, Tenn., in the 1950s and '60s. Jewell stayed in that same class from the third grade through the 12th.

Walker introduced her to everything from algebra to diagramming sentences. She showed her how to be an independent thinker.

She collected butter pat dishes. Her husband taught at the University of Tennessee. She encouraged Jewell and loved her like a daughter.

Years later, at her funeral, the minister who delivered the eulogy mentioned Jewell in the same breath as Ruth's own daughters. They were that close.

Jewell became a teacher herself, and once invited Walker to Macon to speak to her gifted students at Springdale Elementary and show her off for show-and-tell.

After living in Macon for the past 40 years, including 26 years as a teacher in the Bibb County public schools, Jewell is moving back to Knoxville in a few weeks to live next door to her sister.

There aren't nearly enough boxes to pack all the memories and move them 294 miles up to Rocky Top. There are poems and freckled-faced drawings her students made for her.

She has sold her house. She has always found joy in nature and will miss the yard where she became a master gardener and identified more than three dozen species of birds.

When Denny Jones, of Fickling and Co., presented the offer on her house with a closing date of Sept. 17, Jewell said it was all meant to be.

"That is the birthday of my guardian angel," she said.

Ruth Walker was that guardian angel. She turned out to be one of many.

Jewell was born in Tazewell, Tenn., about 45 miles northeast of Knoxville. Her family was so poor her mother, Leetie, cut up old petticoats to make diapers.

Her father was in and out of the family's life, mostly out. They moved to Knoxville to live with her Aunt Thelma.

In 1950, when Jewell was 3, she and her 2-year-old brother, O.D., contracted polio a few days apart. She remembers being in the same hospital room with him, an iron lung next to her bed. He scooted his crib over to be close to her. The only part of her body she could move was her left hand. Her father abandoned the family during the time she and her brother were in isolation.

O.D. made a full recovery from his polio and later became a Navy pilot who flew with the Blue Angels.

The disease left Jewell crippled. One day, when she was 4, her mother was taking her to physical therapy on the city bus. A woman noticed the braces on Jewell's legs and back. "What awful sin did you commit to have a child like that?" the woman asked.

The following year, Dr. Jonas Salk invented the polio vaccine, which was made available to the public in 1955.

But, by then, she had developed scoliosis and was placed in Ruth Walker's special education class after spending three years in a homebound program. It was a rag-tag class of misfits the school system did not mainstream.

"Most of the kids were mentally challenged or terminally ill," Jewell said. "We never felt like we fit in. We were so isolated we even had our own lunchroom. I guess the way we talked was disturbing. And we drooled when we ate."

Her mother, who had only a fifth-grade education, worked in a hospital kitchen at night to provide for the family. When her father reappeared for a brief period of time, they moved into the housing projects. She read books from the bookmobile by the dim light of a 25-watt bulb dangling from the ceiling.

On several occasions, Jewell went to Warm Springs for physical therapy or to have surgery. Some of her happiest memories and strongest friendships were forged there.

She became a poster child for the Shriners and the March of Dimes. "My 15 minutes of fame," she said. She also made public appearances for Easter Seals.

When she left for college at Lincoln Memorial University, one of her relatives said to her mother: "I don't know why you're sending her over there. They're going to send her right back."

Said Jewell: "They did — four years later as an honor graduate. If I had known she said that, I might have come out a valedictorian."

She spent her first two years teaching in Jacksonville, Fla., then left for a teaching opportunity in Macon because it was halfway home to Knoxville.

She never intended to stay 40 years, and it's a wonder she didn't pack up and leave after her first year in the Bibb County public schools.

It was 1970, and the first year of county-wide integration. Her first assignment was teaching science at the Ballard B Middle School.

"It was jumping from the skillet into the fire," she said. "Ballard had formerly been the all-black school. There was nothing to work with. Parts of the blackboard were missing. There weren't any blinds on the windows."

She was there for three years, then taught children with behavior disorders in the system for five years. She would cry every morning and drink Mylanta antacid straight from the bottle.

But she didn't quit. She didn't give up. By 1979, she was teaching gifted elementary school students. It would be her passion for the next 18 years.

Many of her students had never been around an adult in a wheelchair, much less had a teacher who rolled to work in one. They adored being around her as much as she loved teaching them. She would let them sign up to push her to lunch, and she would allow them to take turns riding in the wheelchair when they graduated from the sixth grade.

When she won the Ms. Wheelchair America in 1988, it was the first time she had ever competed in anything. She had seen an announcement in *The*

Telegraph about the statewide contest in Warm Springs. She entered and won, then went on to the national competition in Mobile.

Her mama came to live with her in 1982, and Jewell was her mother's caregiver late in life when she developed Alzheimer's. (She died in 2008.) Jewell called taking care of her mom one of her "greatest privileges." She learned to change her mother's bed with one hand holding on to a wheel and the other for balance.

Capable hands.

And now it's time for Jewell to go back to Knoxville, leaving the tug of one home for another. She has been an inspiration to so many folks in this town. She left me with one of her favorite quotations, often attributed to Will Rogers.

"I want people to know why I look this way. I've traveled a long way, and some of the roads weren't paved."

Life in another man's skin

February 5, 2005

CRAWFORD COUNTY — Danny Yaughn's skin is rumpled and flaky, like a pie crust that has been baked in the oven too long.

When he goes out, he knows strange looks will follow him everywhere. At the grocery store, he can feel the stares. They burn like the sun that will kill him if the rays touch for too long.

Yes, he allows himself to wonder what it would be like to walk around in another man's skin.

He is 58 years old and has always lived with this rare skin condition. He was born without sweat and oil glands. After every bath, he must cover his body from head to toe with petroleum jelly.

Every day, his skin flakes and peels. Every two weeks, he has pockets of squamous cell carcinoma, a type of skin cancer, surgically removed from his body.

He has been diagnosed with congenital ichthyosiform erythroderma (CIE), a skin disease so rare it afflicts only 1 in every 3.3 million people in the United States.

It's a type of ichthyosis. It gets its name from the Greek root "ichthy," which means "fish." His skin is marked by dry, cracked and often-discolored scales.

Yaughn grew up in Byron. His family was poor, and his classmates teased him unmercifully about his birth defect, calling him names like "Little Red Monkey" and "Lizard Boy."

"It was rough," he said. "I felt different and unwanted. I was shy and had only a few friends."

His family took him to hospitals from Augusta to Alabama to Tennessee. "I was a guinea pig," Yaughn said. "They tried to find ways to help me, but there was nothing they could do."

He once saw 48 doctors in a span of two hours at a meeting of dermatologists at Emory University in Atlanta.

He now lives on a fixed income with his daughter, Jennifer, in a small house near the Crawford and Peach County line.

At first glance, Yaughn looks like a guy who might have spent too many days at the beach. His skin appears blistered and peeling. "I always look this way," he said.

There are days when he sheds enough skin to fill a small dustpan. He has to keep the dead skin cleared from inside his ears so he can hear. His fingernails no longer grow back.

He hasn't held a job in more than 20 years. He once worked in factories. His last job was as a dispatcher and jailer for the Crawford County Sheriff's Office.

His profession is now a "homebody." When he works outside, it is usually in the morning or evening. "I can't perspire, so it builds up and feels like it will explode, like a pressure cooker," he said.

Yaughn's disease has been known to carry with it an alarming suicide rate. There have been times when he has felt that way, too. But no longer.

Friends and family tell him he is an inspiration to them. Even a psychiatrist in Warner Robins was impressed with Yaughn's ability to cope with his condition.

"There are mornings when I don't feel like getting out of bed," he said. "But the Lord has given me the courage to get through each day."

Another man's skin?

Sometimes he wonders what it would be like, if only for a little while.

Danny died on October 12, 2007. He was 60.

Not everyone can see the beauty

March 19, 2006

The window in her apartment catches the rays of morning sun, but Mary Wiley does not see the light.

She usually hangs a pink bow on her patio during the Cherry Blossom Festival, even though she has no clue what it looks like.

"I go out and feel it," she said.

As we reflect on the beauty of another springtime in Macon — a season dropped straight out of heaven — we could easily take it for granted.

Mary has never witnessed the cascade of loveliness on the Cherry Blossom trail. She has never seen pink poodles prancing down Mulberry Street or watched the firefighters flip pink pancakes at Central City Park. She has never had her breath stolen under the glow of hot-air balloons tethering against the night sky.

Mary has been blind since she was 8 months old. She is now 63 and lives alone.

She has no concept of shapes, sizes and colors. Her only frame of reference for a Yoshino cherry tree is touching the petals with her fingers.

If you woke up this morning, but the sun never did, at least you could claim to have witnessed one of the great visual wonders of our city.

In her dark corner of the world, Mary has no concept of the 300,000 flowering cherries that grace our landscape.

"I've heard people talking about the festival, but it has never meant that much to me because I've never participated in it," she said. "I'm glad it makes other people happy, though."

She grew up in Sparta. She was adopted by Sam and Mary Wiley when she was 5 weeks old. Retina blastoma, a form of eye cancer, robbed her of her sight.

She moved to Macon in 1948 to attend the Georgia Academy for the Blind, where she learned to read Braille. She moved back to Sparta in the seventh grade and attended public school. She rode the school bus with the other students, was mainstreamed in the same classes and graduated in 1960.

For several years, she worked as a stenographer at The Medical Center of Central Georgia. She now spends her time listening to library books on tape and playing the piano and accordion for social functions and nursing homes. Sometimes, she tunes in to hear the local TV news and to what "Judge Judy" has to say.

She uses "echo location" by snapping her fingers to navigate her way around a room. She "sees" her friends by the sound of their voice. She rarely forgets a voice.

The friend's voice that has been with her the longest is Esther Boyer, who now lives in Macon but remembers when Mary was a young girl in Sparta.

"I've always admired her," Boyer said. "She has the ability to cope. She has never known sight, so she doesn't miss it."

You probably know folks like Mary, and might even wonder what you can do for them.

I told Mary I was going to call her one day next week and take her down to Third Street Park. There, we will stand in line for some cherry ice cream beneath the beautiful canopy of blossoms.

I will do my best to try and describe the surroundings to her.

The best way to enjoy the festival is to share it with someone else.

Some fires can never be put out

December 7, 2007

CORDELE — For years, the words did not come easy for Ed Kiker Williams. They stuck in his throat. He carried his grief like heavy luggage.

Folks in Cordele understood why he could never talk about the early hours of Dec. 7, 1946, when he was a 17-year-old high school senior on a trip to Atlanta with his family.

That was the night a fire broke out at the Winecoff Hotel in Atlanta and 119 people died in the smoke and flames. It remains the worst hotel disaster in U.S. history.

In a small community where most everybody knows each other, they shared his sorrow. A town's tears fell like soft rain in the watermelon fields. And every Sunday, he would go with his grandmother to the cemetery and place fresh flowers on the graves of his mother and sister.

For most Americans, today is a day of remembrance. It is the 66th anniversary of the attack on Pearl Harbor. More than 2,300 people lost their lives on the day that marked America's entry into World War II. It was a war that killed more people, destroyed more property and changed the world more than any military conflict in history.

Somewhat forgotten in the shadows of that somber anniversary is a tragedy that struck much closer to home on the same date five years later.

The 15-story Winecoff, the tallest hotel in Atlanta, was supposed to be "fireproof" in the same way the *Titanic* was supposed to be "unsinkable."

But 280 guests filled the 195 rooms that night, and 119 of them did not live to see the sunrise the next morning.

It broke the heart of a state and nation. They came from towns like Cordele, Thomaston, Bainbridge, Fitzgerald and Barnesville.

They were fathers, mothers, teachers, secretaries, traveling salesmen, bus drivers and soldiers who had returned home from the war.

Perhaps most tragic were the deaths of 30 high school students chosen as delegates for a YMCA youth assembly at the state Capitol. Seven were from

Bainbridge, including 14-year-old Patsy Griffin, the daughter of Marvin Griffin, who later became governor of Georgia.

Also among the victims was 64-year-old E.B. Weatherly of Cochran. A graduate of Mercer University law school in Macon, he had returned to the farm during the Great Depression and become one of the premier cattlemen in the South. He was a frequent visitor to the Winecoff when he traveled to Atlanta to meet with state legislators about the beef industry.

Williams not only lost his 40-year-old mother, Boisclair Williams, and his 8-year-old sister, Claire, he also lost his 36-year-old aunt, Dorothy Kiker Smith of Fitzgerald and her three children — his cousins Fred, 14, Dotsy, 12, and Mary, 4. They were staying in a room on the same floor.

Williams is now 78 years old, one of only a handful of Winecoff survivors who are still living. Tonight, he will attend a special gathering in Atlanta to remember the fire's victims and their families. The ceremony will take place in the Ellis Hotel, which opened in October in the refurbished Winecoff building at the corner of Peachtree and Ellis streets.

He can talk about it now. Time has healed his wounds. He is at peace knowing his mother and sister "are in a better place."

Although more than 100 people died, he said he believes thousands more lives have been saved as the result of revised fire codes.

The Winecoff was hailed as being fireproof, but it was fatally flawed. It had been designed and built in 1913 without fire escapes, fire alarms or a sprinkler system because none of them were required by law. Ladders from the Atlanta Fire Department could reach no higher than the seventh floor of the 15-story building.

On that first Friday of December six decades ago, Williams recalls being excited about the trip to Atlanta. He had been just one other time. A few months earlier, he and a friend had hitchhiked to the big city to watch a Georgia Tech football game.

On the morning of Dec. 6, 1946, he loaded the car with his mother, aunt, sister and three cousins. They had planned to do some Christmas shopping at Davison's and Rich's department stores. They also were going to the premiere of Walt Disney's "Song of the South" across the street at the Paramount Theater.

Williams wasn't exactly overjoyed with the prospects of seeing the movie or having to go shopping. What thrilled him was the chance to drive his Aunt Dot's new 1947 Buick.

Since it was long before the days of Interstate 75, they headed up U.S. 41 through Vienna, Perry, Macon, Forsyth, Barnesville, Griffin and Jonesboro. It was a four-hour trip. They saw a matinee of the movie at the Paramount across Peachtree Street and ate supper at a nearby cafeteria.

The family was staying in Room 1520 on the 14th floor, one floor from the top. (In keeping with superstition, the hotel listed no 13th floor.)

Williams doesn't remember going to bed that night. He just remembers his mother waking him. The room was filled with smoke, and they soon realized they were trapped by an inferno several floors below.

For more than an hour, they kept vigil at the double windows, trying to breathe.

"The smoke was so thick I could not see down," he said. "But I could hear the sirens. It was like being in a chimney. The heat was like somebody holding a blow torch to my back."

At one point, he reached through the darkness to embrace his mother and sister. They were not there. They were on the floor, passed out from smoke inhalation. He checked his mother's pulse. He could not feel one. He lifted their lifeless bodies to the window, hoping to revive them.

"I never felt like I was going to die," he said. "I did a lot of praying."

As he leaned out the window, his lungs gasping for air, he held onto the mullion between the windows. Then, he lost consciousness.

He doesn't remember falling.

He could have been one of the estimated three dozen people who died from either falling or jumping. But he miraculously landed on top of a ladder about 25 feet below. It had been extended horizontally across the alley to windows in the Mortgage Guarantee Building. A firefighter was able to rescue him.

"My head was cut and my heel was hurt, but I could still walk," he said. "They wanted to put me in an ambulance. I told them others needed it worse than I did. I took a taxi to St. Joseph's Hospital."

It was there his father, John Williams, and two uncles found him the next day.

At one time, fire investigators believed the fire might have been started on the third floor by a careless guest dropping a burning cigarette on a mattress. Later, several arson theories emerged. Other details surfaced about an all-night poker game on the same floor.

Regardless, no one can bring back the dead. About 80 percent of the guests who died were staying on the eighth floor or above or on the back side of the building. Photographs taken that night show haunting images of people trapped on the upper floors, with bed sheets tied together and dangling from open windows.

Williams was very close to his mother, who taught Sunday School and was a pillar of the First Baptist Church in Cordele. She never got to see him graduate from high school and become a well-respected member of the community.

His connection to the Winecoff fire has been laced with its own ironies. He did not meet his wife, Marylene, until later in life. It was then he learned she was supposed to have been at the Winecoff that same night.

She and her sister played basketball at R.E. Lee in Thomaston. They both had been selected as delegates to the Hi-Y and Tri-Hi-Y (YMCA service clubs) convention at the Capitol. But their coach insisted that he needed them for the next game, and two other girls from Thomaston went to Atlanta in their place.

Those two girls, along with two others and a popular teacher from R.E. Lee, all died in the fire. They were staying in Room 1430, directly below his aunt and cousins, who also perished.

Williams has never seen "Song of the South" since that night. But his brother-in-law and his wife, Riley and Lanelle Frost, help run the Uncle Remus Museum in Eatonton.

"And I still sing 'Zip-A-Dee-Doo-Dah,'" he said, smiling.

Today, he will pause, reflect and remember.

There are some fires you can never put out.

The day the weather changed

March 8, 2009

Jeanetta Jones remembers the weather that Thursday morning in 2006. It was clear and a pleasant, late-November cool. The sun was hanging like bright wallpaper above Cobb Parkway in Marietta.

There wasn't much traffic on the road because of the holiday. It was Thanksgiving Day, and most folks had already gotten to where they were going. Since she had to work, she and her family celebrated their Thanksgiving meal the night before.

Jeanetta left her home in Smyrna for the 15-minute commute. She was almost at her office.

Of course, she remembers the weather.

It was her job.

For 20 years, she had worked at The Weather Channel. She would stand in front of bluescreen weather maps surrounded by cameras, cables and monitors. Between smiles, she could tell millions of viewers the barometric pressure in Bakersfield and the wind chill in Chicago.

In an instant, she saw the other vehicle racing across the corner of her eye. It flew through the traffic light and struck her Mazda Tribute on the passenger side.

The rest of what happened is like deleted files she can no longer recover.

Her small SUV flipped several times. Because she did not hit the brakes, the air bags never engaged. Although she was wearing her seat belt, her head still went through the windshield.

She was conscious when she dialed her cell phone to call her husband, Lenny, and daughter, Rebecca. A woman who had stopped to help told her not to move for fear her neck might be broken.

Someone recognized her as being that "gal from The Weather Channel."

There was glass in her face, even pressed against her teeth on the inside of her mouth. The rescue team used the Jaws of Life to pry her from the vehicle. They told her they usually saw wrecks like that only when the weather was bad.

But the weather was fine. She remembers that.

The emergency room was packed. The flu was going around. They took some X-rays and sent her home.

"I kept telling them my head was killing me," said Jeanetta. "They said I would be fine and that I would probably be back at work in a few days."

It has been 836 days, and Jeanetta still hasn't returned to work. It has been 29 months, and she is still finding slivers of glass in her skin.

Jeanetta grew up in Macon, the daughter of Tommy and Barbara Jones. Tommy is celebrating his 50th year as a local minister. She graduated from Stratford Academy in 1978 and received her journalism degree from the University of Georgia. She worked at both WMAZ in Macon (1982-84) and at a TV station in Spartanburg, S.C., before being hired by the Atlanta-based cable network.

Jerilyn Leverett was among the first to notice something wasn't right with her older sister. Jeanetta's behavior was not normal. She was forgetful. Even the simplest tasks would frustrate her. She was transposing numbers in her checkbook.

"We were watching the show '24,' and she couldn't remember who Jack Bauer was," said Jerilyn. (Nobody who watches the popular drama on Fox would ever forget the name of the show's hero.)

Jerilyn, who is executive director of Disability Connections in Macon, has a form of muscular dystrophy and is in a wheelchair. She often deals with clients who are suffering from brain injuries. So she began to suspect Jeanetta might have suffered a mild traumatic brain injury. She suggested to her sister that she consult a doctor and undergo testing.

Jeanetta went down a checklist at The Shepherd Center in Atlanta. Difficulty concentrating? Yes. Difficulty processing information? Yes. Irritability? Paranoia? Fatigue? Ringing in ears? Yes. Yes. Yes. Yes.

"I had thought I was going crazy," she said. "It was frustrating doing simple tasks, like putting on my makeup. I couldn't do anything fast. I was so tired that I was taking three naps a day. I went down the symptoms on the list and flunked every one of them."

Soon, a parade of therapists were tracking through her living room like a storm on Doppler radar. Physical therapy. Occupational therapy. Speech cognitive therapy.

She no longer drives. She has to have help chopping food because she is afraid to be around knives. She doesn't leave the kitchen when she's cooking, either. She is fearful of forgetting to turn off the stove.

The injury has been debilitating. She walks with a slight limp. It has wreaked havoc on everything from her balance to her depth perception to her ability to sit down and read.

"It has affected every aspect of my life," she said. "My brain tries to process everything, but it's like all my filters are broken."

Inner-ear problems have kept her away from crowds. And that's not easy for a "people person." She used to love to shop with her 13-year-old daughter but now stays away from malls. It is difficult to attend church, go to the movies or have lunch with friends in a busy restaurant.

"It's like having vertigo all the time," she said.

The accident was on Thanksgiving. Despite her difficulties, Jeanetta remains thankful.

"I'm so grateful my life was spared," she said. "I wake up every day and thank God."

The MVP of FPD

November 7, 2008

Austin Childers has spent what seems like half his life in hospital rooms.

This morning, he is on the third floor of the Children's Hospital at The Medical Center of Central Georgia.

He hopes the doctor will release him later today. If not, Austin has a backup plan.

From his hospital bed, he gestured toward the window and grinned.

"I'm going to tie some bed sheets together," he said, laughing.

Austin is a senior at First Presbyterian Day School. He is anxious to "escape" because the Vikings open the first round of the GISA Class AAA play-offs tonight against Deerfield-Windsor in Albany.

Austin is a member of FPD's varsity team even though he has never made a tackle or caught a pass.

His teammates voted him one of the team captains. He will earn his fourth varsity letter in football this year.

On the Vikings' roster, he is No. 31 on your program, No. 1 in your heart.

"In a world where we need heroes, Austin is as close to one as I've seen in my lifetime," said FPD coach Greg Moore. "He deals with obstacles every day that most of us can't even fathom."

Life has been tough ever since he came home from football practice one day in the seventh grade, complaining of a headache and nausea.

That marked the beginning of a long and painful journey of pills, needles, tubes and machines that go beep in the night. If Austin got bonus points for every time his head has been on a hospital pillow, he would be a rich man.

Last year alone, he spent 70 days in the hospital. His family has taken him to a string of doctors from California to Chicago to Milwaukee searching for answers.

"We have had to put the puzzle together slowly," said his mother, Ashley.

Austin suffers from a mitochondrial disorder. It occurs when mitochondria — the enzymes that provide power to each cell in our bodies — fail to produce enough energy for normal cell and organ function.

When you're 18 years old, you should be more worried about charging your cell phone than charging the cells inside your body. You shouldn't have a feeding tube dangling at your side and an IV following you around like a puppy dog. You shouldn't have to brag about having had your eighth porta-cath removed this week.

But Austin is always sunny side up. He must have been born with a smile on his face.

"I'm not going to let this illness get the best of me," he said. "I'm going to keep right on being Austin."

Said Ashley: "He keeps getting knocked down, and he keeps getting back up."

Austin selected a quote from Winston Churchill for his senior section in the FPD yearbook. "A pessimist sees the difficulty in every opportunity. An optimist sees the opportunity in every difficulty."

He grew up playing football, until his health problems began keeping him off the field. He went to Moore and asked to be part of the team.

"I wanted to be involved," he said. "But I wanted to be more than just a water boy."

When he is able, Austin attends every FPD practice. He is on the sidelines on Friday nights, sometimes in a wheelchair. Every now and then, he gets to ceremoniously snap the ball to the quarterback in practice.

"I know my role," Austin said. "I'm fine with my role."

His father, Chris Childers, is convinced a team full of Austins would go undefeated every year.

"As his father, I'm supposed to be his role model," Chris said. "But it's the other way around."

Being an MVP has taken on another meaning.

Most valuable person.

The friends of Ed R.

August 22, 2008

Ed Rowe's obituary said he was born in 1930 and died on Monday. It noted that he is survived by his wife, daughter, son-in-law, sister and two grandchildren. A memorial service will be held this afternoon at St. Paul's Episcopal Church.

It also mentioned he was a "faithful friend of Bill W. for 47 wonderful years."

Most folks won't know how to read between those lines.

Bill W. was Bill Wilson. He was named one of *Time* magazine's "100 Most Important People" of the 20th century. He was the co-founder of Alcoholics Anonymous and its famous 12-step program. He died in 1971.

To be identified as a "friend of Bill W." is the universal code for a recovering alcoholic.

That's why Ed's obituary could never begin to tell the story of this remarkable man who loved life and laughter. He always was obsessed about the weather. Had cancer not claimed him so quickly, he would no doubt be tracking Tropical Storm Fay, calling friends along the projected path and urging them to batten down the hatches.

He was a pretty fair baseball player in his day. He was known as "Fast Eddie" because he could really run. He also was quite a rarity at his position. You don't see too many left-handed third basemen. He played professional baseball for seven years in the St. Louis Cardinals organization.

His father and brother both battled alcoholism. The demons stalked him, too. He mostly got fun-loving drunk, never violent drunk, but that could never justify his actions.

Drinking ended his promising baseball career and nearly cost him his family. With two young children, his wife, Anabel, issued him an ultimatum, then helped him seek help.

"He was strong enough," she said, "to know his weaknesses."

A friend named "Horizontal Harry" introduced him to AA. Harry got his name because horizontal was how he usually ended up after he'd been drinking. He clung to Ed like a shadow, making sure he didn't backslide. He would send him chocolate-covered cherries to curb the cravings for alcohol.

Ed became a salesman for Lee Jeans and spent most of his life in Oklahoma City. There were times when he attended AA meetings every day. After 1961, he never sipped anything stronger than a Coca-Cola. Every Christmas, he had his photograph taken holding a Coke can, a personal symbol of victory.

Recovering alcoholics never consider themselves cured. They are always recovering.

While saving his own life, he began saving others. His daughter, Cindy Gonzalez, remembers the phone would sometimes ring in the middle of the night, and her father would slip into the darkness to go help somebody.

The heartaches were still there, though. His son, Randy, was killed on Father's Day in 1981. Randy was hit by a train while driving across railroad tracks. Alcohol was involved in the accident.

Cindy and her husband, Fred Gonzalez, moved to Macon with their children, Kaylee and Brady. Three years ago, Ed and Anabel followed them here. In a short time, Ed grew to love Macon and became involved with local AA groups.

At the hospital, Cindy did not recognize several men who stopped by to visit her father. But when they introduced themselves as a Frank G. or a Bob M., she nodded to acknowledge that she understood. They told her how much he meant to them.

He was a friend of Bill W.

They were friends of Ed R.

When happy hour really comes

September 20, 2009

I met a buddy for a drink after work the other night.

He got there early and ordered iced tea. I came in out of the rain, pulled up a chair and ordered a Coca-Cola.

After he got to the bottom of his glass, he decided to switch to the harder stuff. He had the waitress bring him a Coke, straight up.

We laughed. This was our happy hour. Two wild and crazy guys, huh?

When I had seen him a few weeks earlier, I almost didn't recognize him. He told me he had stopped drinking. He was working again. There was a bounce in his step.

I asked about his wife.

"She has a new husband," he said. "Me."

My friend has spent more than two-thirds of his life bending elbows and breaking hearts.

There were times when he was guzzling a case of beer every day. He would pop open his first can before lunch and keep himself wasted until long after sundown.

In almost every photograph or video of himself for the past 30 years, he is holding a beer can, like an extension of his hand.

"I was out of control," he said. "I was killing myself, and I knew it. But I couldn't stop."

He quit smoking several years ago. He kicked his two-pack-a-day habit in the butt and moved on.

Snuffing his cigarette habit was easy compared to the demons of alcohol. He could never go cold turkey on the cold beer.

His wife wore out her knees praying for him to stop. One day last year, he sat next to her on the porch.

"I told her I needed to get help, and a beautiful smile came over her face," he said. "She started crying. I don't know if I've ever seen her so happy, and I hadn't done anything yet. I had just told her that I needed help."

He now realizes the importance of that first step. Recognition. It was followed by admission, then action.

So he checked himself into a rehabilitation hospital in another city. He has not had a drop of alcohol touch his lips in more than a year.

The temptation is always there, though. He teeters on the edge of a cliff, where one beer is too many and a dozen are never enough.

My friend is 61 years old. It all started when those numbers were reversed. At age 16, a friend snuck out with some of his father's vodka, and they mixed it with cherry ice drinks from Dairy Queen.

He spent a year in Vietnam, where he "brought up the rear with the gear." The rest of the time he soaked his brain with liquor like the monsoon rains.

He returned home, vowing to make up for lost party time. He moved to the Georgia coast. He would stay out half the night drinking, then somehow manage to drag to work the next morning with a Category 5 hangover.

Marriage settled him down for a while, but then the tap started again, this time almost nonstop.

He quit working. He struggled with back problems, then had knee surgery.

He used beer to wash down all those pain killers. He even kept it in his hospital room following his surgery.

He remembers being angry after his 30-day stay in the rehabilitation clinic.

"They had taken away my best buddy," he said. "And I was never going to see him (the beer) again."

Not even visitation rights.

My friend now attends Alcoholic Anonymous meetings and takes one day at a time.

That's all he can do. And, for right now, that's enough.

Brighten the corner

Merry Christmas, forever and ever

December 18, 2005

When I called Bill Meriwether the other day, I knew what he was going to say before he answered the phone.

"Merry Christmas."

It's like that everywhere he goes. "Merry Christmas" in the cereal aisle at the grocery store. "Merry Christmas" at the gas station and the drug store.

Meriwether and his wife, Betsy, are regulars for supper at the S&S Cafeteria in Macon's Bloomfield neighborhood. He extends his trademark "Merry Christmas" greeting to every server on the line from the Jell-O to the corn-bread.

"If I come in and don't say it, everyone will say it to me," he said, laughing.

It makes no difference whether it's May 18 or Dec. 18. It doesn't matter if it's 98 degrees in the shade or his frosty front yard is as white as Santa's beard.

With Bill Meriwether, it's never hello, goodbye or how's it going?

It's "Merry Christmas."

Forever.

"Whenever you say 'Merry Christmas,' you're usually thinking about what you can do for others," he said. "If everybody practiced the spirit of Christmas all year, it would be a better world."

Meriwether is 86 years old and among the wisest of wise men. He has substituted life's standard greetings with "Merry Christmas" for the past 55 years.

Every introduction. Every handshake. Every phone call.

There is no way to measure the happiness he has brought and the smiles he has produced by reciting those two little words.

By now, thousands of folks around town are familiar with his story. In December 1950, at his photography studio on Cotton Avenue, he extended Christmas greetings to every customer. After the holidays, he kept repeating it. He has never stopped.

Sometimes children will come up to him and ask why he's wishing every-one a "Merry Christmas" on the Fourth of July.

Because every day should be Christmas, he tells them.

There has been plenty of reaction and over-reaction to the Merry Christmas muzzle that has been placed on some schools and businesses. Society has been hijacked by political correctness, and many folks are plain fed up.

If anything, I believe the controversy has energized those who truly believe in the spirit of the season. This year, I've heard more people making an effort to say "Merry Christmas," and to say it more sincerely than ever before.

"I've never offended anyone," Meriwether said. "I once went to a synagogue to take photographs for a wedding. I had Jewish people coming up and telling me 'Merry Christmas.'"

A framed cross stitch with the words "Merry Christmas" was given to him by one of his former photography students, Amy "Shortcake" Yow, in 1983. It hangs on his living room wall year-round.

His son, Bill Meriwether III, and Bill's wife, Jeanene, named their second daughter Meri Christmas Meriwether. She is 16 years old, and answers to "Christie."

"We are not going to change her name to 'Happy Holidays' and call her 'Holly'!" said her dad.

Merry Christmas.

I'm never going to get tired of hearing it.

Bill Meriwether died on September 28, 2008, three weeks after his 89th birthday. I miss Merry Christmas.

Where the sun is always shining

January 11, 2008

There are days when the air gets warm beneath the brim of her school crossing guard hat.

Other days, when it's cold enough to see her breath, the orange or white gloves are a welcome part of the dress code.

Wind, rain, foggy mornings and sultry afternoons. It really makes no difference to Angellisa Spears.

The sun is always shining at the corner of Oglethorpe and College streets. That's the forecast for today and every day. Plenty of sunshine.

Angellisa's job is to help students at Alexander II Elementary cross at the busy intersection.

In one hand, she holds a small stop sign. In her other hand, she embraces the world as it passes by.

She waves to everyone. Not just one red car or two yellow school buses. Not just one sweaty jogger or one tired construction worker.

Not just one homesick college student or three desperate housewives trying to keep their kids from spilling crumbs in the backseat of the minivan.

Angellisa doesn't single out Buicks or Beemers. She doesn't discriminate against bicycles, baby strollers or pickups. She makes no distinction between an Avalanche and an Escalade.

She smiles and waves to everything and everybody.

"Nobody wants to be left out," she said. "While I'm waiting, I figure I might as well wave to people. If I smile, they smile back. It makes me happy to make them happy."

Being amiable is certainly encouraged, but not necessarily included in the job description for crossing guards in the Bibb County school system.

It goes beyond the call of duty. It's the call of howdy doody.

Angellisa does more than simply brighten her corner. She believes friendliness is contagious. Maybe folks will take the simple gestures she extends and spread them several blocks in every direction.

Cheerfulness knows no boundaries.

Every morning and afternoon, she watches — and sometime directs —the school traffic from Alex II, Mount de Sales Academy and Mercer University.

She also sees her share of downtown commuters, as well as those headed for Tattnall Square Park, several churches and the Bear's Den restaurant.

"Some people have told me they come this way just so they can wave to me," she said.

Of course, there are challenges. Frowns at the red light. Long faces in the turn lane. Dump trucks and grump trucks.

"If they see me smiling, maybe I can make them smile," she said. "Maybe I can make them forget their troubles. If I'm having a bad day myself, I can come out here and smile and wave to people, and I feel better. It's therapeutic. It makes me happy to make them happy."

Folks appreciate her. They send her thank-you notes, bring her candy and remember her at Christmas.

Angellisa is 42 years old and a 1983 graduate of Mount de Sales. She received her art degree from Spellman College in Atlanta and married Ken Spears in 1994. They have two children — Ken Jr., 12, and Beau, 6 — both students at St. Peter Claver Catholic School.

She was a stay-at-home mom for 11 years, then began searching for a part-time job when both children began attending school. She considered becoming a substitute teacher for Bibb County, but became interested in a position as a school crossing guard in October 2006 because her aunt, Christine Willis, is a crossing guard.

Angellisa works the corner from 7:30 to 9 a.m., then heads to her part-time job as a sales associate at Kohl's department store. She is back from 2:20 to 4 p.m. at Alexander II, the oldest school building (106 years) in continuous service in Georgia.

She wanted a job where she could get off by mid-afternoon to be with her children when they got out of school. It hasn't quite worked out that way. But her mother, Elizabeth Tasker, picks up Ken Jr. and Beau at St. Peter Claver.

"Sometimes she drives them by so they can wave at me," Angellisa said.

I can't begin to tell you how many times Angellisa has sent her sunbeams in my direction. I have never seen her without a smile.

So I had to ask her a question many of you probably have wanted to ask her, too.

"No," she said. "My arm never gets tired."

He salutes life as it passes by

May 3, 2009

He is a man of many hats, some of them tall as a stovepipe and others snug and flat against his head.

He wears them to keep his head warm and the sun off 89 years of living. But also because they represent who he is and what he does.

George Cox is in the business of putting smiles on people's faces. He sits in his wheelchair every morning and most afternoons — saluting and waving to cars, trucks, minivans and bicycles traveling along Forsyth Road.

Twice a day, he travels to the corner of North Wellington in his motorized wheelchair. He rolls past mailboxes and tidy lawns at the blazing speed of 5 mph. There is enough battery life and torque to get him up the short hill.

George is doing his part, as the old gospel song instructs us, to "brighten the corner where you are."

He salutes every man.

He waves to every woman and child.

He has had his photograph taken from moving vehicles. Women have been known to slow down to blow kisses.

He likes that.

George spreads his sunshine "just to be doing something" but also to help pass the long, lonely hours since his wife, Claudia, died in January after a heroic battle with cancer.

His son, Deane, believes his father's daily ritual began more out of goodwill than boredom and grief.

"My dad never meets a stranger," he said. "It's what keeps him alive. It lifts his spirit and gets him through each day."

To celebrate Cinco de Mayo on Tuesday, George will wear a sombrero with a brim wide enough to provide shade for a pack of Chihuahuas. It's authentic, too. He bought it in Mexico.

His hats are a tradition, especially during the holidays. It began when a neighbor, Bonnie Jenks, gave him an elf's hat at Christmas. He added a top hat for Groundhog's Day, an Uncle Sam hat for the Fourth of July and bunny ears for Easter.

"If I'm not wearing a hat, people will ask me about it," he said.

George spent part of last year in an assisted living facility in Tampa, Fla. He gained such a following for his gestures of waving and saluting along Bayshore Boulevard that he was written up in *The St. Petersburg Times*. It delighted him to salute so many military personnel on their way to MacDill Air Force Base.

George is a retired Air Force colonel. He was born in Scotland and moved with his family to Dayton, Ohio, as a child. It was there he developed his love of aviation — Dayton was the home of the Wright Brothers. He was a pilot for eight different aircraft and more than 60 missions in the Pacific Theater during World War II.

When he's not waving and saluting on the corner, George is passing out "smiley face" stickers at Forest Hills United Methodist Church, where he sometimes comes home with lipstick on his face from all the kisses.

Neighbor Bonnie finds inspiration in George's calling to spread cheer on his corner. "He wants to reach out and touch people, and this is one way he can do it," she said. "It's his instrument."

George Cox died on April 1, 2010. He was 90.

Santa was the real 'Story'

December 16, 2007

Santa Claus is buried beneath the pine trees on the gentle slope of a hill.

Inscribed on his grave marker are the dates that served as the bookends for his life. Born: May 4, 1893. Died: Aug. 9, 1967.

He was laid to rest 40 Christmases ago, not far from the small chapel at Macon Memorial Park.

His name was Alfred King Story, but a generation of Maconites never knew his real name. They only knew him as Santa Claus.

For 30 years, he was the face and voice of Christmas in Macon. He walked the walk and talked the talk.

No one could "ho ho ho" like Story. He had no rivals.

He would dress in his Santa outfit and climb aboard a float in the annual chamber of commerce Christmas parade on Cherry Street. He would wink and wave to every wide-eyed child shouting his name atop their father's shoulders.

And every Christmas Eve, he would broadcast from the studios of WMAZ radio. In the days before television and mall Santas, his audience would gather around their radios and listen to weather reports from the North Pole. He read letters from children asking for dolls and bicycles. In the background, you could hear the scurrying of elves and reindeer getting ready to deliver those toys all over the world.

He was in the hospital the Christmas before he died. The radio station made arrangements for him to do his final Christmas Eve broadcast from his hospital bed.

Although he was never a rich man, when he died, someone announced the "wealthiest man in Macon" had passed away.

His name was A.K. Story, and this is his story.

"He was the most wonderful man I have ever known," said Carolyn Reagan, one of his 19 grandchildren. "He waved in that Christmas parade as long as I can remember. For years, I never knew that was my granddaddy. But as I grew older there were tell-tale signs. ... One year, I noticed Santa's hands were just like my granddaddy's hands. ... I can't say I was surprised. Who else would this wonderful grandfather be but Santa?"

He was born in Culloden and grew up in tiny Wellston, which later became Warner Robins. He married his wife, Lizzie, on June 21, 1914, in what was the first formal wedding ever held at Mabel White Memorial Baptist Church.

He and Lizzie raised nine children in the house on Piedmont Avenue in south Macon. He worked for the state employment office and was responsible for organizing the first WPA program in the city.

Story was not a large man. In his early years as Santa, he had to tuck a pillow into his midsection to fill the role. Later, after the years and biscuits piled up, the Santa suit with the 50-inch waist began to fit.

He was larger than life, too, with a strong personality and firm grip on the moral compass.

His voice could fill a room, and often did.

The man who would be Santa was certainly qualified in spirit. He was compassionate and caring, often reaching into his own pockets to help those who were down on their luck.

"He didn't just worship on Sunday and forget about it for the rest of the week," said his daughter Mary Ruth Holt. "He also reached out to people of different faiths. He was ecumenical before anyone even knew what it meant."

He had a pencil-thin mustache and wore his derby hat with white shoes. When he wasn't wearing his trademark attire — railroad overalls and an engineer's cap — you might catch him in his Sunday trousers. He called them his "ice cream britches," and he would warn you to be careful not to wrinkle them when you climbed on his lap.

Story grew more than 100 varieties of irises and gave them away to folks all over town. He raised chickens and rabbits in the backyard. He loved to tell stories from the front-porch swing at the house where he lived for 53 years.

He was bitten by the stage bug and acted in a number of plays at Macon Little Theatre when it was located downtown. He had several roles opposite Susan Myrick, the *Telegraph* columnist who was friends with Margaret Mitchell and served as a technical adviser for the movie production of "Gone With the Wind" in 1939.

Myrick tried to persuade Story to audition for the part of one of the Tarleton twins in the movie, but he declined. He never traveled far from Macon. In fact, he never owned a car or had a driver's license. He took the city bus to and from work every day.

Mary Ruth remembers running to the bus stop in the afternoon to meet her dad. Her friends would sometimes tag along. They would giggle when he would "ho ho ho," just like Santa Claus, but they never suspected he really was.

Macon's Leonard Grace played Santa for many years himself on stage at Macon Little Theatre's "Holiday Spectacular." Story was his inspiration.

"My father was his insurance agent," said Grace. "When I was about 8 or 9 years old, we went to see Mr. Story. When we left, I told my father that man sounded just like Santa Claus! And he did. He had this smooth, velvety bass voice. It was beautiful."

"He was very believable," said Mary Ruth. "He loved the season. It concerned him when I got older and started having doubts about whether there really was a Santa Claus because I was the youngest of his nine children.

"He told me we were going to test Santa. We poured out some salt on Christmas Eve because reindeer like salt. On Christmas morning, there was a hoof print in the salt. My daddy was a craftsman, a woodworker, and he had made a reindeer hoof out of wood."

She finally blew his cover when she snuck into the kitchen after her bedtime and saw all the letters from children spread across the table. He would stay up late at night, reading them and making notes in the margin.

He then began to allow her to go with him to the radio station on Christmas Eve. She would help out with some of the sound effects — the wind from the North Pole howling in the background and the mischievous elf, Tiny Tim, turning over a chair in the background as he delivered a big sack of mail from Georgia.

Mary Ruth said, to her knowledge, her father never received a dime for playing Santa Claus. It was his gift to the community.

"Everything he did was about making a life, not a living," she said.

He died six weeks after his beloved wife, Lizzie, in 1967. He closed what was his final Christmas Eve broadcast with these words:

"The spirit of Christmas will live as long as good moms and dads live the kind of life God wants us to live. I pray that you will foster that spirit in your daily lives so that my little friends can appreciate why we celebrate this wonderful season of the year."

He may not have been the real St. Nick, but the man was a saint.

The lessons of Eulan

January 8, 2010

Eulan Brown never traveled far beyond his hometown of Reynolds. The corners of his world went to the edges of wherever his bicycle would carry him.

Most folks in Taylor County knew him. He always seemed to be several places at once. Every patch of road was his personal highway — from North Liberty to Whatley Street to Little Vine Road.

He delivered *Grit* newspapers, making 4 cents on each one he sold. He had other odd jobs, too, like mowing people's yards. He usually smelled of sweat, motor oil and fresh-cut grass.

Eulan was a simple fellow, with a wave of close-cropped hair and the calloused hands of a working man. He lived with his mother in an apartment next to the bank. He would talk on his CB radio to every trucker who rolled through Reynolds. His antenna was a mop handle wrapped with telephone wire.

Bruce Goddard remembers Eulan. How could he forget the character he has now made famous?

As a youngster, Bruce and his buddies would sometimes make fun of Eulan. He was an easy target. He had a number of physical problems. He would often lose his balance and crash his bicycle into the ditch. Newspapers in the basket would go flying everywhere.

The boys were a little scared of him, too. They would hear things go bump in the night, and wonder if Eulan was scratching at their bedroom windows.

One day, when he was 12 years old, Bruce was sitting at the lunch counter at Hicks Trussell's grocery store, which served the best hamburgers in town. Before Bruce could take a bite into his pickle, Eulan walked in and sat on the stool next to him.

At first Bruce was frightened. He sat frozen, not saying a word. Then Eulan spoke up. He knew Bruce's name. He asked about his mom and dad, his sister and brothers. He was kind, considerate and caring, not some freak show from a traveling circus.

The next time Bruce saw him wrecked in the ditch, he stopped to help him gather his newspapers.

From that day on, something spoke to his heart.

"I never forgot Eulan Brown," he said. "And I never forgot the lessons I learned from his life."

Eulan died on an August day in 1985. He was 46 years old. Bruce, who was a fourth-generation undertaker at Goddard Funeral Home, served as the funeral director. Eulan was laid to rest at the Mount Olive Church cemetery in Potterville, on a hill rising above the old mill town.

Nobody might have believed that almost 25 years later, Eulan would have his name in the title and his photograph on the cover of Bruce's new book, "The Legacy of Eulan Brown."

Bruce, 55, is now a popular inspirational speaker and humorist who travels the country. He lives in Warner Robins and works in the Macon office of Service Corporation International, the largest single provider of funeral, cremation and cemetery services in North America.

He has spent much of the past three years writing about his adventures in a blog he calls "View from a Hearse" at www.brucegoddard.com.

Many of those wonderful slices of life are about growing up in a small town. They are about being a son, father and now grandfather. In the 241-page collection, he pays tribute to many of the people who shaped his life.

Bruce has an outgoing personality, ongoing curiosity and remarkable powers of observation. That's why there are tales of his many travels — meeting a cab driver in Chicago, a waitress in Tennessee and a shoeshine man at the airport in Atlanta.

His philosophy — both spiritual and Southern-rooted — is taking the time to get to know folks. He seeks the positive in people, then revels in the storytelling.

And then there is the gift of Eulan, a mockingbird who lived in the moment. He never complained. He never quit. He always picked himself up and pulled himself out of the ditch.

It's a powerful message that already has been delivered to a group in Oklahoma City, where Bruce recently gave a speech. The words have been lifted up to Alaska, where a man ordered the book last week.

Part of Eulan Brown still lives on. We should listen.

Absent friends

His words live on

March 14, 2010

There are days when the words float on the page like clouds across the sky.

I do not have to reach to find them because they are there, gifts from above.

And then there are days like today, when I struggle, even though I've known for a long time I would have to write this column.

I'm gonna miss Ol' Boyd.

I will miss his wise counsel, that tough-and-gruff voice of experience in my ear. I will miss the curiosity with which he approached everyday life and the passion with which he wrote about it.

Bill Boyd, who died Tuesday, was blue-collar to the bone and proud of it. The man was not afraid of hard work. He had the miles on his odometer and the ink stains on his shirt to prove it.

He never had a journalism degree. He earned his battle stripes on the field.

He prided himself on being more of a blacksmith than a wordsmith. He rarely reached for the dictionary to try and impress readers with fancy adjectives. In the words of Mark Twain, he never wrote "metropolis" for seven cents when he could get the same price for "city."

Still, he could turn a phrase and keep you nibbling on a story right down to the last crumb.

He would gather 650 words and make you laugh, cry, think and believe in something greater than yourself. His writer's toolbox carried the virtues of the very best. He was a gifted storyteller.

He understood the power of a newspaper story and its capacity to connect.

He became *The Telegraph*'s goodwill ambassador. For 25 years, he was the face at the top of the page, the guy you invited to pull up a chair at the kitchen table.

Ol' Boyd.

We took many trips together. We shared plenty of adventures. We ordered cheeseburgers over lunch counters, and he introduced me to back roads that can't be found on any map.

For several years, our desks were separated only by a small cubicle. I could hear his hearing aids squealing over the top as he tried to adjust them.

Vintage Boyd.

I went to visit him on a recent Sunday afternoon. I told him people were always asking about him. They wanted to know how he was doing.

"They have never forgotten you," I told him.

They never will.

The three people who most influenced my newspaper career — Billy Watson, Harley Bowers and Bill Boyd — are now gone. Heaven must have one heckuva newspaper staff.

It was Billy Watson who once described the subjects of Ol' Boyd's folksy columns as common people who "otherwise get their names in the paper only when they are born, get married or die."

Bill looked for the extraordinary in the ordinary. He wrote about Burma Shave signs and being "fat, dumb and happy down in Georgia."

He penned anthems to little ladies who kept the oven at 350 degrees, baking cookies for the hungry and the heartsick.

He befriended nearly every animal species on the planet, including his pal Muley (Durwood Rainey) and the legendary Goat Man (Charles "Ches" McCartney).

He rocked on front porches with aging soldiers who told him they had never been on an airplane or seen the ocean until their country called them to serve. He understood what it meant to wear the uniform. He was a Marine himself.

Semper Fi.

Readers got to know his family — a cast of characters who lived inside the margins of his columns.

There was Marvalene, the devoted wife of 43 years, and Joe and Wanda — the now-grown kids who "adopted" him.

He had an abiding respect for seniors. He drew strength from listening to their life experiences. He started the "Bill Boyd's Over-80 Birthday Club" parties at the Macon Coliseum. It soon became the "75-and-Over Happy Birthday Club," a feature that still runs in *The Telegraph* every Sunday.

It's sad to realize he died before he got to see his own name listed. He would have turned 75 on Aug. 7.

Bill had an appreciation for the untold stories he would find when he visited nursing homes. Walking in the door was like opening a history book. He once told me those folks didn't want his job, his money, his car or his wife. All they wanted was his time. And he gave it freely.

He drew inspiration from writing about people who had overcome obstacles — an illness or injury or just plain down on their luck. He encouraged them. He often held their hands through their struggles. He rejoiced at their triumphs. He cried at their funerals.

Bill always had a lot of explaining to do, how the son of a sharecropper from Okmulgee, Okla., landed on the banks of the Ocmulgee River in Georgia.

Another guy by the name of William Boyd was an actor who gained fame as Hopalong Cassidy. The movie character got his nickname after being shot in the leg outside a bank in 1935, the same year Ol' Boyd was born.

There wasn't a job at this newspaper he couldn't handle. He cut his teeth snapping photographs and pounding out sports stories on deadline. In the days before cell phones, he could dictate a breaking news story from a phone booth in Cochran or Thomaston in the middle of the night.

The greatest journalistic lesson I learned from Bill Boyd was to put a human face on every story. He once spent the night at the Macon Rescue Mission, along with several homeless men, so he could better understand the piece he was writing.

He took a job as a carnival worker at the state fair. He volunteered to babysit 2-year-old triplet boys and wrote about his experience. He spent so much time with the Mennonite farmers in Macon County, he could have had his own plow.

I am convinced he knew every hole-in-the-wall restaurant from Ocilla to Flovilla. He tracked down stories at barber shops, truck stops, pool halls and Wednesday night church suppers. He hit all the Saturday yard sales, too. And he didn't need a GPS to locate nearly every flea market from here to Ohio.

When he retired in 1998, I knew I was stepping into some mighty big shoes. As a parting gift, he left me with a long, wooden dowel with a spaghetti spoon drilled onto the end. It had been given to him by a loyal reader — a homemade back scratcher. I still use it every day.

After he was diagnosed with prostate cancer three years ago this month, he told me the Boyd family always had been more concerned about the quality of life than the quantity.

"You get to the point where you live as good a life as you can right up to the last," he said. "There is no fear of death on my part. It comes to everybody."

His words live on.

Bo Whaley kept 'em grinning

July 28, 2006

I still keep his note framed in my office.

"Welcome to the wonderful world of book writing."

It is dated March 20, 1998, and signed by Bo Whaley, the legendary newspaper columnist from Dublin.

I had just published my first book, *True Gris*, and Bo was welcoming me to the fraternity. He was familiar with the lines. He, too, had experienced the joy.

His byline appeared on more than 1,800 columns for *The Courier Herald* in Dublin. He was the author of more than a dozen books. I'm not sure of the exact number. It didn't say in his obituary that appeared after he died Saturday at age 79.

Long before there was a Jeff Foxworthy, Bo was cranking out redneck humor across the universe. Just look at his book titles: *The Official Redneck Handbook. Field Guide to Southern Women. Redneckin' Made Easy. Why the South Lost the War. Kudzu Don't Cover Everything. How to Love Yankees with a Clear Conscience.*

You could hardly walk into a Cracker Barrel without seeing a book bearing Bo Whaley's name in the gift shop. He served as master of ceremonies during the early days of East Dublin's annual Redneck Games.

Ludlow Porch, the Atlanta radio personality, once said when Bo wrote about the South, he made you "want to hide behind a Stuckey's and mug a Yankee."

Bo was a friend and mentor who helped me grow into my role as a columnist. He had me as a guest on his radio show. One afternoon in Dublin, we could hardly eat lunch because so many folks were coming up to shake his hand.

He once snuck me backstage at Theatre Dublin to meet world champion fiddle player Randy Howard. It was Howard's final performance in May 2000. A few weeks later, Howard died of cancer.

Bo was born the son of a preacher man, a dozen miles east of Dublin in the Johnson County community of Scott. He claimed to have "fought like hell in World War II but the authorities caught him and drafted him anyway."

He swallowed every drop of life. He played minor league baseball. He was a high school coach, principal and history teacher. He was an FBI special agent for 20 years. He sold insurance and managed the restaurant at the Holiday Inn. He loved riding motorcycles and taught Sunday School at the Methodist church.

Bo had the perfect dynamics for a columnist. He was a self-professed "people watcher." He considered himself an "authority on nothing with an opinion on everything."

He claimed to have set the English language back a hundred years. He might not always have issued the right words, but he was never at a loss for them.

Bo engaged his readers. He made them laugh. He made them weep. There are desk drawers all over Laurens County full of clipped columns that carry the name of the late, great Bo Whaley.

He once wrote a column where he listed a few things he wished he "could have done."

He said he wished he could have eaten fried chicken with Col. Sanders and watched him lick his fingers. He wished he could grab the wheel of a Greyhound bus and tell the driver to relax and leave the driving to him.

He wished he could dance — up close — with Dolly Parton as the band played the "Tennessee Waltz."

But most of all, he said, he wished he could hear his daddy preach one more time.

The day she was remembered

July 10, 2009

There was no gold casket in the sanctuary at First Baptist Church on Thursday morning, only a gold picture frame.

There were three dozen roses and two candles at the altar. A needlepoint bookmark, made by Ruth Cheves, rested against the pages of an open Bible.

There were no TV cameras on the steps, no paparazzi at the top of Poplar Street. Nobody pulled out a Blackberry to dispatch details of the funeral on "Twitter."

There was no hearse because there was no casket, gold or otherwise, at Ruth Cheves' memorial service.

In her will, she had requested her body be sent to Mercer's medical school to be used in research.

I sat in the third pew, with my wife and mother, and listened to the tributes, scripture readings, beautiful music and heartfelt eulogy.

If only the world could have seen this, too, I thought.

Four days ago, the planet paused to watch Michael Jackson's memorial service. About 30.9 million viewers tuned in — more than for Ronald Reagan's funeral but less than Princess Di's — as if it were a ratings contest.

Only about 100 people attended Ruth's service. About 20,000 (out of 1.6 million requests) had the required tickets for Jackson.

I'm sure Miss Ruth never would have approved of turning her farewell into a box-office attraction, anyway. She had everything already planned and scripted, from the songs sung and scriptures read. To the very end, she was set in her ways.

I did not watch the memorial for the "King of Pop." Although I applaud his humanitarian efforts, his rather bizarre lifestyle was hardly worthy of hero worship. (Frankly, he lost me after the Jackson Five.)

He was, however, an extraordinary talent. I've never seen anybody move like M.J. in his "Captain EO" video in 3-D at Disney World.

Miss Ruth never married and lived alone. I once served as her deacon. For years, my family invited her to join us at Thanksgiving.

She was born in 1918, grew up in Fort Hill, went to school at Fort Hawkins and joined First Baptist Church when she was 6 years old.

She never caused a ripple of trouble, except for some mischief the time she and a few childhood friends waxed the trolley tracks with soap, causing a slight derailment.

(I still think they will let her into heaven when the rail ... er, roll ... is called up yonder.)

Ruth was a pioneer in working with special needs children. Her studies in the field were among the first published in the U.S. She spent 16 years in the Christianity department at Mercer.

She was an avid reader and served as our church librarian. She loved crossword puzzles and classical music. She never needed a dial on her radio. She kept it planted on FM-89.7, the local public radio station.

In 1974, she was the only Georgia woman (and one of 132 in the country) asked to contribute a needlepoint panel for the United Nations in New York. She put 40,000 stitches into her square, which represented Russia.

No, I wasn't much of a Michael Jackson fan, but I did belong to Ruth's fan club. Her memorial service replicated the way she lived her life. No fanfare. More substance than glorification.

She was one of those saints who lived her life, served her Lord and would have been proud of the way she was remembered.

The man behind B.C.

April 11, 2007

Johnny Hart first found his way through their door.

Sure, he had a New York accent and put sugar on his grits. But Wiley and Fran Baxter could forgive him for that.

After all, he made them laugh. He entertained their children with his drawings. He fell in love with Fran's sister and became part of the family.

Next, he found his way onto their walls.

Over the years, they framed his caricatures of prehistoric cavemen and hung them from their sheetrock. Who needs a Picasso or a Rembrandt when you can have an original Hart?

"Everywhere we look in our house, we see something of Johnny's," said Wiley.

That will never change, even in these numbing hours after Hart's death four days ago.

Although the grief is overwhelming, at least they can wrap themselves in the happy memories of their brother-in-law, better known as the man who created the comic strip "B.C."

Many of those seeds were planted right here in Macon more than a half century ago. Hart was a photographer for the public information office at Robins Air Force Base in the early 1950s. He met his future wife, Bobby, at a dance on the base. She was a lab technician at the old Macon Hospital.

We must turn back the pages even more to connect all the dots.

Wiley grew up in L.A., better known in his neck of the woods as Lower Alabama. Fran was from Boston, but not the big city in Massachusetts. Boston is a small community in Thomas County near Thomasville.

The Baxters were married June 28, 1942. Wiley was sent to Europe with the 3rd Infantry during World War II. He lost his right leg while engaged in heavy fighting in France. An artillery shell hit his bunker, killing the two men in the bunker with him.

Wiley was discharged in 1947 after spending more than two years in military hospitals. The Baxters moved to Macon in 1951, where he began working with munitions at the Naval Ordnance Plant on Guy Paine Road.

Fran's younger sister, Bobby Hatcher, was already living on Pine Street in Macon, not far from the hospital. When the Baxters got an apartment on Cherry Avenue, near Montpelier, Bobby moved in with them.

Fran won't ever forget the night Bobby came home from the dance at the base.

"She told me she had met the cutest boy," Fran said. "That's all I heard about. Then she brought Johnny over to meet us. The minute I saw him, I liked him."

Wiley wasn't as impressed with his future brother-in-law. He barely looked up from his newspaper when Hart introduced himself.

"Johnny used to say he was going to win Wiley over," said Fran. "And he did. They became like brothers."

They found common ground in two of their shared passions — fishing and New York Yankees baseball.

Hart didn't have to work nearly as hard to gain the approval of the Baxters' three children — Herky, 6, Hank, 4, and 3-year-old Suzie.

He would draw silly things for them.

"They adored him," said Fran. "As soon as Johnny walked in the door, Hank would take him a piece of paper and a pencil. And I would say: 'Let him sit down first!'"

The Harts were married April 26, 1952, in the chapel at Robins. As newlyweds, they lived in an upstairs apartment of a house on Georgia Avenue in Macon. The house is no longer there. It was located down the hill from the old Wesleyan Conservatory (now the main post office) and up the hill from the old Pig 'n Whistle drive-in restaurant (now the site of Church's Fried Chicken.)

It was in the apartment that Hart began to doodle and dream up some of his earliest ideas for comic strips. After he returned from Korea, he and Bobby moved to her family's farm in south Georgia.

He eventually sold his first freelance cartoon to the *Saturday Evening Post*. He admired the work of "Peanuts" creator Charles Schulz. Because Hart loved to draw cavemen, a friend jokingly suggested that he start a strip that took place in prehistoric times.

On Feb. 17, 1958, the day before Hart turned 27, "B.C." made its debut in the *New York Herald Tribune* and 30 other newspapers. Two years later, he created "The Wizard of Id" with fellow cartoonist Brant Parker.

Hart based many of his "B.C." characters on family members and friends. Among the more prominent was Wiley. Since Wiley had lost his leg in the war, Hart honored him by making him the peg-legged poet and assistant coach of the football and baseball teams.

The main characters often look up the definition of words in "Wiley's Dictionary" on top of a large rock.

Actually, the real Wiley is a man of few words — except when you get him talking about Auburn football or the Yankees baseball team. And the grubby comic character Wiley, who has an aversion to bathing, is the opposite of the 84-year-old Baxter, who is clean and well-groomed.

Hart created the main character, "B.C.," to most closely represent himself. Bobby was the inspiration for the "Cute Chick."

Peter, Thor, Grog and Clumsy Carp were all composites of others Hart chose to immortalize on the comics page.

Bobby and Fran's mother, the late Janie Hatcher, was a small, thin woman. But Fran is convinced she became the model for the "Fat Broad" after Hart once watched her kill a snake with a stick.

Fran's middle son, Hank, has an ant named after him in the strip. Her oldest son, Herky, who works at Robins as his uncle once did, said he believes Uncle Johnny created the pig, Oynque (pronounced "Oink"), to characterize him.

"B.C." appears in more than 1,300 papers worldwide, including *The Telegraph*, and reaches more than 100 million readers. Hart's combined work on both "B.C." and "The Wizard of Id" inspired *Time* magazine to call him the world's "most syndicated comic author." In 1999, *The Washington Post* hailed Hart as "the most widely read writer on earth."

The shocking news came this past Saturday from Ninevah, N.Y. Hart died of an apparent heart attack. He was working at his story board in his studio overlooking a large lake.

Bobby found him when she returned from grocery shopping. Hart had been preparing a Sunday School lesson for Easter Sunday. He taught a class of high school students at Ninevah Presbyterian Church. Funeral services are Friday.

"He was one of those people you never expect to pass away," Fran said. "Everybody who ever met him, loved him. He was a very special person in our lives."

She said his daughters, Patti and Perri, gave their father a trombone two months ago for his 76th birthday. Fran said she told Hart she was looking forward to hearing him play "76 Trombones."

Some of Hart's loyal fans found irony that his death came one day before Easter. In March 1996, *The Los Angeles Times* refused to run several B.C. strips containing Christian messages during Lent.

His Palm Sunday strip featured Wiley resting against a tree, holding his stone tablet and writing a poem called "The Suffering Prince."

Then, on Easter Sunday 2001, Hart took the heat again when the cartoon depicted a menorah (a seven-branched Jewish candelabrum) being transformed into a cross with the text of Jesus Christ's last words.

Fran said she doubted Hart would have ever retired. "That comic strip was like a child to him," she said. "He brought it into this world. He wasn't going to give it up."

She expects Hart's most recent book, "50 Years of B.C." still will be published in October. The golden anniversary of "B.C." is in February 2008.

This is what Wiley wrote for his section of the book:

"Johnny Hart is my brother-in-law, my dear friend and Yankees buddy. I feel honored to be a member of his comic strip. B.C. has brought much pleasure to my family, especially my grandkids, who enjoy seeing Papa in the funny paper. God bless you, Mr. Johnny. I love you."

Making a difference

Not your average Papa Joe

June 21, 2009

There are many days when Papa Joe Bullard practically meets himself coming and going on the road.

That's when there are almost as many miles as there are minutes in the day. He must keep his eye on the gas gauge in the Taurus so he won't have to make an unscheduled stop somewhere.

He shuttles young people from The Methodist Home for Children and Youth to their jobs, summer camps and various other appointments.

He tries to keep all their arrivals and departures in his head.

It works. Most of the time.

Occasionally, he misses one.

"Oh, I've forgotten a few," he said, laughing. "But I always go back and get 'em."

It certainly brings new meaning to "no child left behind."

If anyone can be forgiven, it is Papa Joe Bullard — a living, breathing sermon of a man.

They never forget him.

He is an institution at the Methodist Home — a gentleman admired and respected for his boundless energy, enthusiasm and tireless work ethic.

He is 75 years old, too, with no signs of easing his foot off the gas pedal.

"The head is gray, but the heart is young," he said.

That heart, appropriately enough, arrived in the world on Valentine's Day in 1934.

It has not only stayed young, but it also beats as one with the children who must come here to rebuild their broken hearts.

He has been a father figure to hundreds of young people. He is both a patriot and a patriarch. And he understands it takes a village to raise them.

"It's like soup," he said. "You can't just put in peas. You have to have a lot of ingredients working together."

The Methodist Home has a Daddy Rick, the nickname given to the Rev. Rick Lanford.

Behind the scenes, there is a Papa Joe, too.

He's not your average Joe, either.

A few years ago, his wife, Shirley, cooked some of her famous spaghetti and took it over to the home.

He can't remember which one of the boys started calling him Papa Joe that night, but the name stuck like dried pasta to the side of the dish.

It is a term of endearment.

"Kids are honest," he said. "If you're a bum, they'll let you know it."

His own father was never really a part of his life. He was dropped off at his aunt's house in Jamaica, Long Island.

His aunt and uncle taught him the meaning of elbow grease and the value of sticking his nose in a book. He was in church every time the doors were open.

He spent three years in the Air Force and another 27 in the Army. He met Shirley, who was working in New York, and they married in 1964.

Shirley's apron strings ran all the way back to Macon. So that, along with a huge helping of Southern hospitality and a couple of bites of Fincher's Barbecue, were enough to lure him just above the gnat line.

A paratrooper, he was assigned to two tours of duty in Vietnam. His own children — Joseph Jr. and Stephanie — were born while he was 9,000 miles away in Southeast Asia.

He never got to pace outside the delivery room door.

But he has held them dear ever since.

He spent three years as an ROTC instructor at Georgia Tech, and eventually planted his feet at Central High School in Macon. He served as an ROTC instructor with David Carter, a former Macon mayor and longtime city councilman.

He later met Steve Rumford, president and CEO of the Methodist Home, who was so impressed he offered him a part-time position as a weekend "house parent."

Although Papa Joe retired from teaching in 1998, his teaching days were far from over. At the Methodist Home, he now serves as "college coordinator," helping young people prepare for college.

He tutors them, helps coach them on taking the standardized tests, travels with them on their college visits and then sees them at least once a month after they start college.

He has so many moving parts, folks at the Methodist Home can hardly keep up with him. He is part chauffeur, part cook and bottle-washer and full-time friend and disciplinarian.

The kids have his number on their speed dials. And they use it.

"I try to set an example," he said. "When you see them grow, you grow, too. I tell the boys to pull up their pants and open the doors for ladies. I want them to have manners, to say 'yes sir' and 'no sir.' "

He is not mean. He just means what he says.

He teaches them to show others the same care and compassion that has been demonstrated to them. That's why the youngsters will sometimes ask him to stop so they can give the last dollar in their pockets to a homeless man. Or head back to the Methodist Home, so they can run into the kitchen and get a plate of food for a woman who is starving on the street corner.

One day, Papa Joe dreams of hiking the entire Appalachian Trail from Georgia to Maine.

But for now, he saves all those steps for this journey.

"I tell people I want to die on the job," he said. "I want them to put me in the (Methodist Home's) van, and roll me up to the cafeteria and have the service right there."

He laughed and said he'll probably have to remind Bentley and Sons about the discount they promised on his casket.

Stick around for a while, Papa Joe. We need more like you.

Oh yeah, I almost forgot.

Happy Father's Day.

Jesus Dollars keep his memory alive

September 24, 2006

The letter crossed my desk last week, a heartfelt note from a reader.

She enclosed a photograph of a 3-year-old boy jumping in a pile of hay, his arms outstretched.

Below was the name of William Christopher Bush III.

Born: May 15, 1979.

Died: Aug. 7, 2001.

The picture was taken almost 25 years ago in an Alabama field by Will's mother, Terry Everett. Terry has been a public defender in Houston County for the past 17 years.

The picture remains one of Terry's favorite photos of Will as a child. And the reader, a close friend of the family, said it perfectly captured Will's "zest for life."

Enclosed with the note and photograph was a $1 bill. There was a large "J" inside the Federal Reserve Bank seal. There was a smaller "J" at the beginning of the serial number.

I realized I had been sent what has become known in the area as a "Jesus Dollar."

It was one of many letters and e-mails I received after my Monday column about two retired Macon men, Larry Myers and Kenneth Dobson. They had started a "Jesus Dollar" ministry to help needy people with everything from hospital bills, groceries and car payments.

Myers had told me he first learned about "Jesus Dollars" after reading a story written by Chris Morrison in "His Voice," a Christian news publication in Warner Robins.

A young man with cancer had asked for his $20 allowance in $1 bills. He then used the "J" bills to help others and perform random acts of kindness.

However, Myers could not remember the name of the young man.

Now I know. It was Will Bush.

It made the story hit closer to home. I had written a column about Will in July 2000, a little more than a year before he died. It was an inspiring story about him meeting former Atlanta Braves first baseman Andres Galarraga, who also was battling cancer.

At the time, Will was a junior at the University of Georgia. During his senior year at Warner Robins High School, he was diagnosed with synovial sarcoma—a rare, soft-tissue cancer.

Will began his "J Dollar" campaign that same summer he met Galarraga. He was too sick to return to classes at UGA in the fall, so his new ministry became one of the focal points of his life.

"When he was in college, I would give him $20 every week," said Terry. "It wasn't really an allowance, but it was money he didn't have to account for. He could spend it however he wanted.

"After he got so sick and couldn't go back to school, I didn't have the heart to stop giving him the $20. Then, one day, he asked me to give it to him in $1 bills."

Will explained how he was going to earmark every bill that started with the letter "J." It would be designated as a "Jesus Dollar" and used to serve others."

The "J" is actually a symbol that represents the 10th District, Federal Reserve Bank in Kansas City.

But to Will, it stood for "Jesus."

"Even when he kept getting weaker and weaker, he told me that no matter how sick he was, he still felt he could help somebody," Terry said.

"God's not finished with me yet," Will told her. "There's still something I can do."

She watched him put those dollars into motion during the last 12 months of his life. At the funeral home, people she had never met came up and told her ways Will had helped them.

Sometimes he had given a donation. Other times he bought food. He once sent flowers to someone's mother in a nursing home. Another time he simply offered an encouraging word to a young black man who told Terry: "He would always talk to me when no one else would."

Terry made a promise to herself to carry on Will's ministry. She began keeping every "J" dollar that floated her way. It became her special fund. She now carries a few "J" dollars with her wherever she goes.

During the past five years, the money has been used to purchase toys and school supplies for children and buy McDonald's gift cards for homeless people. It assisted a young man studying for the ministry. It has gone to fund research for cancer and to help victims of Hurricane Katrina.

Often, Terry makes her contribution in the amount of $22. It is symbolic of the number of years Will spent on this earth. He was 22 when he died.

Although Terry has done it without a lot of fanfare, word of the ministry has spread through grass roots and word of mouth.

A number of times, people have wanted to give her a history lesson about the "J" dollars.

"I already know," she tells them politely. "Will was my son!"

There are times she believes that son is looking down on her with a clipboard in his hand.

He's grading me," she said, laughing.

No, there can never be enough "J" dollars.

"When I grew up in north Alabama, we had what we called 'making up money,' " she said.

If someone was down on their luck, people would rally together, pass the hat and make up the difference with Washingtons, Lincolns and Jeffersons.

That's the way it worked. In some places, it still works that way.

"Will would be very happy about all this if he were here," Terry said. "But it's not so much the dollar amount. It gives people a chance to interact with each other and to show compassion.

"When you lose a child, you always wonder if he will be remembered," she said. "Of course, I will never forget him. But what about other people? He was only 22. He didn't graduate from college, get a job, get married or become a father. This was his contribution. It lets me know he will never be forgotten."

'I hope to God I ain't too late'

November 1, 2009

MCRAE — Rhett Lee had forgotten his drink at lunch that Friday, so he went back through the cafeteria line at Telfair County Middle School.

He had just settled in his seat when his friend, Allie Holland, punched him in the arm.

"I didn't think much about it," he said. "She hits me all the time. I knew she wasn't kidding when she almost broke my arm."

He turned to see her face flush with fear. Her skin was a shade of purple. Her eyes were red and filled with tears.

Allie was desperately trying to speak, but the words would not come. She made a gesture by holding her hands to her throat.

She was choking.

Rhett is 13 years old with a birthday coming up in December. He has known Allie since they used to hang out in diapers. They are in every class together at Telfair Middle. They killed their first deer while hunting on the same day.

Allie had taken a bite of hamburger steak. She said it was too hot to chew but she was trying to show good manners and not spit it out. Suddenly, it lodged in her windpipe. She was terrified.

Rhett sprung from his chair and grabbed her from behind. She is taller than he is, but he lifted her with the strength and adrenaline of at least a dozen eighth-graders.

He wasn't exactly sure what to do next. After all, he had never performed the Heimlich maneuver. But he had seen it demonstrated on television. He had studied it on a wall poster at a local restaurant.

Rhett has suffered from severe asthma all his life, so he understands what it's like not to be able to catch your breath.

One thought crossed Rhett's mind when he grabbed Allie, clenched his fists against her abdomen and squeezed.

"I hope to God I ain't too late."

A teacher, Elaine Page, noticed Rhett had gotten out of his assigned seat. But she did not immediately realize she was witnessing a young hero in action.

"He is always so playful," she said. "When I first saw him jumping up and down behind her, I told him to sit down."

Rhett's quick actions saved his friend. Although they were able to giggle about it later, they also have been giving thanks to a multitude of guardian angels for watching over them.

"I was shaking," said Rhett. "I could barely finish my lunch. I don't think I calmed down until halfway through fifth period."

Rhett's mom, Wendy Lee, teaches gifted students at Telfair Middle School. She did not learn about her son's heroics until later.

She said he was quiet on the way home from school that day a few weeks ago, so she asked him what he was thinking.

"Mama," he said. "Allie could be gone right now."

Wendy felt nine years of emotions come rushing back.

"It's something that is a part of our lives every day," she said. "We are keenly aware of things like this. Rhett understands how quickly life can be taken away."

The grief keeps Wendy and her husband, Jonsey, and the rest of her family in its grips. She wears a silver necklace around her neck. It is a figure of her 15-month-old daughter, Sailor Kate, in a hat and beads.

Sailor Kate died in February 2001 when Wendy's father, Clif "Randy" Yawn, accidentally backed over her with his car in the driveway. Rhett, who was then 5 years old, witnessed the tragedy.

Randy and his wife, Betty, were taking Rhett and Sailor Kate to the cemetery to place flowers on the grave of Betty's mother, who had died a week earlier. Marie "Mama Rie" Fowler had a grocery store in Helena for more than 40 years.

The day of Sailor's funeral, there were pink bows and teddy bears spread across every corner of the county. Some businesses even closed their doors.

In big cities, death often comes and goes without serving notice. But in small communities like McRae and Helena, the sadness paces every front porch and sits together in every church pew.

Rhett got his name partly because of his grandmother's love of "Gone With the Wind." Sailor was given her name because her grandfather was an old Navy man who loved anything nautical, even though he lived in landlocked McRae.

Randy — his grandkids called him "Poppy" — was one of Telfair's most respected citizens. He worked as a nurse at the Veterans Administration Hospital in Dublin.

He was commissioned to carve a replica of the Statue of Liberty that has become a landmark in downtown McRae. He did other work as well, creating an Indian from a tree in nearby Little Ocmulgee State Park.

He later built a memorial gazebo in the driveway where the accident took place. He filled it with carvings of ducks, hearts and baby angels.

Randy lost his battle with cancer two years ago, but ask anybody in this town and they'll tell you he really died of a broken heart.

Rhett was close to his grandfather. "Poppy" had used his medical knowledge to walk Rhett through what he should do in the event of an asthma attack. Wendy is convinced her dad might also have coached Rhett about what to do if someone stopped breathing or was choking.

Rhett is outgoing, athletic and loves the outdoors. His mother compares him to Huck Finn.

He also has what she calls "impeccable balance." Randy once bought a unicycle at a yard sale. Rhett picked it up one day, knocked off the rust and learned to ride it. He did so well he advanced to a "giraffe" unicycle. It is 5 feet off the ground — as tall as he is. He has to climb a ladder to mount it. No broken bones yet, either.

A year after Sailor Kate's death, Wendy gave birth to another daughter, Randi Chele, who is now 7. They named her Randi, after Wendy's father.

In two weeks, Sailor Kate would have celebrated her 10th birthday. Wendy has seen the circle of life take shape around her. She and her family started the Sailor Kate Ministry (www.sailorkate.com).

The ministry sends homemade quilts to families who have experienced similar tragedies. It also donates "Sailor's Snuggles" teddy bears to law enforcement agencies, hospitals and children's homes.

Wendy has shared her testimony in a number of local churches. This past spring, during Mother's Day, Wendy traveled with her mother and sister-in-law to California to present a quilt to a grieving mother.

The woman had returned from work one day and accidentally ran over and killed her 5-year-old daughter, who was riding her tricycle in the driveway.

Wendy has always considered Allie to be "a member of our family."

She hugs her son every day and tells him: "God put you in the right place."

Give my regards to Broadway

July 30, 2006

His nickname is Broadway. His last name is Cotton. And he lives on Cherry Street.

Willie "Broadway" Cotton can hardly drive his truck, "Old Faithful" — the 1983 Ford with two bullet holes in the side — in any direction downtown without seeing his name on a street sign.

He has traveled broken roads to get here. Easy Street? Never saw it on the map.

If you ask some of the old folks at the Dempsey Apartments, they will tell you Broadway isn't just a resident. He's a saint.

Up on the ninth floor, where the sounds of trains float through open windows and electric fans push and sway the air, Broadway is only a phone call or a door knock away.

At 5-foot-2, it is easy to miss him.

At 292 pounds, it is not.

On any given day, he takes as many as a half-dozen residents to the doctor, the grocery store, the bank. He's a one-man courier, a cheerful chauffeur.

They call him when they're sick, lonely or when they fall in the bathroom in the middle of the night.

He delivers their lunches for Meals on Wheels. He fetches them Dr Peppers from the drink machine.

If someone doesn't have money to buy a newspaper, he dips into his emergency fund — a row of change on the ledge beneath his window sill.

He is 65 years old, lives on his disability checks and doesn't hide from his checkered past. He speaks openly about the time he spent in prison and when he was addicted to crack cocaine.

"I lost everything," he said, his voice tilting. "Even the clothes on my back."

He quit school in the fifth grade to help his single-parent mother put food on the table. They lived on First Street Lane. He dreamed of becoming a professional wrestler. He would head for the rail yard to lift the only set of weights he knew — the wheels from the railroad cars.

He was tagged with the nickname "Broadway" after years of shining shoes at the Paramount Barber Shop on Broadway.

He bounced to other jobs, where his only wealth was experience. He worked at the Douglass Theatre, repaired shoes, poured concrete, raised scaffolding, pulled cloth in the cotton mills, and worked as a custodian and a grave digger.

Seven years ago, his niece, Cynthia Cotton, took him to church at Lizzie Chapel Baptist, where he got a fresh start.

"God was somebody I needed, but I didn't know how to get in touch with him," he said.

His life began again in 1999 A.D. The A.D. stands for After Dempsey. He attended a chapel service in the apartment building's basement on a Thursday night, stood up and gave his testimony.

He told them about Broadway — who he was and the dreams he had stuffed away.

It was a confession, warts and all. It was a promise, too. He vowed to help those who could not help themselves. Folks like Mary Sue Jackson, who wears oxygen tubes around her neck like silver lockets.

"He's about my best friend in the whole world," she said.

He takes out the trash and makes his rounds every night before bed. Sometimes folks offer to help out with a little gas money, but he mostly runs Old Faithful on "trust and energy."

The Rev. A.E. English, who died last year at age 102, once gave him a silver dollar and told him to keep it in his wallet and he would never go broke.

I'll give my regards to Broadway any day.

Giving him a leg to stand on

October 4, 2009

MARIETTA — This is the story of how three special people came together.

It is a story of faith and compassion. It is a story of hope.

The characters are two physicians and a 7-year-old Iraqi boy named "Babou." It is the tale of a man who never gave up on his dream of becoming a doctor, a seasoned marathon runner and a child who could barely lift his foot to walk across the room.

It spans three generations, two cultures, almost 7,000 miles and 4 inches of a little boy's left leg.

It is a story that has changed lives.

I don't believe in coincidences. Albert Einstein once said coincidences are merely those times "when God chooses to remain anonymous."

So it was no coincidence that Dr. Bill Terrell was introduced to Dr. G.B. Espy this past January. Although they were both physicians practicing medicine just a few miles apart in Marietta, their paths had never crossed.

Terrell, 46, is an orthopedic surgeon who grew up in Macon. Espy is still delivering babies and running in marathons at age 74.

A chance meeting? I think not.

No, I don't really believe it was a coincidence that Espy, while out on one of his runs, fell and busted both of his knees. And that when he went for an appointment at Pinnacle Orthopedics, his regular doctor had been called out to see about a case at nearby Kennestone Hospital.

That's how Espy ended up in Terrell's office, where he couldn't help but notice all the certificates on the wall. Terrell was well-traveled and well-trained in his field.

In fact, he was recognized as one of only 15 doctors in the world qualified to perform a special kind of deformity correction surgery and limb-lengthening known as Ilizarov, a technique developed by a Russian doctor.

Of course, not everyone has a need for that kind of specialized procedure.

But Espy knew a kid with a big smile who did. His name was Mohammed Mustafa, and everybody called him "Babou."

Terrell saved Babou's left leg.

Along the way, Babou stole Terrell's heart.

He arrived special delivery, all 44 pounds and 45 inches of him. He had been fighting the fury of infections in his leg since he was 2 years old.

His leg was severely infected and 4 inches shorter than his right. He had surgery a dozen times back in Iraq, and the doctors there were prepared to amputate the leg at his hip.

Espy had traveled to Iraq for humanitarian work. He had learned about Babou through a missionary named Heather Mercer, who was there helping the Kurdish people of Iraq. With assistance from the First Baptist Church of Woodstock, Espy arranged to bring Babou and his father, Kader, to the U.S. from their village in northern Iraq.

At the time, Espy was unaware of a physician who could help Babou.

But he took a spill, and his unexpected tumble landed him in Terrell's office.

He had found his man.

Terrell performed the five-hour surgery in June, cutting away the dead bone at both ends, then stabilizing Babou's leg with a rod and special brace.

This week, Babou will begin the nine-month process of turning a screw on the brace with a wrench 1 millimeter each day to begin lengthening the bone. Over time, there are hopes it can be increased at least 3 inches.

By next summer, maybe he won't wobble any more. He and his father can return to Iraq and be reunited with his mother and three brothers.

Babou does not know how it feels to run and play with the other children.

Over the summer, the story caught the attention of a local newspaper in Marietta and an Atlanta television station.

Through all the media publicity, Terrell was quick to point out he stands on the shoulders of others.

He may have a degree in medicine, but he holds a Ph.D. in modesty. He also gave credit to the big boss upstairs.

"I shine from reflected light," he said. "I have a lot of good people around me. One of my favorite quotations is what Ben Franklin wrote in *Poor Richard's Almanac.* 'God heals, and the doctor takes the fees.'"

Terrell always wanted to be a doctor, and he received plenty of support from his parents, Dean and Nina Terrell, who still live in Macon, and sister, Ruth.

He wondered if it would ever happen, though.

When he was 15, he worked at Wansley's Texaco Station at the corner of Vineville and Holt avenues. He pumped gas, checked oil and cleaned windshields.

One of his heroes was the late W.O. "Spike" Williams Jr., a Macon doctor who, for more than 50 years, organized father-son fishing trips to St. Marks, Fla., every spring.

Williams would bring his Chevy Blazer, one of the first SUVs in Macon, to the gas station, and Terrell developed a friendship with the good doctor.

"I admired him," Terrell said. "He worked hard, played hard, loved what he did and helped other people."

As a teenager, Terrell coveted a job working at The Medical Center of Central Georgia but was convinced most of those jobs "went to doctor's kids." Although his father was a pharmaceutical salesman, that apparently didn't qualify.

After he was not hired, he asked when he could re-apply for the next year. He marked his calendar for Dec. 9 at 9 a.m. and showed up at 6 a.m. After completing another application, he wandered around outside the hospital. A man stopped to see if he was lost. "Who are you looking for?" the man asked.

"I'll know him when I see him," said Terrell.

The man was the late Lamar Taylor, who was an administrator with the hospital. It wasn't long before Terrell had a job scrubbing floors in the operating room.

He worked his way through the ranks, doing whatever tasks he was told to do whenever he was told to do it. He often had a front-row seat observing doctors, nurses and other medical staff members. He was drawn to those who were passionate about their work.

He affirmed his life's calling when he was moved to the orthopedic operating room. The action didn't move nearly as quickly as it did in the emergency room, but he was fascinated with the premise.

"They didn't just treat people," he said. "They fixed them."

He now tells other orthopedists he is not competing with them. In fact, he doesn't mind taking their worst cases.

Still an avid car enthusiast, he often talks in automotive terms. He wants them to send him their wrecks.

That is why his workload is among the most challenging. And he considers Babou's situation one of the "most severe I've ever seen."

By spring, he hopes Babou will be able to return home. He would give anything to watch him greet his mother on two good legs.

Just another coincidence, I guess.

You never stop being an angel

March 9, 2008

There are many things Betsy Cleveland remembers about her daddy.

How she sat in his lap as a little girl. How proud he was the day she got married. How his grandchildren all called him "B-da-B."

Bobby Butler was a wonderful man, full of love and life. I count myself among those honored to have known him. He was a friendly, engaging and well-respected insurance agent in Barnesville.

For all of Betsy's joyful memories, there was also sadness in watching her father's long struggle with stomach cancer. He was only 58 when he died on a spring day three years ago, just as the dogwoods were blooming.

Through it all, he never stopped teaching her. And she never stopped learning.

Betsy and her mother, Linda, would take him for his chemotherapy treatments at Emory Healthcare in Atlanta. They would wait with him and hold his hand. He was blessed to have them there to take care of him.

One day, in the chemo room, a woman arrived for her treatment. She was alone.

"She was like a skeleton," said Betsy. "I looked over at my dad and tears were streaming down his face."

"Pray for that lady," he told his daughter.

And they did.

Betsy never could erase that image. It bothered her when she realized many patients have to go down that difficult road with little or no support.

So she typed "helping people undergoing chemotherapy" into a search engine on the Internet.

And that's how she became an "angel."

Betsy signed up with an organization called "Chemo Angels," a collection of more than 4,000 volunteers from 12 countries. Many are either cancer survivors or have been touched by cancer in some way through friends and loved ones. Their common denominator is "a desire to brighten the lives of cancer patients while they are going through this challenging time."

Betsy lives in Macon with her husband, Blair, a local attorney. They have two children, Ellie and Knox.

Her first "angel" assignment was a boy named Danny, who lived in New Jersey. He was 3 years old, the same age her daughter, Ellie, was at the time.

The simple acts of kindness made their relationship special. Although she never got to meet Danny, he was always in her thoughts and prayers, especially when his little body was enduring those brutal chemotherapy treatments.

Each week, she would send him cards and gifts in bubble mailers. She decorated them with bright stickers. She would buy coloring books from the dollar store. She had a list of his favorite toy, cartoon and ice cream flavor. His family sent her a Christmas photo with him on Santa's knee.

Danny died on March 23, 2004. This Easter Sunday will mark the fourth anniversary of his death.

Her father died a year later, on April 14, 2005.

Betsy is now on her fifth patient. All have been children. All are still alive, except for Danny. Her newest "angel" is a 7-year-old boy named Ryan who lives in Ohio.

"I've never met any of them," she said. "But I feel like I know them all."

She still thinks of Danny. She e-mails his mother, Ellen, almost every day.

She's a lot like me, except she's a Yankee," Betsy said, laughing.

In a few weeks, Betsy and her family are traveling to New York. They have arranged to meet Danny's family for the first time.

"I do this in memory of Daddy," she said.

You never stop being an angel.

Mr. Willie's final ride

January 4, 2006

For the past six years, Willie Nesbitt has orbited downtown Macon 27 times a day in a big, green box-shaped trolley.

On the three-mile loop from the foot of Cherry Street to the top of Coleman Hill and back, there are 19 traffic lights, a combination of 12 streets, eight left turns and seven right turns.

Each weekday, the route has taken him past schools, churches, libraries, parks, loft apartments and historic homes. He would turn sharp corners and ride along bumpy brick streets with a practiced familiarity.

There have been times when I'm sure "Mitsi" could have been re-named "Monotony." But Willie never got bored.

"This city has so much history," he said, following the pink center line up Cherry Street. "I learned something new almost every day."

If downtown has had a face since the turn of this century, it has been that of Mr. Willie. His photograph, with his broad smile flashing a gold front tooth, has appeared in newspapers, travel magazines and *Southern Living*.

While driving the Mitsi trolley for the Macon-Bibb County Convention and Visitor's Bureau, he has shuttled thousands of folks from the Terminal Station to the Hay House, around to the music and sports halls of fame and all points in between.

He has given accelerated history lessons to visitors from six continents who travel to Macon to learn about everything from cherry trees to Civil War history. He has been asked by many of the tourists to pose for photographs.

Sadie Crumbley, a representative with the bureau, said Willie has helped "show off" Macon by charming folks with his "genuine Southern hospitality."

If it's true, it ain't bragging.

"He has been a wonderful asset to our historic city," she said.

Unfortunately, Willie turned in his keys a few days ago. He retired Dec. 31 from his familiar day route, although he will still help NewTown Macon with special events.

It has been a wonderful ride, he said, but he wants to spend time with his three young grandchildren. They are the children of his son, Willie "Tre" Nesbitt III, who died in March.

Although Willie will be replaced by another driver, I'm going to miss watching him circle clockwise around the central business district every day.

Notice I said clockwise and not clockwork. Laid-back Willie has been known to drop off folks at a downtown restaurant for lunch, then return later to pick them up. So you can't exactly set your watch by him if you're waiting for a scheduled trolley stop.

"The joggers always wave to me at lunch," he said. "Sometimes I stop and tell them if they get tired, they can always put in a quarter and get on board."

He called his circuit as much a ministry as a job. He never hesitated to tell passengers how much God has worked in his life. Other times, he ministered to them simply by listening.

On slow days, when the 12 rows of double seats on the bus were empty, he often would pause for a few minutes at the top of Coleman Hill, overlooking the city where he was born 57 years ago.

"It was my prayer closet," he said. "I would thank God for a wonderful life and a wonderful job."

He considered his route a personal trip down memory lane. He passed houses along College and Bond streets, where he once cut grass with a push mower as a youngster. He passed downtown markets and stores where he worked as a young man. And the old Young Drug Store, now Lawrence Mayer Florist, where he would buy a pimento cheese sandwich for 35 cents.

Growing up the oldest of his family's 10 children in the Fort Hill neighborhood, he always fancied a career driving a bus. He joined the Army after high school and was sent to Vietnam. He held several jobs after the service, including driving a school bus.

He became a regular route driver for the Macon Transit Authority in 1992. He even got his father, the late Willie Nesbitt Sr., a job there.

In 1999, the transit authority recognized the need for a downtown shuttle. Willie was assigned to Mitsi, which is short for Macon Intown Transportation Service Inc.

Last week, when I learned his driving days were numbered, I jumped on his trolley Friday afternoon. I dropped in my quarter and made two final loops with Willie. I thanked him for his service to our city, and told him how much he would be missed.

"Have a blessed day," he told me as I was getting off the trolley. "And watch your step."

I will, Willie.

You do, too.

Almost famous

Welcome to Munchkinland

December 4, 2005

DUBLIN — Karl Slover has told the same stories more times than there are bricks in the yellow brick road.

Stories about little people with bright felt costumes and striped socks with curly toes. Stories about wicked witches, emerald cities, Dorothy and Toto, too.

He's 87 years old, and the lines on his face are bunched together like rings on a dwarf maple.

The tiny, squeaky voice is unmistakable.

We wish to welcome you to Munchkinland.

Now the stories can be heard in the lobby and hallways of an assisted living home in Dublin. He has lived there only two months, but he has quickly become the resident celebrity.

I visited him last week. He was delightful, polite and witty, with a face forever locked in a smile.

He is 4 feet, 4 inches tall and weighs 85 pounds. When he reached to shake my hand, the top of his head barely came to my belly button. I thought I was prepared for his miniature size, but I was still somewhat startled by a man so small I was almost afraid I might step on him.

It was an honor and pleasure to meet him. I cannot think of another movie with the personal staying power of "The Wizard of Oz."

It has been on the marquee in my head since I was old enough to remember. We used to look forward to it coming on network television every year around Thanksgiving, Christmas and Easter.

I still know most every line in the movie and, of course, all the songs. I can never seem to remember my niece's birthday, and I sometimes forget my computer password, but I have "Over the Rainbow" and "If I Only Had a Brain" committed to memory.

Of the 124 "little people" hired for the cast of the movie, Slover is one of only nine still living. He appeared in four Munchkin roles — a soldier, the first of the trumpeters announcing the death of the wicked witch, the only boy "sleepyhead" in the nest and one of the Munchkins who led Dorothy to the start of the yellow brick road.

It took two months to film the scenes from Munchkinland, and Slover never got to see any of the filming of the rest of the movie. He admits having doubts about its potential at the box office.

"We didn't think it was all that fantastic when we were making it," he said. "But after we saw the rest of the movie, we really enjoyed it."

Karl Kosiczky was born Sept. 21, 1918, in Prakendorf, Germany, with a deficient growth hormone. He was the middle of five children, with four sisters. His father was a policeman and stood 6-foot-6. At age 9, Karl was barely 2 feet tall. He could hardly reach the knobs to open doors. He joined a touring troupe, where he was billed as the "world's smallest midget."

When Karl left home, he was hurt by something his father said. As he was putting his son on the train, his father told the agent he was glad to get rid of him because of his small size.

He was 10 when he came to the United States, where he continued to sing and dance in the vaudevillian shows. He got his big break in 1938, at the age of 20, when Leo Singer was contracted through MGM Studios to provide the 124 little people to inhabit the magical village over the rainbow. They became known as "The Singer Midgets."

Although he has seen the movie thousands of times, Slover can't remember every little detail — no pun intended — of the film's production.

"That was a long time ago," he said, rolling back his head and laughing. "I know I didn't like having four parts. I was having to change clothes so much."

He had several off-camera conversations with Judy Garland, who was only 15 years old when she was cast as Dorothy. He also has fond memories of the lovely Billie Burke. She played Glinda, the good witch, and was married to Florenz Ziegfeld, of Ziegfeld Follies fame.

Margaret Hamilton, the wicked witch of the west, was a kindergarten teacher from Cleveland, Ohio, and a very kind woman, he said.

"I remember the first day we toured the MGM Studio," Slover said. "It was 9 o'clock in the morning, and we were walking by the fruit trees they used in the scenes on the yellow brick road. I told my friend one of the apple trees made a face at me, and the only thing I had to drink that day was coffee. Then, he saw it, too. They told us there were men inside those rubber trees."

After Oz, Slover landed roles in five other movies, including "The Lost Weekend," with Jane Wyman (President Reagan's first wife), "Bringing Up

Baby," with Katharine Hepburn and Cary Grant, "Block Heads" with Laurel and Hardy, "They Gave Him a Gun" with Spencer Tracy and "The Terror of Tiny Town," with a cast of other little people.

He eventually went to live with a couple named B.A. and Ada Slover. He changed his last name to Slover when he became a U.S. citizen in 1943. He later went to live with the Slovers' son, James, and his wife, Marion. They recently relocated to Dublin from Tampa, Fla.

At the Sheridan Senior Living home in Dublin, executive director Gina Ensley and business manager Wendy Douglas have worked to protect Slover's privacy.

After all, having a munchkin-in-residence has the potential to bring out curiosity seekers.

Slover travels a lot, attending various "Wizard of Oz" and Judy Garland festivals, where he signs autographs. Since coming to Dublin, he has been to Charlotte, N.C., Kansas City and California.

He has never married. He reads and watches "Jeopardy!" and "Wheel of Fortune." He has joined the other residents for exercise and devotional.

And he wishes there could be more movies like the Wiz.

"There's no swearing or filthy language," he said. "People come up to me and say it's the best movie they've ever seen. If they made more movies like that, it would be wonderful."

The most famous rear end in the world

January 21, 2007

WARNER ROBINS — At a routine traffic check a few years ago, Al Hortman rolled down his window to show the police officer his driver's license and insurance card.

The police officer noticed a decal on the window of Hortman's truck. It was the famous logo of a Shriner carrying a child in his left arm and holding her crutches in his right hand.

"It's not the first time I've seen that," the officer said to Hortman.

Hortman smiled.

"Yeah, but I bet it's the first time you've ever seen the man who is on that decal sitting behind the wheel of a truck," he said.

Al Hortman is a modest fellow, even though he has been asked for his autograph many times. He prefers to be a household name only in his own house.

He has been a Shriner for almost 40 years. He now belongs to the 1,500-member Al Sihah Temple in Macon.

Yes, he does wear one of those funny-looking hats with the long tassel, sometimes known as a fez.

But even though he is a celebrity, of sorts, his head hasn't swelled to the point of having to change hat sizes.

"My fez still fits," he said, laughing.

Most folks in Middle Georgia probably don't realize there is a man living among us whose image has been seen all over the world.

His likeness can be found on letterheads, mosaics, tie tacks and stained-glass windows. His profile has been immortalized on larger-than-life statues at Shriners Hospitals from Colorado Springs to Dallas, Texas, to Chicago to Virginia Beach, Va., to Greenville, S.C.

It also stands outside the International Shrine Headquarters building in Tampa, Fla. Plans are now being discussed to put one at the Al Sihah Temple on Mecca Drive in south Macon.

(Hey, maybe they can just go ahead and change the name from Al Sihah to Al Hortman. Just a thought.)

Hortman grew up on a farm in Crawford County, fought in the Korean War, lived for 20 years in Evansville, Ind., and has spent the past 35 years in Warner Robins. He is retired from Robins Air Force Base and will be 77 years old on Feb. 14, which happens to be Valentine's Day.

His famous image, shown from behind, is a symbol that has been seen by millions.

"I've got," he said with a grin, "the most famous rear end in the world."

When his daughter, Laura, was born in 1956, her hip joints were not formed properly and she required medical attention. The family was living in Evansville at the time, and Laura was treated at the Shriners Hospital in St. Louis. (She is now Laura Little, lives in Cochran and later became an avid runner.)

Hortman was so impressed with the care and treatment his daughter received that he dedicated himself to becoming a Shriner. He joined the Hadi Temple in Evansville in 1968.

Every summer, the temple rented a local amusement park and invited area children who had been patients at one of the 22 Shriners Hospitals in North America.

On Saturday, June 13, 1970, Hortman attended the event at the amusement park with Laura, who was then 14. He noticed a 5-year-old girl struggling to walk with crutches on the gravel paths.

So he reached down, picked her up and carried her.

Her name was Bobbi Jo Wright. She had been born with cerebral palsy.

Fate stepped in to join hands when Randy Dieter, a photographer for the Evansville newspaper, spotted them in the midway.

Because Dieter was using a telephoto lens, his subjects were too close for him to focus for a picture. When he hurried past them to get into a better position, his camera jammed. He had one last shot at the end of his roll of film. He snapped it as they walked by.

Back at the newspaper office, an editor made the decision to run the photograph even though it did not show their faces. It appeared on the front page of Sunday's *Evansville Courier & Press*.

"I didn't even know it was in there until a friend called me about it," Hortman said. "When he told me the photo was taken from behind, I asked him how he knew it was me. He said he recognized the keys I always wore on my belt."

Hortman said the image has become an icon for the Shriners Hospitals because of its universal appeal.

"The image represents every Shriner and every crippled child," he said. "It just happened to be me."

The famous photo has been called the "Editorial Without Words." The statue is known as the "Silent Messenger." And the rallying cry for Shriners has become "No Man Stands So Tall As When He Stoops To Help a Child."

Hortman, Dieter and Wright have been reunited for dedications of statues at Shriners Hospitals, which have been called the "world's greatest philanthropy." Since 1922, medical services have been provided for more than 800,000 children at no cost.

Wright still lives in Evansville, works at a hospital library and teaches Sunday School. Dieter is a graphics editor at the *Kentucky Post*.

Hortman said he once asked Dieter if his camera had really jammed.

Dieter teased him.

"You just looked better going than coming," he said.

In January 2008, the famous Shriners' statue was dedicated in front of the Al Sihah Temple on Mecca Drive in Macon. The 9-foot statue can be seen from Interstate 75. Hortman died in December 2009.

Stop that man on the lawn mower!

April 29, 2007

I have devoted at least a portion of my writing career to uncovering bits of obscure local trivia.

I once interviewed a Dodge County woman who had a part in an Elvis Presley movie.

I did a story on a Barnesville man who wrote a country ballad called "Lester Goes to Ludowici." It was about former Gov. Lester Maddox and the famed speed traps of the tiny southeast Georgia town.

After months of extensive research, I confirmed Richard Nixon once owned a Macon Whoopee T-shirt.

Now I can add another item to the list. Last week, I met a man who pulled over country singer George Jones for driving his lawn mower down the middle of a busy Tennessee highway.

Don McClain is a sergeant with the Bibb County Sheriff's Department. He also has one of the most unique résumés in Middle Georgia.

He plays the bagpipes for special events in the area. He once took banjo lessons from the legendary Earl Scruggs. He has held jobs as a cook, an electrician, a carpenter, a police officer and a studio musician. He once managed the Regal Rivergate Cinema theaters in Macon.

He has performed on stage at the Grand Ole Opry. Remember the hit song "Desperado," by The Eagles? That's McClain playing the dobro in the background.

There was a time when he and singer Don McLean, of "American Pie" fame, used to get each other's mail by mistake.

No joke, but Donald Earl McClain was born on April 1, 1946. April Fool's Day.

He inherited his musical genes from his mother, Heather, who has had a long career in show business and once brushed elbows with Shirley Temple.

His career took off when he realized there were thousands of banjo players in Nashville but only a handful of musicians who could play the dobro, a type of resonator guitar.

So he learned to play the instrument and soon found himself recording with the likes of The Stanley Brothers, Dickey Betts (of The Allman Brothers), Bonnie Bramlett, Melanie, Del Reeves, Kris Kristofferson and The Kendalls.

He even formed his own band — Donald Earl and the Foggy Mountain Bluegrass. His mother played stand-up bass.

In the summer of 1974, he was moonlighting with the police department in Hendersonville, Tenn., a suburb of Nashville. One day, while on patrol with fellow officer Butch Woodard, they noticed someone riding a lawn mower on Highway 31.

At first, they thought it was a teenager. When they pulled over the driver, they discovered it was the popular country singer.

McClain said Jones had been drinking, but the officers only gave him a citation for operating an illegal vehicle on the road.

His wife, Tammy Wynette, had hidden the car keys, and Jones had hopped on the mower in search of a liquor store. (It was not the only riding lawn mower incident for The Possum.)

Two years later, McClain found himself in the studio with Jones and Wynette. Jones did not recognize him, and McClain was self-conscious about mentioning their previous meeting. He performed as a studio musician on the song, "Golden Ring."

After 12 years with the sheriff's department, McClain said he is retiring in June and moving with his mother back to Nashville.

But he'll forever be connected to a trivia question.

If it ever comes up in "Trivial Pursuit," you'll know the answer.

The house that Hubert built

April 10, 2005

CUMMING — I expected a certain amount of show-off in a man who is building a $35 million home in north Atlanta that is twice as large as the governor's mansion.

I expected arrogance to follow like the echo of his footsteps as we moved from room to unfinished room — from the bowling alley to the miniature Fox Theatre to the 12-car garage to ceilings so high you would swear there were stars in the attic.

But I found none of this in Hubert Humphrey, a marketing tycoon who — since you probably will ask — is no relation to the late vice president.

I didn't find a trace of pompous in his personality, no in-your-face braggadocio in his voice.

If anything, his name could be Hubert H. Humphrey. His middle initial could stand for "Humble."

No, he has never forgotten those humble beginnings in south Macon where, if he didn't grow up dirt poor, at the very least he was gravel poor.

He has never forgotten working as a soda jerk at Hogg's Drug Store on Houston Avenue, where he made cherry cokes to impress the girls. And pumping gas at T. Louie Wood's Texaco station, where he whetted his love for cars. (He now owns one of the most impressive collections of antique cars in the country.)

He has never forgotten, as a young boy, sweeping the floor at Brown's Grocery in Houston Heights, then being promoted to making deliveries on a bicycle. "My legs hardly touched the pedals," he said. "People had to help me off when I got to their house."

And he has never forgotten those early years of his marriage, trying to provide for a wife and four children while working for the railroad. There were times when there was too much month at the end of the money. He felt like a conductor waiting for the tracks to lead him out of a dark tunnel.

He is now "63 years old going on 30," a man who insists the journey itself has been more important than the acquisition of wealth.

"It's not about how much money you make," he said. "You can't take it with you. I'm going to work harder at giving it away than I ever did working for it."

The 48-room house, being built on 80 acres south of Ga. 20, has raised eyebrows even in Forsyth County, where folks are accustomed to multimillion dollar homes.

Construction began two years ago, and Humphrey said he expects to move into the house in October. I toured it a few weeks ago with Kenneth Smith, who grew up with Humphrey in south Macon. We both gave it a "10" rating on the "gee whiz" scale.

How could we not be impressed with a home almost as large (44,000 square feet) as the White House? How could we not be amazed at a mansion with so many windows it took two boatloads to import them from Europe?

Humphrey is even constructing a five-hole golf course on his property, with a replica of No. 12 at Augusta National.

"We have closets bigger than the house we lived in on San Juan Avenue back in Macon," he said.

His roots still run deep through his hometown, a place he will always cherish because it is "filled with good, special people who influenced my life."

He was born in 1942, three months after the attack on Pearl Harbor, and calls himself the "product of a special era."

His parents were Steeley and June Humphrey, who began their marriage in debt after his father borrowed his brother's car for their honeymoon. On their way to Florida, he swerved off the road and into a pasture, where he hit and killed a farmer's prized cow.

When he was an infant, Humphrey's mother entered him in a baby contest sponsored by Carnation. He won a year's supply of diapers and milk. "I paid for the first year of my life," he said.

In the third grade, he met an "angel." Her name was Norma Patrick, and she would later become his wife. "The most wonderful woman in the world," he said. "She raised me."

Growing up, there were no silver spoons on the place mats at the Humphreys' supper table.

"Some people are born into affluence," he said. "But I found a deep appreciation in hard work."

Those jobs as a stock boy, soda jerk, service station attendant, bakery worker, shoe store employee and plumber's assistant developed in him a work ethic that would serve him well. He graduated from Macon's Lanier High in 1960 and enrolled at Georgia Tech with the intention of becoming an electrical engineer.

He married Norma in July 1961. By the following summer, she was pregnant. He decided to return to Macon and find a good-paying summer job.

He was hired by the railroad and put off going back to school until after the baby was born in December. Before he knew it, the couple was expecting their second child. The "summer job" would last 17 years.

"I enjoyed my first four years with the railroad," he said. "I spent the next 13 trying to figure out how to get out."

As a brake man and later a conductor for Southern Railroad, he escaped death and serious injury several times. It was dangerous work, running those ribbons of steel. On a summer night in 1973, a friend named Larry Hinson, who had helped him get the job with the railroad, offered to work his shift while Humphrey attended a meeting in Warner Robins. Hinson was killed in a head-on train collision between Macon and Columbus.

"Working for the railroad shaped the rest of my life," Humphrey said. "I wouldn't trade anything for those ups and downs and challenges. But I just knew I had to get out. I had four children and no college degree. Somehow, some way, I wanted to be my own boss. I didn't have any money or experience to go into business. But I wanted to control my own future."

Feeling "trapped," he looked at several business opportunities. In 1968, he took a part-time job selling with Amway, an international multilevel marketing company, while he continued his job with the railroad.

"It cost $15 to sign up," he said. "I had never heard of it. But it was a chance."

He worked 25 to 30 hours on the side as an Amway distributor, learning the basics of recruiting and building an organization. It wasn't the most lucrative paycheck in the world, but it was a start.

He almost stretched himself too thin by also volunteering as a Little League coach and serving as a bishop at the Church of Jesus Christ of Latter-day Saints on Williamson Road.

"It really put my family behind the eight ball," he said. "I wanted it to work out so badly. I was trying to hold it together. My oldest son needed braces, and I felt so guilty. It was almost like my arms were up three-quarters of the way to surrender. But I didn't want to be average and ordinary. I snatched my arms down. I told Norma I loved her, and that I could not stop trying."

The day after his mother's funeral, Humphrey was approached by a fellow Mormon church member who was a local piano salesman. He was selling term insurance part-time for A.L. Williams. He explained the company's marketing concept and the opportunity for commission. It wasn't long before the train conductor climbed aboard.

For Humphrey, the timing could not have been more perfect. He made more money working part-time for the A.L. Williams office on Riverside Drive than he did in a year working for the railroad. So, in 1978, he left.

"I escaped from the railroad," he said. "I cut loose from the caboose."

The rest is one of those great, rags-to-riches, Horatio Alger tales of the business world. Encouraging clients to purchase term life insurance and investing the difference, he established sales records.

By 1982, he was a millionaire. A.L. Williams named him "most valuable leader of the decade" in 1987.

Humphrey honed a successful model for recruiting employees and building leaders. As Williams' field general, he launched his own company within the company — first the Humphrey National Network, then the Humphrey Worldwide Network.

"The reason I loved the business so much was because the more I shared it, the bigger it got," he said. "I pulled people up the ladder with me."

In 1989, Williams sold the company to Primerica, now part of CitiGroup. Two years later, Humphrey resigned as senior national sales director. He formed his own company, World Marketing Alliance, a financial services marketing company, then rode the bull stock market of the 1990s.

At its peak, WMA was the leading marketer of mutual funds in the industry and the leading marketer of term insurance in the world. He retired in 2001 but has since founded World Leadership Group, a marketing, financial services and mortgage company based in Forsyth County.

Like his hero Alexander the Great, Humphrey believes you have to conquer men's hearts before you can conquer the world. His faith has helped him understand that, to whom much is given, much is expected.

One of his personal profile slogans is "from box car to business star."

Of course, he really wanted to be a rock star. As a teenager, he used to drive down to the Pig n' Whistle in Macon to hear the singing car hop. Then the car hop changed his name to Little Richard and cut a record called "Tutti Frutti."

"You've got to have wild ambition," Humphrey said. "You've got to dare to dream. But you can't fly a Piper Cub to the moon. You have to get in a rocket ship."

Critters

Chip off the old dog

August 29, 2008

SAVANNAH – His fur is as white as a South Georgia cotton field. His shoulders are broad, like the hood ornament on a Mack truck.

While the Bulldog Nation has sweated, the Dog Almighty has been vetted. We do take our bulldogs seriously. He comes from the most scrutinized bloodline of mascots this side of the hedges.

Not just any bulldog can be ordained as Uga, the "demidog" of this religion in the South we know as college football.

This week, the University of Georgia's athletic department will release the first official photograph of Uga VII. There won't be any 3 a.m. text messages. Georgia fans have been waiting with belated breath.

After all, it has been 61 days since Uga VI died of heart failure. The suspense behind naming his successor has been nail-biting. The new pup has been kept under lock and key. It has prompted a few rumors of a possible black dog candidate. Photographs of imposters have been circulating on the Internet. It also has created a paparazzi-like buzz around the family of owner Frank "Sonny" Seiler.

"Stakeouts," said Seiler's daughter, Swann, laughing. "Daddy has told Mama to make sure she has on a nice nightgown when she goes out to get the morning paper."

Uga VII is putting on his game face. He has been pronounced ready to knock the slobber out of Georgia Southern. He will make his field debut in a "passing of the bone" ceremony Saturday, when he finally gets to see where his father worked on all those sun-splashed autumn afternoons.

Sonny is confident Uga VII is equal to the task, even though he's going where no dawg has gone before. He will be a "true freshman" on the nation's top-ranked college football team.

"I'm concerned about how he will react to the crowd noise," Sonny said.

He has some big paws to fill. His pop was the school's all-time winningest dog, and perhaps its most personable. Uga VI also was the heaviest (65 pounds) and the loudest (he barked so much, opposing fans often begged him to shut up).

Still, his bark was never as loud as his bite. He had a reputation for chewing up everything from TV cables on the sideline to wicker baskets in the living room. He once emerged from a hotel room at 6 a.m. with Swann's orthodontic retainer in his mouth.

And he hated to dress in his game jersey. "Once he had it on, he was fine. But he didn't like for you to pull it over his head and legs," Swann said. "It was always a battle. He would draw blood. We used to flip a coin to see who had to dress him."

Swann, the oldest of the four Seiler children, grew up with every bulldog mascot as the family pet. She was born in 1956, the year Uga I — a wedding gift to her parents — made his stage debut. As a student at Georgia, she would often keep Uga III at her apartment and chauffeur him around in her red AMC Pacer.

Uga VI's untimely death stunned the Seilers, but they were nevertheless prepared.

Dogs go four-deep on the depth chart.

"We always have an heir and a spare," said Swann. "My family has been doing this for a long time. The line is secure."

Sonny is proud of the "orderly change" that has taken place.

"It wasn't a beauty contest," he said. "We had three to choose from, and we took our time. We've got an excellent dog. We're not going to put a puppy out there to fill that collar. He is 3 years old. He is Uga VI's son. And he is almost full-grown (56.5 pounds)."

The world won't see his mug until this weekend. In the meantime, the best sneak peek is a picture of his famous daddy.

"He's the spitting image of VI," Sonny said.

A chip off the old dog.

Uga VII died unexpectedly of heart failure on Nov. 19, 2009, two days before Georgia's final home game of the season. His record in two years as mascot was 16-7.

Lt. Bobby was no ordinary dog

July 13, 2008

The dog is buried just a bone's throw past the entrance to Rose Hill Cemetery.

The headstone is small, and the years have leaned against its gray, chiseled granite.

Lt. Bobby's family plot is located in a section called "Triangle Square" along Central Avenue in the historic cemetery.

His marker bears this inscription: *"Lieutenant Bobby. Just a brown dog. Loyal Pal and Pet of Captain D.C. Harris. Mascot of Company C, 121st Infantry. Died Jan. 29, 1936. Age 12. Faithful to the Last."*

Every bit of it is true. He was faithful. He was loyal. And, believe it or not, he was a lieutenant.

But he was not "just a brown dog."

When Uga VI died two weeks ago, it was front-page news. Thousands mourned his passing. The beloved University of Georgia mascot was laid to rest with his jersey and collar in a marble vault inside the main gate at Sanford Stadium.

When Lt. Bobby died on a blustery winter day 72 years ago, it was front-page news, too. And his death prompted one of the most unique funerals this city has ever witnessed.

Like Uga, this was no ordinary dog.

At a time when America was between world wars, he became the first dog to receive a commission in the Army. The commission was signed by President Calvin Coolidge while the brown fox terrier faithfully attended training school for a dozen years at Fort Benning with his master, Capt. D.C. Harris.

Harris had been overseas with the Rainbow Division during World War I and served as commander of the famed Floyd Rifles for almost 20 years.

His dog led a storybook life and, lest we forget, Lt. Bobby was 84 in dog years, so he was an octogenarian canine.

He served as the official mascot of the 121st Blue Bonnet Infantry of the Georgia National Guard. He was well-known for the miniature sword he wore on his leather harness. He appeared in many parades with Capt. Harris.

Yes, he was somewhat of a top dog around town.

Sadly, he did not die a storybook death. Lt. Bobby tragically fell down the elevator shaft at the Hotel Dempsey while Harris was there visiting friends.

Harris was heartbroken, and an entire city joined in his grief. Flowers were sent from all over the country. The dog was embalmed and placed in a tiny, white, silk-lined casket. There was a viewing in the parlor of a local funeral home.

Lt. Bobby received a military funeral with four honorary pallbearers. A 21-gun salute was given by the Floyd Rifles. A U.S. flag was draped over his casket. An Army chaplain delivered a brief eulogy, and taps was played by an Army bugler as the casket was lowered into the ground.

Several "newsreel" cameras were there to record the event. That's how people got their news and information — at the movie theater — in the days before television.

Lt. Bobby is buried in the company of the city's founding fathers, three governors, two U.S. senators, a congressman, 31 mayors, 1,474 Confederate soldiers, famous musicians and athletes.

Harris died 65 years ago this past week, and he is buried next to Lt. Bobby in the family plot.

We do love our dogs, don't we?

The forecast from Weathering Heights

February 1, 2008

LILBURN — Gen. Beauregard Lee isn't much of a conversationalist.

He's the chubby, silent type. He mostly squeaks and grunts, like a 14-year-old boy trying to wake up in the morning.

Yes, the art of chitchat is lost behind Beau's whiskers and gray fur. He ignores those common denominators of conversation — politics, sports and religion.

The weather, however, is a different story.

In many ways, Beau is Georgia's most famous weatherman. He's cute. Maybe not as cute as WMAZ weatherman Ben Jones, but he does have his meteorological moments.

For 364 days, he leads a hermit-like existence on his "Weathering Heights" plantation at the Yellow River Game Ranch. He is neighbors with 600 other animals, including one of the largest herds of buffalo east of the Mississippi River. He eats, sleeps and keeps a low-to-the-ground profile.

But every Feb. 2, the whole world wants to know what Beau knows.

Did he see his shadow?

On Saturday morning, by the dawn's early light, the phone will start ringing along the banks of the Yellow River.

It's the only day of the year when Beau actually works or gives a toot about global warming.

Folks call to find out if the sun was peeking through the poplars as Beau was being stirred from his winter's nap by a clanging bell and plate of hash browns from Waffle House.

That scenario, of course, means six more dreadful weeks of winter.

If it's cloudy or overcast, there's a bit of rejoicing from the hundreds of folks who gather in the dark and cold. Get out the short sleeves. Make way for the daffodils.

There are those who don't ascribe to such superstitions. They think it's a bunch of groundhogwash.

So they probably don't believe Col. Art Rilling, the founder of the Yellow River Game Ranch, when he claims the groundhog is a real ham.

"When he comes out, it's almost like he's posing for the cameras," Rilling said, laughing.

The reliability of Beau's long-range forecast ranks right up there with Doppler Radar and the *Farmer's Almanac.* He has twice been commended for the accuracy of his predictions by the National Weather Service. He received honorary doctorates from the University of Georgia ("Doctor of Weather Prognostication") and Georgia State University ("Doctor of Southern Groundology").

Of course, Beau doesn't have a monopoly on forecasting. His more famous cousin, Pennsylvania's "Punxsutawney Phil," is the rock star of all groundhogs. They have never met and rarely even acknowledge one another. Their relationship is, pardon the expression, a bit chilly.

Several other groundhogs will be holding court Saturday. There is Staten Island Chuck in New York City, Sir Walter Wally of Raleigh, N.C., Pardon Me Pete of Tampa, Fla., and Jimmy the Groundhog of Sun Prairie, Wis.

Beau weighs about 12 pounds and is built so low to the ground he looks like a speed bump in the parking lot. Rilling describes his head as being shaped like a torpedo.

He lives in the lap of luxury. He dines on fresh vegetables and dry dog food. He has his own library and a mailbox for all his fan mail.

There is a satellite dish outside the white-columned "mansion." Rilling jokes it's so Beau can watch his favorite show, "Dark Shadows."

He also hints there is a wine cellar inside, which may explain why Beau sleeps a lot.

The Saturday forecast for Lilburn is sunny. I'm not exactly thrilled about having six more weeks of winter.

But I do believe in Beau, beyond a shadow of a doubt.

Eulogy for a fish

April 6, 2005

I buried McGill at the corner of the house. I wrapped him in tissue, placed him in an Altoids can and dug a small hole beneath the down spout. When it rains, he'll be right at home.

I've buried plenty of family pets over the years. This was the first time I've buried a fish. They usually get flushed down the toilet.

But McGill deserved a memorial service. He was a desktop companion for four years at *The Telegraph*. He never whined or complained. The only times he would raise his gills in anger was when I accidentally bumped my knees against the desk and disturbed his watery world.

He seemed to sense my arrival every morning because he knew it was time for breakfast. Four tiny pellets. His diet never changed.

He was somewhat of a newsroom institution. He even had his own nameplate. I mentioned him in my column from time to time. He had been here longer than many of the reporters and editors.

Since I got him in the spring of 2001, I have written more than 800 columns. McGill was there for every one of them, looking over my right shoulder.

A eulogy for a fish may seem trivial in a daily newspaper. McGill, though, was a part of my daily life that is now gone. He was a sounding board, a welcome diversion and a conversation piece for the dozens of folks who drop by during any given news cycle.

He also was the perfect cure for writer's block. I would watch him swim, free from the pressures of headlines and deadlines. I placed a miniature typewriter in the bottom of his bowl.

In the spring of 2001, Paulette Fountain, our newsroom receptionist, bought a betta (Chinese fighting fish) and named him "Wrapper" after fish wrapper, one of a newspaper's many uses.

It wasn't long before I wanted my own fish. McGill was a bright, beautiful blue, which made him stand out from the others at the pet store. I named him after Ralph McGill, one of the South's great newspaper editors.

I also bought each of my three sons a betta that day. One fish died in less than a week. The others lived less than a month.

I don't know how old McGill was in fish years, but I suspect he outlived his life expectancy. (Paulette is now on Wrapper III.)

Every Monday afternoon, the high school editors for the "Fresh Ink" page have come by to check on McGill. They have tapped on his bowl and told me he didn't look so good. Finally, I put up a sign: "No, Kathy, Megan and Jacqueline! I'm not dead ... yet!!!"

And then he did die, while I was taking a few days off last week. We had moved his bowl to the front desk to visit his cousin, Wrapper III. He did an unexplained high dive, and metro editor Oby Brown found him on the floor. Paulette said he must have tried to follow me out the door.

So now there's an empty bowl in my office. I expect there will be a McGill II real soon. You're not supposed to grieve over a fish. I still miss him, though.

The dog that answered the phone

June 11, 2008

Seven summers ago, the late Earl Zimmerman called me at my office.

It was a delight to hear from "Mr. Z," the longtime county commissioner and insurance salesman. He knew just about everybody in town. He always was sending me anecdotes, story ideas and encouraging letters and cards.

"Call this number," Earl said, giving me the home number for Dub Simmons and his wife, Nina. "Be prepared, because a dog is going to answer the telephone."

Sure enough, a dog named Nick barked and yelped into the receiver. Not being fluent in poodle, I waited until someone who wasn't wearing a flea collar picked up the phone. Dub came to the rescue, laughing and apologizing at the same time.

"We've got a four-legged answering machine," he explained.

Who needs Caller ID when you've got Collar ID?

I had to see this for myself, so I rushed over to Rice Mill Road.

Thus began my friendship with Nick, Dub and Nina. Nick became somewhat of a "celebrity" dog after being the subject of one of my columns. I included his story in one of my books in a chapter called "If the dog answers, don't hang up."

He was later featured on the "Georgia Gazette" program on Georgia Public Radio. They played some sound bites (or is that dog bites?) of Nick barking on the phone. Dub estimates he made about 300 copies of the recording and sent them all over the country.

On my office wall, I have a photograph of Nick sitting at the computer with his "autographed" paw print.

So I got a lump in my throat when I called the Simmonses last week and Nick didn't answer the phone. All I got was the answering machine.

Nick died May 30.

"His heart just gave out," said Dub.

It has been a trying month for the Simmonses. Nina has been under the weather, and they both were hit by the rough weather that swept through south

Macon on Mother's Day. They lost several trees. High winds ripped off part of their roof.

Their loyal pet of 15 years died three weeks later. Two days after that, their church closed its doors forever. They were charter members at Glenwood Hills United Methodist, which was built in 1956. The final service was June 1.

Dub and Nina celebrated their 60th wedding anniversary in February. They have no children, so their dogs always have been important to them. First, there was Chipper, then Onyx, Chico, then Nick.

Nick was a stray found by a man in Monroe County. He was covered in red clay when the Simmonses took him home in December 1993. It was the week before Christmas, so they named him Nick, after St. Nicholas.

They believe his previous owner must have been hearing impaired. Nick had been taught to pick up the phone with his mouth and bark into the mouthpiece.

Answering the phone became his life's "calling," and the humor wasn't lost on Nina, who was retired from Southern Bell.

Nick once hit the speed dial on Dub's car phone and accidentally called the burglar alarm company. Dub still isn't sure they believed him when he blamed the dog for dialing the number.

When Nina and Dub would eat supper at the S&S in Bloomfield, the servers in the cafeteria line knew to take Nick's order first. It was usually the baked chicken or chopped steak.

Those same servers fought back tears when Dub told them about Nick's passing.

Nick had lost some of his teeth in his later years, but he had learned to nudge the phone receiver with his paw.

Now, every time the phone rings, there is a curly-haired hole in their hearts that can never be filled.

Business is picking up

June 9, 2006

Michael Rentz and Randy Johnson always dreamed of starting their own business together.

They waded through details and weighed options. They studied supply and demand. They considered location, overhead and the labor pool.

It all paid off. Things are beginning to ... er, pick up.

They now wear royal blue shirts with their company logo stitched above their hearts. They have placed the company emblem on the door of a silver Ford Ranger pickup.

Their new business, you might say, keeps them down in the dumps.

I've been trying very hard to write this column with a straight face, but it's no use.

Randy and Michael have started a new "poop 'n' scoop" service for pets. After weeks of brainstorming, they have settled on a name.

"Call of Doody."

Coming soon to a back yard near you.

OK, I know some of you are reading the newspaper at the breakfast table this morning, so I am going to spare many of the details. (But you might want to go ahead and put away the prunes.)

Michael and Randy have been friends since they were at Mary Persons High School in Forsyth. They both work at Publix grocery.

Since Michael is getting married this summer, and Randy is saying his vows next spring, they decided they needed a little — pardon the pun — disposable income.

After months of careful research and planning, they now believe they have found a niche. There were businesses that offered pet grooming, pet photography, pet training and pet sitting.

But they couldn't find another company providing such a specialized service.

And it's a job most folks don't like to do themselves.

You might say they found their calling.

Along the way, they have collected a few slogans.

Got Poop? We Scoop!

We Do Our Best To Clean Your Pet's Mess.

These guys are having way too much fun.

They acquired a business license. They carefully studied all the environmental regulations regarding proper waste disposal. And they finally found an insurance company that didn't laugh when they mentioned their occupation.

They also stocked up on supplies: a small rake, two types of shovels and a dust pan.

It's all in the wrist.

They owe a debt of gratitude to Bud and Coco, two Labrador retrievers who belong to Randy's brother, Scott. Bud and Coco supplied piles of training material in the back yard.

Randy and Michael admit to getting a few curious looks when folks see the name of their business on the side of the truck. But they also get some "thumbs up."

I was most impressed when I learned they wear their khakis and collared shirts when they go out on a job. They are dressed for success. Maybe they're on their way to making their first million.

The hours are flexible, and the job isn't all that bad — if it's not too hot. Or raining. Or you don't have a keen sense of smell.

There definitely are some fringe benefits.

Said Michael: "We get to meet a lot of dogs."

Food for thought

Blessed be the pie that binds

March 3, 2009

I asked John T. Edge, in front of God and about a hundred people, what his last meal would be if he was sentenced to die in the electric chair.

"The warden has requested your final menu selection," I instructed him. "Don't worry about calories or cholesterol. What would you order?"

He was standing in the pulpit, like a Baptist preacher with apron strings. I had certainly given him some food for thought during a lecture at Mercer's Newton Chapel.

He chuckled at the idea of being sentenced to — pardon the culinary expression — "fry." And especially on an Ash Wednesday night.

He had been asked the same question earlier in the day while speaking to a Southern Foodways class taught by assistant English professor David A. Davis.

"Barbecue," John T. said to the surprise of no one in the chapel.

Then he smiled. "And I hope to God I don't get incarcerated up North."

He was practically raised on Old Clinton Barbecue. He would ride his five-speed Schwinn bicycle from his home near Gray and wash down a pork sandwich and Brunswick stew with an Orange Crush. (For supper on Wednesday night, his father ordered take-out from Fresh Air.)

John T. has the gift of making an audience laugh and think. And he can write and talk about Southern food in a way that will make your mouth water the garden.

The *Miami Herald* once hailed him as the "Faulkner of Southern food." Just imagine William Faulkner writing "Southern Belly" instead of "Absalom, Absalom!"

John T. now resides in Oxford, Miss., the town Faulkner made the literary capital of the South. He serves as director of the Southern Foodways Alliance, an institute of the Center for the Study of Southern Culture at Ole Miss.

His life's work is documenting the South's "fried-chicken cooks," "row-crop farmers" and others by telling their oral histories. He has helped celebrate America's diverse food culture with portraits of people and places rather than simply listing how many teaspoons of cinnamon are in Aunt Jane's sweet potato pie recipe.

He is a guy after our own stomachs, eating and writing his way through the South with a grub bag of books on everything from fried chicken to apple pie. I keep a signed copy of "A Gracious Plenty" in my kitchen.

After graduating from Macon's Tattnall Square Academy and the University of Georgia, John T. spent nine years in the corporate world of Atlanta, then followed his curious heart to Oxford where he wrote his master's thesis on potlikker.

His quick rise among food historians made him somewhat of a Forrest Gumbo. He is now the "culinary curator" for National Public Radio's weekend edition of "All Things Considered." *The New York Times* and The Food Network routinely get his take on everything from buttermilk biscuits to black-eyed peas.

The greasy spoon restaurants and other forks in the road are an affirmation. Food brings us together like notes in a sweet song. We may argue about politics and differ on our religious beliefs, but we can still sit down and break bread.

Blessed be the pie that binds.

"Food is an event," he said. "It's not what is on the plate but who we share it with."

He later confided he might request some coleslaw with that barbecue. And some sweet tea, so long as it wasn't 40-weight on the sugar.

"I'm never looking at the last meal," he said. "I would rather look forward to the next one."

Variety is the spice of life

June 28, 2009

When his hands aren't busy rolling crêpes or stuffing quiche, Paul Harpin might be tempted to take his thumb and fingers and pinch himself.

Even after 61 years on his remarkable journey, it still seems like a dream.

His eyes twinkle when he talks about the places he has been and the people he has fed along the way.

Paul is co-owner of Harpin's Restaurant with his wife, Hazel. He is chief cook and bottle washer, while Hazel bakes cakes, takes orders and runs the cash register.

When the soup is on and the salads have been prepared, Paul's apron strings often pull him out of the kitchen for handshakes and hugs.

It has become his favorite part of the job. He sure has some serendipitous stories to tell, boasting a colorful culinary history.

It also serves to explain how someone who grew up in a steel mill town in England has found happiness running a small restaurant on the edge of an old cotton mill village in Macon.

Variety is the spice of life.

Paul once served as Mick Jagger's personal chef.

Judy Garland gave him her recipe for egg salad a few months before she died.

He brushed elbows with Frank Sinatra, Elton John and Sammy Davis Jr.

He danced with Carol Channing and went swimming with Olivia Newton-John before she became famous.

He prepared meals for Andy Warhol, Bette Midler and Jimmy Carter.

This month marks the 35th anniversary of Paul's arrival in a place he had never been before. Of course, he never dreamed it would one day become his place setting.

His destiny certainly hasn't followed a straight line. There have been plenty of white tablecloths and a few crumbs under the table.

He has kept the faith, though. Still does.

"You make a life," he said. "You never forget where you came from. You never let it go. And it never lets you go."

Paul was born in August 1947, one of six children to Mary and Matthew Harpin in Consett, County Durham, England.

Consett was a steel town north of London and holds the distinction of having the world's first Salvation Army band in 1879.

His father died when he was 12, and Paul quit school to help his mother. Those were troublesome economic times in England, and he mostly found work running errands and doing odd jobs in the neighborhood.

He had always loved cooking, and he learned from two of his favorite cooks ever to put on an apron — his mother and grandmother.

He would watch the Fanny Cradock children's show on the BBC, which included a segment on cooking, and built his own grill out of a fireplace grate.

He also found it fascinating to read the labels on cans and food packages. He could recite the ingredients for just about anything in the pantry.

In July 1963, his aunt took him with her to live in London. He got on the bus with a 10-shilling note, a candy bar, a copy of the *Daily Mirror* newspaper and most of his worldly possessions.

He stayed with his cousin in London and was hired to stock shelves in a local market, the perfect job for a label-lover. His big break came when he got an apprenticeship in the kitchen at Scott's, one of London's most famous restaurants.

He began to taste life, too. Even though he had dropped out of school, he was able to self-educate himself. London was his classroom. He read books and visited museums.

"One day, Princess Margaret came into the restaurant," he said. "I had never seen royalty. The kitchen was upstairs, and they let me peek through the curtains."

He worked such long hours, his bosses practically had to shoo him from the ovens. On the night of June 6, 1966, he reluctantly went home from work. After a few hours of boredom, he dressed in a pinstripe suit and headed to a nightclub on the West End.

The first young lady he asked to dance turned him down. Then his eyes fixed on Hazel across the dance floor.

For Paul, it was love at first sight.

For Hazel, it was a case of mistaken identity. (She thought he was Peter Noone, lead singer for the Herman's Hermits.)

Hazel worked as a switchboard operator. They married three years later. Their daughter, Trudy, was born in 1970.

Those newlywed years brought several rounds of job hopping. Paul worked in the executive dining room for Kodak and served ice cream in a bingo hall.

He then became chef at the Revolution, a nightclub that brought him toe-to-toe with many celebrities.

He was hired to cook meals for the Rolling Stones while the band finished an album at Mick Jagger's country estate. Jagger extended an invitation for Paul to become his full-time chef and travel with the group.

By then, however, Paul was being tugged in another direction.

Frank Fenter, a successful music executive in London, had co-founded Capricorn Records in Macon with Phil and Alan Walden.

As Macon became the epicenter of Southern rock 'n' roll in the 1970s, Fenter hired Harpin and manager Peter Marriott to open a restaurant in downtown Macon that would cater to the city's vibrant music scene.

"It was a leap of faith for me," said Paul. "It was an opportunity in unknown territory. I had never been to the United States. Hazel and I were both young and didn't think about the consequences."

His perception of America had been formed by television and books. "I thought it would be glamorous, with lots of skyscrapers," Paul said.

In June 1974, he flew from London to Washington, D.C., and then to Atlanta. A few miles south of the airport on Interstate 75, Paul realized he was a stranger in a strange land.

"Nothing but pine trees," he said. "I kept looking for the skyscrapers."

He called Hazel when he arrived in Macon.

"How is it?" she asked.

"Hot," he said.

Le Bistro opened in September 1974 in what is now the Downtown Grill on Mulberry Street Lane.

It was a different fare from the customary cornbread and collards.

"We brought food here some people had never eaten before," he said. "It was continental food like veal, lamb and kidneys. We served trout with the head still on."

He also introduced the European concept of having a couple of booths with curtains for private dining. He was in the restaurant the night Greg Allman proposed to Cher in one of the booths. (Paul later called the *Telegraph* with the scoop.)

Le Bistro eventually fell victim to Capricorn's financial difficulties and closed in 1977. At the time, Hazel was pregnant with their son, Matthew.

Paul started a small restaurant on Cherry Street before becoming the head chef at Leo's, which opened in the former Le Bistro building in the alley. He was there for 17 years.

When Leo's closed in 1995, Paul led a nomadic cooking life, jumping from the old Radisson Hotel to Beaches on Northside to Caper's on Ingleside and Paul's Bistro on Arkwright Road.

Four years ago, another leap of faith led him across the railroad tracks to Payne City. The old cotton mill village provided him with a fresh start.

Hazel had retired from her job as a record-keeper at Piedmont Orthopaedic and Sports Medicine, and she joined him in the venture.

Paul was familiar with several other businesses that had prospered on the same ground where the mill once operated — The Shamrock, Milltown Market & Dawson's Kitchen and Payne City Antique Mall.

"We had very little money," Paul said. "We just believed. We had faith God would take care of us. God helps those who help themselves."

A Payne City business license now hangs on the wall, and the 36 chairs in the dining room are often filled for weekday lunches and Friday night dinners.

Just about everyone has their own favorite dish. Steak au poivre (pepper steak), one of Paul's specialties. Or the chicken salad. Or the salmon cheese-cake.

Paul will sometimes slip home in the afternoon for a cup of hot tea. It's a change of pace from the sweet tea he serves to his loyal customers at Harpin's.

His British accent has never completely left him. Still, he can pronounce Harpin's with a slight Southern drawl.

Hah-pins.

He can also say: "Y'all come back."

He fought the slaw, and the slaw won

April 8, 2009

Ray Mills lived in the margins of life.

Anyone who followed him kept an eraser at the end of their pencils. He lived under so many different roofs, he would often head home trying to remember which key fit the lock.

The one place that was always home, though, was the Nu-Way Weiners at 430 Cotton Ave. For 32 years, Ray clocked in six days a week and saved his odd jobs for Sunday.

Oh, there were pockets of interruptions. He spent some time in jail. His personnel file was as thick as his fist.

But Nu-Way co-owners Jim Cacavias and Spyros Dermatas helped him clear his name, pay his bills and knock back the demons. After all, Ray could handle the workload of three employees. And nobody took greater pride in their calling.

If you've ever eaten a chili dog or a slaw dog from Nu-Way, then you should bow your head in a moment of silence for Ray.

He made the chili and slaw for all the Nu-Way restaurants. He cooked nearly a half-ton of chili every week. He diced some 300,000 pounds of cabbage in his lifetime.

Yes, he fought the slaw. And the slaw won.

"I doubt anyone else in Georgia can make that claim," Centenary Methodist pastor Tim Bagwell said at Ray's funeral. "There aren't many people in Macon who have not at some point eaten Ray's cooking."

Ronnie Marshall worked side-by-side with Ray for more than 20 years. They shed a lot of tears together, mostly when they chopped onions. Ronnie would chew on a wooden matchstick to ward off the watery eyes. But Ray would always tough it out.

There were plenty of tears — hold the onions — a few weeks ago. Ray's three-pack-a-day cigarette habit caught up with him, and the lung cancer ended his life at age 58.

He had blue-collar roots in south Macon. He once worked for the circus putting up tents and rides. Then he and his wife dined at the Nu-Way one spring evening in 1977, and his life changed forever.

Dermatas can still remember where Ray sat (third booth from the door) and what he ordered (two burgers all the way with hot sauce).

More importantly, he remembers it was the night Ray asked him for a job.

"He was like a jack rabbit, energetic and full of life," Dermatas said. "He was always eager to please."

"There were no limits to his work ethic," Cacavias said. "He would get things so clean, he would almost wipe the paint off the finish."

It was Jim's father, the late John Cacavias, who developed the local restaurant's famous secret slaw recipe in 1980.

But it was Ray who made 250 tons of the stuff over the next 29 years. On July 4, 2002, the dining edition of *The New York Times* hailed it as the "best slaw dog in America.'"

Ray didn't own a car. He either caught the bus or walked. He knew every shortcut and every downtown alley. He was scrawny but strong, and he always tried to appear tougher than he was. He would sometimes arrive at work with tall tales of switchblade-wielding attackers.

He never traveled far. If he ever told you he went to the beach, he usually meant Lake Tobesofkee.

He always looked forward to going to Atlanta for the annual Taste of Macon during the state legislature, too. Whenever someone would rave about the chili or slaw, he would raise his hand, thump his chest and proudly boast that he made it.

Ray couldn't read, so it never really mattered that Nu-Way's neon sign has intentionally misspelled "weiners" since 1937.

He didn't have any teeth, either, but the man could chew up an apple and gnaw down a piece of fried chicken.

Bagwell called Ray one of those "unknown faithful servants" who was "happy to the core."

Despite his flaws and imperfections, he was genuine.

"He was a character," Cacavias said. "One of a kind."

Head-over-meals in love

June 17, 2009

WARNER ROBINS — Don and Ann Hetzner celebrated their 55th wedding anniversary Saturday night.

You might wonder if Don took his wife to a fancy restaurant for a candle-light dinner, with a white tablecloth and violin music.

But Ann had a special request.

"Let's go to Chick-fil-A and get one of those new peach milkshakes," she suggested.

A chargrilled chicken sandwich with waffle fries and a sweet tea might not sound like a romantic anniversary meal. But the Hetzners count themselves among Chick-fil-A's most loyal customers. They have been known to eat three meals a day there.

They often plan their trips to the post office around lunchtime, when they might happen to be in the neighborhood of the Chick-fil-A at 1867 Watson Blvd.

They have been eating those famous chicken sandwiches for 42 years. Gosh, it's a wonder they both haven't sprouted feathers.

Ann showed me her arm.

"Those aren't freckles," she said, laughing. "They're chicken nuggets."

So, on Saturday night, Don took his No. 1 chick to the Chick-fil-A for one of those peach milkshakes.

They were treated to a nice dinner — compliments of the house. Julian Lashley, the restaurant's service manager, showed up on his day off just to serve them in the dining room. He reserved a special booth with a red table-cloth and a couple of cow dolls dressed in a tuxedo and bridal gown.

"They're always in here with a smile on their faces, and you can tell they love each other very much," Julian said. "We wanted to do something special for them."

Ann said they eat there so often, they should probably have their name on the marquee. Or at least have a sandwich named after them.

No special table would be necessary, though. They usually sit wherever they can find an open booth.

Their love affair with Chick-fil-A began not long after they fell head-over-meals for each other.

Ann grew up near Grant Park in Atlanta, not far from where Chick-fil-A founder Truett Cathy opened the first Dwarf (House) Grill in Hapeville in 1946.

She met Don in 1952 when they both were working at Rich's department store downtown. He took her to Leb's restaurant in Atlanta on their first date. She was wearing a blue dress with her hair pulled back.

It was love at first bite.

They were married June 13, 1954.

For years, they ate regularly at the very first Chick-fil-A, which opened at Atlanta's Greenbriar Mall in 1967. They moved to Warner Robins in 1972, where Don worked in civil service at Robins Air Force Base.

Those original Chick-fil-A restaurants were located only in malls and shopping centers. So the Hetzners would take their daughter, Amy, to the Houston Mall every Friday night for a family supper.

It wasn't until 1986 that the company began building free-standing restaurants. The popular location in Williams Plaza on Watson Boulevard opened in 1991.

They were married on a Sunday in 1954, but it's probably a good thing June 13 didn't fall on a Sunday this year. Chick-fil-A restaurants are closed, a policy admired and respected by many folks, myself included.

If that had been the case, they would have simply celebrated a day early or a day later.

Yes, they will cross the road to get to that chicken on the other side.

Everything made from scratch

William Grant still rises, like the yeast in his famous cakes, and heads to his pastry shop.

While most of the city is sleeping, he drives across the hills — from Pleasant Hill to College Hill across Shirley Hills to the edge of Fort Hill.

At 4 a.m., the only thing darker than the night is the coffee in his cup. And he swallows about a gallon of it to keep moving.

On winter mornings, it helps keep him warm, too. It is chilly back in the kitchen until he can get the ovens going.

There's not much insulation in the ceiling, either. But at least the prayers float upward a little faster.

He has a lot to be thankful for, because he turned 80 years old in December and still works 12-hour days at Grant's Pastry Shop on Hall Street, near the foot of Gray Highway.

Grant carries around a bullet in his leg from the Korean War. Three years ago, doctors took out one of his lungs after a bout with pneumonia.

But the man can still make some mean brownies on four hours sleep — thanks to the gallon of coffee, of course, and a work ethic that has guided him for 71 years.

Yep, that's right. Grant has been working at pastry shops since he started sweeping the floors for $7 a week at Wilder's on Pio Nono Avenue when he was 9 years old.

He makes everything from scratch — you won't find a preservative on the premises — and he won't hesitate to tell you his secret ingredient.

"Love," he said. "You have to love what you're doing. You work to make a dollar, but you have to care about what you're doing to make it come out right."

Welcome to Grant's Pastry, where there are no millionaires. The only thing rich here is the calories.

Let me fill you in on another little secret. And this one may surprise you.

A confession among the confections.

"I don't like sweets," Grant said. "I don't think I've eaten two dozen dough-nuts since I've been in business."

He was born in Juarez, Mexico, just across the Rio Grande from El Paso, Texas. His mother never told him much about his father, who was killed in a fight.

Grant lived with a succession of relatives — an aunt in Philadelphia and his grandmother in Crawford County — until he moved to Macon with his mother when he was 8.

The next year, he went to work at Wilder's. His weekly take-home pay was $6.87 (13 cents went for Social Security). He spent $2.50 a week for tuition at a small, private school he could attend at night.

"Growing up, I never played cowboys and Indians like the other children," he said. "I never shot marbles. I got up and went to work at 2:30 every morn-ing, then went to school every afternoon from 5:30 to 10 at night."

The Army drafted him in 1952 and sent him to Korea, where it was so cold he couldn't feel the trigger of his M-1 rifle.

"I was in the infantry, a foot soldier," he said. "Then I told them I could cook, and they put me to work in the mess hall."

He opened his first pastry shop in Warner Robins in 1969, staying there three years. He eventually opened in Macon on Second Street.

It was at the corner of Poplar. It should have been renamed Popular. After all, it was next to a bus stop, and folks could put on a few pounds just standing there waiting for the next bus to Napier.

When the city moved the transfer station from Poplar to the Terminal Station in 2003, a lot of his business went away.

He closed up shop but stayed retired only six months. His loyal customers urged him to relocate. Where else were they going to get those petit fours, pies, cakes, biscuits, breads and brownies?

There are other bakeries in town but only one Grant's.

This past Christmas, the same week he turned 80, he stayed so busy he didn't leave the shop for four days, sleeping on a bed in a back room.

He may not be much of sweet tooth himself, but not to worry.

Others have made up for it.

Mr. Grant died on Feb. 7, 2010. I was glad I was able to honor him while he was still living.

Flour child hits the big time

December 5, 2008

MARIETTA — Johnnie Gabriel's recipe for life came at a young age.

Cakes. Cookies. Pies. Yes, she was a flour child of the 1950s.

Growing up in Macon, she would rush home from elementary school to tug on her grandmother's apron strings. Kate Howell could make your mouth water just anticipating what she might be cooking.

"I would come in, and she would be pulling a hot pound cake or a layer cake out of the oven," said Johnnie. "I would hang off the side of the table watching her."

Of course, there was plenty of sugar and spice and everything nice. If you can't stand the sweet, get out of the kitchen.

It was all made from scratch with real butter and whole milk. Nothing skimpy about the shortening. Betty Crocker was nowhere to be found around that oven.

Johnnie wasn't old enough to do much of the baking herself. She was, however, allowed to lick the spoon and watch.

"Being the youngest, I got to wash the dishes and set the table," she said, laughing.

A career in cooking came much later in life. Now, Johnnie owns and operates one of metro Atlanta's most popular bakeries, Gabriel's Desserts in Marietta. It was once called the "little shop of wonders" by *Atlanta Magazine*, which has crowned it as the city's best place for desserts on four occasions.

Johnnie has a newly published cookbook called "Cooking in the South," and she admits many of the 150 recipes have her Macon fingerprints all over them.

She has her own cooking show on Atlanta cable television, and she has recently been on the Food Network with her famous cousin, Paula Deen.

Her parents were the late Jimmy and Carol Howell. Her older sister, Kay, went to Miller High School. Johnnie, who was named after her grandfather, graduated from McEvoy in 1963.

She cut her sweet teeth learning from both her grandmothers — Kate Howell and Charlie Heath. Her maternal grandmother and Paula Deen's grandfather were brother and sister.

When Johnnie settled in Marietta, she would buy many of her cakes from Mary Moon, who was known as the "Marietta Cake Lady."

"When she retired, it created a void in the community," said Johnnie. "She left me with six of her recipes. In the South, you either bake it yourself or buy it at the grocery store. It's not like in the Northeast where there is a bakery on every corner. So there was a big demand for home-baked desserts."

In 1989, on a leap of faith to help pay for their daughter's tuition and to supplement their income during a recession, Johnnie and her husband, Ed, began their bakery operation.

Since then, they've tripled in size and now employ a staff of more than 40. Of course, having the exposure on Paula Deen's show has certainly helped.

This time of year always stirs Johnnie's memories of food. Her mother's cornbread dressing and gravy at the Thanksgiving table. Her grandmother's fresh coconut cake. It was also the time of the year when her grandmother would start baking fruit cakes for the holidays, then get ready to make her divinity candy.

"Few things in life extend the hand of friendship like food does," Johnnie said. "In the South, we invite people into our homes and share meals at the table. It's all about relationships."

Call of duty

Every one of them had a name

May 28, 2007

Every one of them had a name. Names their mothers gave them at birth. Names like Judson and Joe, Clarence and Clyde, Dewey and Doc.

They carried those names with them to Cub Scout meetings and birthday parties. Their teachers and preachers called their names in home rooms and Sunday School classes. Their coaches hollered those names from the dugout.

Their combinations of consonants and vowels were typed on report cards, driver's licenses and draft cards. Some of those who were married passed their names down to their children.

Although a few knew each other, most of them didn't. They came from different neighborhoods and different towns. They lived across different generations. They fought in different wars on different battlefields.

But all for the same cause.

Their names have forged them together like a band of brothers.

Along a stretch of grass and trees, in the parking lot of the Macon Coliseum, their names are joined in rows of tiny, raised letters.

They are the names of the more than 600 who were either killed or missing in action from World War I, World War II, Korea, Vietnam and Iraq. They lived in the counties of Bibb, Houston, Jones, Monroe, Peach, Crawford and Twiggs.

It is difficult not to notice the Veterans Memorial, a sturdy row of black-and-red granite pillars at the foot of the Coliseum, near the chamber of commerce.

But, then, so many people emerging from the sea of parking spaces never stop — or even slow down — in their hurry to get to the basketball game or buy tickets for the concert.

Across the grassy quadrangle, near the front doors of the Coliseum, is a statue of Sgt. Rodney Davis, Macon's only Medal of Honor recipient. He died in Vietnam on a September afternoon in 1967, throwing himself on a grenade to save the lives of the men in his company. He was 25 years old. He left behind a wife and two young daughters.

I wonder how many people attending the high school graduations this past weekend paused to reflect at the statue of Davis, kneeling with his weapon resting against his right leg.

Across the river, on the slope of Coleman Hill, there are names like Otis, Ben and Norman. They are engraved on a monument to members of the 151st Machine Gun Battalion and the 42nd "Rainbow" Division killed in World War I.

Farther up the hill, there are Eugenes, Willies and Leos listed on the "Memorial Magnolias." It is a WWII monument to the more than 200 local soldiers who loved home, left home, wrote home but never came home.

It bears this inscription: "In grateful appreciation of those of our own families and friends who gave their lives in World War II that the ideals they cherished more than life might not perish from the earth. We the citizens of Bibb County have caused their names to be engraved upon this tablet and have surrounded it with rare magnolias, a living memorial to their unfaltering devotion."

Today is Memorial Day. Just another holiday, you say? A three-day weekend. The banks are closed. The mail won't run. Huge sale at the mall. Cook burgers out on the deck. The fish are biting at the lake.

Stop. Take a minute. Or more. But at least 60 seconds if that is all you have. Remember their names.

They were somebody's son. Somebody's brother. Somebody's father.

We are here because they were there.

Kilgore was there

September 30, 2007

His name was Thomas Kilgore. He was one of 11 children. After he served his country in World War II, he came home to Macon and built a life.

He worked as an electrician in the maintenance department for the Bibb County Board of Education. He lived in the same house he grew up in on Trammel Avenue in the Peach Orchard.

He never married. He was quiet, and he never talked much about the war.

When he died on Feb. 25, 1982, his 166-word obituary appeared in the back on page 6.

So you might never have known a photograph was once taken of him that became an icon of World War II, appearing on the covers of both *Time* and *Life* magazines.

The image of a battle-weary Kilgore, a bazooka propped on his left shoulder, ran in dozens of newspapers and prompted hundreds of letters to his family back home in Macon.

Time magazine later used the picture as its "Army Man of the Year" for 1944 because it symbolized the loneliness and fatigue of war.

Although it cannot be verified, there are those who believe Kilgore might have even been the inspiration for the "Kilroy Was Here" cartoons.

Now, 25 years after his death, Kilgore is back.

The haunting image of the "cover boy soldier" from Macon has been resurrected for filmmaker Ken Burns' new seven-part PBS documentary, "The War." The photo also appeared on the cover of last week's *U.S. News & World Report*.

Barbara Wood grew up with stories of the famous photo of her Uncle Tom. She remembers it was framed in the living room of her grandparents' home.

Because the photo was first published on Dec. 13, 1944, it struck a chord with Americans because it was the holidays. Someone mailed the family the picture with the words to "(I'm Dreaming of a) White Christmas."

What made the photograph so dramatic was Kilgore's eyes.

"To us, he looked so sad," said Wood, who is the public affairs officer for the Bibb Board of Commissioners. "It was so close to Christmas, and he was so far away from home."

Kilgore was in Company D of the Eighth Division's 121st Infantry, the Gray Bonnet Regiment. Company D landed in France in July 1944, one month after D-Day, and pushed across Europe into Germany, the shouts of Gen. George Patton ringing in their ears halfway across France.

With the Germans in retreat, they engaged in the Battle of Hurtgen Forest, the longest single battle (114 days) in U.S. Army history.

During a lull in the fighting one December day, and knee-deep in snow and ice, several soldiers stopped to rest before entering the forest.

A signal corpsman walked past Kilgore, who was resting against his bazooka. He stopped, pulled out his camera and asked if he could take Kilgore's photo.

"I told him to take it fast because we had to get back on the move," Kilgore would later say.

The photo appeared in *The Stars and Stripes* and hundreds of newspapers across the country. *The New York Times*, not known for running large photographs, reproduced the image at 5x8 inches with a caption, identifying him as Pfc. Thomas Kilgore, of Macon, Ga.

That brought letters from everywhere, even halfway around the world in Australia. A woman in Canada promised him that she and her two children would pray for him at a candlelight service on Christmas Eve.

Perhaps the most touching letter came from a family in Greensburg, Pa., who thought Kilgore might be their own son — another Pfc. Thomas Kilgore — who had been reported killed on D-Day at Cherbourg, France.

Barbara Wood's father, James Kilgore, was the second-oldest of the 11 children in the Kilgore family and worked for the Macon Water Authority for 41 years. He died in 1978. Four of the Kilgore boys were in the service. Tom and Fred were in the Army. Frank and Clarence served in the Navy.

"I remember when the war was over (in 1945), my father took me in the car down to Third Street," she said. "Everybody was honking their horns."

Former Macon Mayor David Carter met Kilgore in 1962, when Carter was named professor of military science at Lanier High School. During that time, Lanier had the largest high school ROTC program in the country.

"He was an electrician for the school system, so I used to see him at the school," Carter said. "He was friendly, but quiet. You might not know he had ever been a soldier."

Carter remembers Kilgore showing him scrapbooks with newspaper clippings that made reference to his name being tied to the "Kilroy Was Here" cartoons.

Kilroy may not be here now. But Kilgore, a little-known Macon soldier, continues to put a face on the greatest military conflict in history.

Five years before Kilgore died, his commanding officer, Gen. Robert Jones, addressed a meeting of the 121st Infantry in Macon. He disagreed that Kilgore's eyes looked sad in the famous photograph.

"Instead, they showed dedication and determination to finish the war and get back home," Jones said. "Kilgore, like all of us, wanted to make this country safe for future generations to come."

When a friend goes to war

July 25, 2005

I remember there was a touch of early fall in the air. I sat with my friend George Fisher in a booth at Nu-Way Weiners on Cotton Avenue, where the chili dogs sometimes bark in the afternoon.

We talked about baseball, politics and barbershop philosophy. We checked each other for gray hairs, a by-product of raising children.

But we mostly talked about going to war. It was a few weeks after the Sept. 11 attacks, the day that changed everything.

I asked him about his chances of going over there.

"It would have to be World War III," he said.

All my life, I've heard talk of World War III. It's the war we think will never come because, if it did, it would probably be the end.

So George went on with his life. A year later, when he turned 40, his friends threw him a surprise party at the Lake Wildwood clubhouse.

He helped coach his son's baseball team, wrote hilarious letters to the editor and snuck past the rooster every morning — driving to Atlanta for his job with the Georgia National Guard.

But, today, my buddy leaves for Iraq.

The war just got a lot more personal for me.

He will join the 48th Brigade — where he cut his teeth — as a logistics officer. For the past three weeks, he has been swatting mosquitoes at Fort Drum in New York. Now it is time, he says, to "fly over the pond" and into the eye of the storm.

He called his mama before he left.

"We have a choice," he told her. "We can either fight the terrorists over there or fight them on Riverside Drive."

George has proudly worn a military uniform since he was 14 years old. Two of his biggest heroes are Gen. Robert Scott (he is co-founder of Scotty's fan club) and retired Army Sgt. Maj. Oscar Sapp Jr., his former Junior ROTC instructor at Central High School.

He became a career soldier but was never thrust into battle. Most of his war moves have come from behind a desk.

The closest he ever got was in 1990 when he was mobilized with the 48th. They made it as far as California. Desert Storm ended, and he came home.

Then came 9/11. Afghanistan. Iraq.

It left him with an empty feeling, like riding the bench in a big game.

"I was always willing to go, but I never got to participate," he said. "I was almost ashamed of myself. I would be wearing my uniform at the grocery store, and folks would come up and thank me. I would go out to eat, and people would see my uniform and buy me lunch. That just added to the guilt."

He was tired of being on the sidelines.

"I believe it's going to kill you — if you don't go," said Susan, his wife of 16 years.

So the summer has been a farewell tour of barbecues, back slaps and choking back tears.

George promises he will continue to sign his letters "George Bailey." That's the Jimmy Stewart character from "It's a Wonderful Life" who realizes he is the luckiest man on earth.

"It's heartbreaking for the wife and (three) kids, yet I actually prayed for something like this to happen for me so I could finally do my part," he said.

Godspeed, my friend.

George Bailey comes ho-ho-home

December 21, 2005

Susan Fisher did not recognize the voice on the phone that told her to go out on her front porch last Tuesday morning.

When she hesitated, the man said: "Trust me."

Her hair was in curlers. She strained to see who was in the truck pulling into her driveway.

She didn't notice the driver was Guerry Bruner, a longtime friend of the family. She was too focused on the person dressed in a bright red Santa outfit.

The man's face was hidden by a fake beard. But, as soon as his Army boots were halfway out the door, you could hear Susan's screams up and down Beaver Oaks, across to Wildwood, over to Tobesofkee and the northern suburbs of Lizella.

George Bailey was home.

George Fisher is her husband's real name. When he turned 40 three years ago, he began signing his letters "George Bailey." That's because he had taken inventory of his blessings much the same way as the Jimmy Stewart character in the classic Christmas movie, "It's a Wonderful Life."

I wrote about my friend, George, when he left for Iraq with the 48th Brigade in July. He is stationed at Balad Air Base, about 40 miles north of Baghdad.

The separation has not been easy for Susan and their three children: Amanda, 15, Joe, 13, and Lyndsay, 10. This is one of the closest, most loving families I have ever known.

George was hoping to come home on leave in February. He figured Christmas would be a longshot, especially with the Iraqi elections last week.

He was not looking forward to being away. Christmas has always been his favorite time of year. After all, he is George Bailey.

So he jumped on the opportunity for a December leave like a kid pouncing on a present on Christmas morning.

He managed to keep it a secret from his family.

On the first leg of his 18-hour flight, he stopped at an Internet cafe in Kuwait and pulled up an e-mail from Susan. She had tried to put the Christmas lights on the tree — that was always his job — and she broke down crying four times.

Guerry picked him up in Atlanta at 6:30 a.m. on Dec. 13. They were in Macon before an unsuspecting Susan had time to get the curlers out of her hair.

This self-described 167-pound "George Bailey Claus" had never even been inside the house. Sue and the kids moved into the new home in October. He had planned and visualized his surprise visit, right down to the Santa outfit.

"I had thought about the whole Norman Rockwell thing," he said. "Kids jumping up and down on the porch. Dogs barking. Neighbors coming out of their homes. It wasn't exactly like that, but it was close. It was good."

Still wearing his Santa suit, he surprised each of the children at school — Lyndsay at Heritage Elementary, Joe at Howard Middle School, then Amanda at Westside High School. George also went to see his mother, Betty Bernard.

Let's just say the Fisher family set a record for happy tears that morning. Son Joe gave him the biggest hug.

"He has really missed me," said George. "He has been living in a sorority house for the past six months."

George gets to stay until Dec. 29. Then he'll head back until the end of May. Christmas is four days away, but my friend already has this one rated.

"The best Christmas ever," he said.

Welcome home, George Bailey.

God called his co-pilot home

February 28, 2006

The sky was blue Monday morning, with a whisper of wind and barely a cloud in the sky.

It was a good day for flying.

I'm sure Scotty would have approved of the day God called his co-pilot home.

It was on such a day 85 years ago Robert L. Scott took his first flight from the roof of a house on East Napier Avenue in Macon.

Imagine an adventurous boy, laughing in the face of gravity with a pair of homemade wings.

Then imagine the boy tumbling to the ground into a bed of Cherokee roses. The state flower, no less.

It was the only time the retired brigadier general ever crashed during his distinguished flying career. The famed aviator and war hero logged more than 33,000 hours in the air, including hundreds of missions over Burma and China during World War II.

To know this man, even from a distance, was to revere a man who was larger than life right up to the end, just 44 days before his 98th birthday.

He was one of the most energetic, enthusiastic and charming men I have ever met. He was an icon in Warner Robins, where the mere mention of his name has always commanded the greatest respect. Even civilians saluted him in the grocery store.

He was a tireless promoter and fund-raiser for the Museum of Aviation. His fingerprints are everywhere in that impressive facility. A six-mile stretch of Ga. 247, near Robins Air Force Base, is named in his honor.

A friend of mine, George Fisher, once called Scotty the "reddest, whitest and bluest American on this planet." George, who is now serving with the 48th Brigade in Iraq, co-founded the Robert L. Scott Fan Club Association in 1975, when he and friends Guerry Bruner and David DeVore were sixth-graders at Lane Elementary School in Macon.

The three boys read a library book about Scott and wrote him a letter. He graciously replied. Then those "snot-nosed boys grew up to become three men who still believe he is the greatest fighter pilot in the world and that he did, as a matter of fact, hang the moon."

A fan club was born. There are now more than 200 members from nearly every state and as far away as France, China, Thailand, Australia and Canada.

It was through George that I got to know Scotty. We nibbled on egg rolls one day at a Chinese restaurant on Russell Parkway. He told me about walking the Great Wall of China. He carried a sand wedge as his walking stick.

He was 72 years old when his footsteps covered the nearly 2,000 miles from Tibet to the Yellow Sea. It took him three months and 1,400 oatmeal cookies. He later wrote about his adventure in *Reader's Digest* magazine.

He reminisced about writing his autobiography, "God Is My Co-Pilot," and the 1945 premiere of the movie at the Grand Theater in Macon, now the Grand Opera House.

He also talked about the embarrassment of getting pulled over for speeding one night in his Ford Thunderbird on the Robert L. Scott Highway. We laughed about that.

Growing up, he was forever fascinated with flying. He dreamed of becoming a fighter pilot. He once rushed to watch Gen. Billy Mitchell, the pioneer aviator, land his plane in Macon. They refueled here on a flight to Miami, but not before he and some of the other Army pilots stopped downtown for a bite to eat at the Hotel Dempsey. Scott tried to stow away in one of the aircraft's compartments, but a mechanic discovered him and sent him home.

Still, by far my favorite Scotty story is the one about that first flight as a 12-year-old working on his Boy Scout aviation badge.

One day, he walked the five blocks from his home on East Napier to the former Tattnall Square Baptist Church, which is now the Newton Chapel at the northwest corner of Mercer University's campus.

He climbed the steeple, captured a few pigeons from the belfry and released them during a particularly fervent prayer at a nearby tent revival. The preacher was not amused. He had the boy arrested for disturbing the peace.

Scotty vowed to get revenge against the "holy rollers and the old preacher." Early one morning, while delivering *The Telegraph* on his bicycle, he used a razor to cut a section of the canvas from the revival tent, leaving a gaping hole.

He hid the canvas in the woods. It came in handy when he decided to build a glider. He designed it like the Wright Brothers' plane at Kitty Hawk. He stretched the cloth across some pine boards and painted an American flag on the "fuselage."

He recruited two friends to stabilize his wings while he launched himself into space from the roof of a neighbor's large antebellum house. It was not far from the home of Viola Ross Napier, who was Georgia's first female state legislator.

When the spar snapped, the wings buckled and he crash-landed in the Cherokee roses. He later claimed the roses probably saved his life, although the thorns left an impression. His father rescued him from the bushes, then ordered him to disassemble the flying machine.

He kept right on flying, though.

We send our own roses today.

He lived a full life, and a remarkable one.

I thought about that Monday as I watched a jet stream disappearing against that blue sky — a perfect day for flying.

I reached for a Bible, turned to II Timothy 4:7 and remembered Scotty with these words:

"I have fought the good fight. I have finished the race. I have kept the faith."

An empty seat, a sense of place

September 11, 2005

When she drives up from Florida — either for a visit or to escape the hurricanes — a strange feeling sweeps over Pat Hogan.

"I feel Cole should be with me every time I go back to Macon," she said. "And he's not."

The seat next to her is empty. She has made the trip alone for the past four years. Four years is also the exact number of years she knew Cole Hogan before he died Sept. 11, 2001.

We all have our ways we remember 9/11. The smoke in the skies. The tears in our eyes. The overwhelming sense that life as we knew it had changed forever.

A song reminds us about the lump in our throats. There was a time when it stirred our patriotism, too.

Where were you when the world stopped turning?

Life changed for Pat Hogan more than most people that horrible morning. Her husband, Maj. Cole Hogan, was one of 125 people killed at the Pentagon after terrorists hijacked American Airlines Flight 77. (Another 64 passengers and crew on the flight also died.)

Three weeks earlier, Cole's offices had been relocated to the section of the Pentagon where the plane crashed. He never had a chance. His area was at the point of impact.

He was 40 years old, just one month shy of his 41st birthday, and Macon was the place he called home. He cut his teeth here, played ball here, went to school at First Presbyterian Day School, rode around town in Jeeps and made his share of lifelong buddies.

In the four years since Cole's death, Macon has become Pat Hogan's second home. An Air Force physician stationed in Fort Walton Beach, Fla., she makes the six-hour drive several times a year.

Jane Hogan has become her "second mom." Cole's sisters, Meg and Kris, are like her own sisters. Some of Cole's closest friends, Andy Greenway and Larry Williams, have been like brothers.

"I had never set foot in Macon before I met Cole," she said. "Now Cole's family has become my family. Cole's friends have become my friends. It's like home to me."

Especially on days like today, the anniversary that is so painful. Cole's dad, Wallace Hogan, died in December 2002. So Pat tries to come to Macon every Sept. 11 to be with Jane.

"It's important for us to be together," Pat said. "It's important for me to wake up in that house. We spend a quiet day talking about Cole. I love to hear those funny stories about when he was growing up. But it's still very hard. It's very emotional for both of us."

It's an amazing story how they found each other. Cole's military career in the Special Forces had carried him all over the map. He was with the Army Jungle Operations Training Battalion in Panama when he met her.

On Sept. 19, 1997, he had a stomach virus. So he made the one-hour trip from Fort Sherman to Howard Air Force Base to see a doctor. Pat was the internist on call. It was love at first dose.

That's a wonder in itself. She was from Thailand. He was from Georgia. She was a Buddhist. He was a Methodist.

But, for all their differences, they shared so much in common. They were both outdoor enthusiasts with a sense of adventure. They loved to travel and ride bikes.

They were married Oct. 9, 1999 — Cole's 39th birthday.

Pat often thinks back to that day they met Sept. 19, 1997. That's because exactly four years later on Sept. 19, 2001 — eight days after the terrorist attacks on the Pentagon and World Trade Center — Army officers knocked on the door of his parents' home in Macon and told the family Cole's body had been positively identified.

Pat is 39 years old now. She doesn't know if she will ever remarry. Time is a great healer, but even a doctor realizes some wounds can never be closed.

Every day carries its reminders of Macon's lone casualty in the Sept. 11 terrorist attacks. A small park was dedicated to Cole at the end of his old neighborhood on Overlook Avenue. In the neighborhood where he and Pat lived in Alexandria, Va., a memorial bench was unveiled in memory of Cole and another neighbor who died in the attack.

An oak tree was planted in Cole's memory on Arbor Day across from City Hall in Macon. There are memorials that bear his name at Fort Benning, Fort Lewis, Fort Bragg and the Pentagon.

Pat often goes to Washington on business trips. She calls those visits "bittersweet." She drives to the home they shared, the house where they were married.

Then she will drive to Arlington National Cemetery, where Cole is buried near a stand of oaks. In the distance, down the hill and through those same trees, there is a view of the Pentagon.

Pat believes in what America is doing to fight the war on terrorism. She was deployed to Afghanistan for a few months.

Her position on the war has not changed. It never will. If anything, it has been strengthened.

She knows if Cole were here, he would be there, too.

"He meant a lot to this community," she said. "I want to live my life in a way that would make him proud of me."

The day bullets fell from the sky

June 11, 2006

Jerry Day found God on a summer morning in a stairwell on the 26th floor of the University of Texas Tower in Austin.

It is during such moments one might expect to reach for heaven. It seems more within your grasp when you're 300 feet in the air and don't know if your next breath will be your last.

The sound of gunfire was closing in on him, and he could not walk two steps without leaving bloody footprints.

He could hear the sniper firing from the observation deck behind a closed door at the top of the stairs.

A wounded man grabbed Day's legs and tried to take his pistol.

"I want to kill that S.O.B.," he told him.

"Don't worry," Day said. "I will get him for you."

Yes, that was the plan.

Find God in this dark moment, then kill this nut before he kills somebody else.

Day said a prayer, although he dared not shut his eyes.

"I don't know you as well as I should, Lord," he prayed. "And I don't know your son, Jesus Christ. I don't want to die. I just want to do my job."

It all happened 40 years ago — a long stretch of road in a dusty rear-view mirror. Although a few strands of gray hair and wrinkles have trailed him, the edges of his story remain sharp.

He just doesn't talk about it much anymore.

"The whole time it was happening, I remember saying to myself this kind of thing doesn't happen in the United States," he said.

It unfolded like a bad dream Aug. 1, 1966. This was years before the horrors of Columbine and the atrocities of Timothy McVeigh. In many ways, it represented the dawn of domestic terrorism in our country.

Three years earlier and 180 miles away, President John F. Kennedy had been assassinated by a gunman perched in a sixth-floor window of the Texas School Book Depository in Dallas.

But no one would have expected a former altar boy and Eagle Scout named Charles Whitman would ascend to the top of the famed tower in Austin and indiscriminately start shooting innocent people. When his guns stopped smoking, he had killed 13 and wounded 31.

Day was the first police officer to reach the top of the tower that day. He was one of three Austin police officers, along with a deputized citizen, who drew Whitman in and then took him out.

The two other officers were credited with pulling the triggers that riddled Whitman with bullet holes. All three men received the Medal of Valor, the highest award for courage given to a public safety officer.

Day found himself appearing at civic clubs and various public functions. He was interviewed by writers from newspapers, magazines and books.

But when the Hollywood types moved in and started asking him all kinds of questions, he told the movie folks to go away. He was tired of talking.

He never gave another interview — until last week.

Day has lived in Middle Georgia for the past seven years. Home is a trailer park in rural Twiggs County.

At age 67, he draws Social Security and considers himself blessed to be alive. Not only did he survive that bloodbath as a young police officer, he battled back from a heart aneurysm in the fall of 2005.

We met one afternoon at Angel's Diner, out on Ga. 57. He stared into a coffee cup, and his words leaned across the table and pulled me with him through his story.

The Austin Police Department was recruiting officers in 1964, and he answered the newspaper ad. He had been in the Air Force. It made sense. At the time, he was married, and the salary was attractive.

He loved the job. It was mostly patrol duty in the black and Hispanic neighborhoods along 12th Street in the Texas state capital.

That morning, he had met another officer, Billy Speed, for a quick breakfast near a bridge along the Colorado River.

Speed was one of his closest friends in the department. He seemed troubled that day, though. He told Day he was considering turning in his badge at the end of his shift.

"He wanted to give it up because he was afraid something might happen, and he might get hurt," said Day. "He had a wife and 18-month-old baby at home. He talked about opening a camera shop down in San Antonio."

Charles Whitman, a 25-year-old former Marine and sharpshooter, was troubled by his own band of demons.

Four months earlier, he had met with a University of Texas psychiatrist. He reportedly told the doctor he had been feeling urges to start shooting people with a deer rifle from the university tower.

The night before the massacre, he began writing suicide notes. Shortly after midnight, he killed his mother by stabbing her in the heart. He then returned home and stabbed his wife five times, killing her, too.

Hiding his guns in a wooden crate and foot locker, he gained access to the tower by posing as a delivery man. He began his killing spree once he reached the top, murdering a receptionist and several tourists. He barricaded the door to the observation deck with a dolly. He then began shooting students and pedestrians on the campus and city streets below.

Day heard the dispatch on the police radio late that morning. Officers were advised to proceed with caution. He headed along Guadalupe Street, then down a back alley to reach the tower, a landmark in the heart of Austin.

He was horrified with what he discovered. A female student lay dead in the street. He stopped to help a man who had been shot in the arm.

"It was wild warfare," Day said. "It was out of control. People were getting guns and shooting at the sniper on top of the building."

Whitman was shooting back at anything that moved. He even fired shots at a small airplane overhead.

Day was unaware his friend, Billy Speed, would soon be counted among the dead. (Speed was the only police officer killed by the sniper.)

Day ran inside the tower and was the first law enforcement official to reach the elevator. He rode to the top with a deputized citizen named Allen "Cookie" Crum. Day called for backup and was later joined by officers Ramiro Martinez and Houston McCoy.

The officers kicked in the door at the top of the stairs. Day and Crum headed to the right. Martinez and McCoy broke to the left.

Day remembers bullets whizzing past his head. They were being fired from below by citizens who did not realize they were shooting at police officers.

In two years with the department, he had never been involved in an exchange of gunfire.

"On patrol, I had knives drawn on me, but I had never been under fire," he said. "I was indignant. I saw blood. I saw death. Why would someone do this to another human being?"

He found God in that stairwell and met providence on the roof, high above the city. Crum fired a shot and his gun jammed. Whitman, who was at the tower's northwest corner, had turned his weapons on Day and Crum when the other two officers unloaded fire on him.

In the end, 13 people died. The death toll was listed at 15 after the bodies of Whitman's mother and wife were found. Some reports place the figure at 17 to reflect a suicide prompted by the attacks and a woman who suffered a miscarriage.

The Austin sniper attacks have been credited with providing the impetus for the formation of SWAT teams within police departments.

The tower was closed for two years following the attacks. After several suicide jumps, the tower remained closed from 1975 to 1998.

It is now open only for guided tours. But it continues to glow "Longhorn Orange" after University of Texas football victories, including the national championship win over Southern Cal in January's Rose Bowl.

Day spent 16 years in law enforcement, and later worked as a street minister and director of a homeless shelter.

He still stays in touch with Speed's widow, who remarried. But he has lost touch with most of the others.

"It took its toll on all of us," he said.

God knows, even 40 years cannot erase the sadness.

Church remembers fallen pilot

October 15, 2006

PINEHURST — There was no need to hear a sermon on hell that morning. The temperature was already climbing the sweaty foreheads of everyone in the pews at Liberty Baptist Church.

It was July 24, 1950, a Monday, and the second day of a weeklong revival. Funeral home fans shoved the air from the front of the sanctuary to the back.

In the churchyard, gnats hummed from their own humid hymn book beneath the pine trees. Less than a mile across the fields, cars and trucks rolled through the south Georgia countryside on U.S. 41.

Dr. L.C. Cutts, the visiting preacher from nearby Vienna, took his place in the pulpit. The congregation stood and began singing. No one can remember the name of the hymn, just the rumble that accompanied it. It sounded like the entire soprano section of the choir had switched to the bass clef.

Most folks assumed it was an airplane circling in the blue skies above. It was common to see and hear planes from Robins Air Force Base, just 30 miles away. There had been increased activity since the United States had entered the Korean War just three weeks earlier.

Suddenly, a loud explosion shook the ground. Flames bolted across the grass and trees. Huge clumps of earth flew through the air. One church member would later describe it as "the world was on fire."

An F-84E Thunderjet, on a training mission from Turner Air Force Base in Albany, crashed into a field of sweet potatoes just 126 yards from the church.

No one at the church was injured. The 21-year-old pilot, a recent graduate of flight school, was killed.

For the past 56 years, members of this small country church at the edge of a cotton field, have believed the pilot, Lt. James R. Greeson, of Hawkins, Texas, did everything within his power to avoid hitting the church. The plane had gone into a steep dive 18,000 feet above Dooly County, a few miles southeast of Pinehurst.

"I remember Dr. Cutts raising his arms and telling us to be calm," said Charles Bowen, now 80, who was in the church that day. "He said there might be another explosion. But nobody listened. Everybody ran outside."

Wayne Peavy, now 67, was 10 years old at the time. He was sitting in the back pews with several other boys.

"I heard somebody say it was a bomb, and the first thing I wanted to do was go find my mama," he said. "I ran into the aisle, but there were so many people running outside they took me right out the door with them."

The crash left a giant crater about 25 feet wide and 15 feet deep. Pieces of the plane were scattered almost 400 feet from the plane's point of impact. Several cars were damaged, and a stoop above a door at the church was destroyed by flying debris.

The plane's engine was never found.

"It's still in the ground out there somewhere," said Bowen. "I worked that field for 15 or 20 years after the crash, and we were still finding pieces of that plane."

The late Howell Porter was one of three eyewitnesses standing outside the church when the plane crashed. He told *The Vienna News* the plane "looked like a rocket heading right at the church."

His theory was an explosion inside the plane about 300 feet above the church caused it to veer off course and avoid hitting the church.

"I think that is what saved the church and everybody in it," Porter told the newspaper.

According to the Air Force accident report, Greeson had a total of 35 hours, 15 minutes of training in the F-80 type aircraft. He had started attending the F-84E transition ground school a week earlier and had scored 100 on his exam.

He and his instructor pilot, Capt. J.M. Vivian, left Turner AFB in two F-84Es about 10:30 a.m. that Monday. Greeson performed a series of training maneuvers for about an hour. The planes began to go into a shallow dive, and Vivian instructed Greeson to cross over from the instructor's left wing to the right-wing position.

He never saw Greeson appear on the right side of his airplane and lost radio contact with the young pilot.

It was estimated Greeson's plane hit the ground at an 85-degree angle and a speed of more than 380 mph.

The crash turned out to be a life-changing experience for Peavy. He was one of four people who joined the church later that day, when the revival resumed. (Thirteen more joined during the week of the revival.)

"I had been wanting to join the church, but I was intimidated so I kept putting it off," he said. "I remember walking around that big hole thinking I almost didn't get a chance to do it. So I went back inside and, as soon as the piano started playing the hymn of invitation, I was walking down the aisle."

Members of the Ladies Sunday School Class later wrote a sympathy letter to the wife and parents of the pilot. A framed copy of the letter is still on display at the church.

A few weeks ago, members of Liberty Baptist placed a memorial to Greeson near the church cemetery, not far from where the pilot's body was found.

The church will officially dedicate the marker at the morning worship service on Oct. 29. Wayne Peavy's son, Jeff, located members of Greeson's family in Texas. Several plan to attend, including a son, Robert Wells, who never knew his father. His mother was pregnant with him at the time.

"We probably should have done this years ago," said Bowen. "If we didn't put something out there, nobody would ever know about it."

* * * * *

For 56 years she had imagined a country church surrounded by fields of cotton whiter than an old man's hair.

"It's just like I pictured it," said Julie Greeson Wells upon seeing Liberty Baptist Church for the first time. "I'm just in awe that a day like today could happen after all these years."

Sunday was splashed with sunshine and crowned by a blue sky, much like it was on the morning of July 24, 1950.

That was the day her first husband, Lt. James Robert "Jackie" Greeson, went on an Air Force training mission and never came back.

Eight members of Greeson's family, who all live in Texas, attended Sunday's memorial service at Liberty Baptist — 56 years and 97 days after the crash. Among them were his widow, Julie, his brother, Bill, sister, Paula Williams and son, Rob Greeson Wells.

Longtime church member Charles Bowen stood after the congregation had sung Hymn No. 243, "Sweet Sweet Spirit," and remembered being in the church that summer morning.

About a dozen others in the pews Sunday were also there that day in 1950. Folks reached to wipe away tears as they reflected on the lives that had been spared — church members who lived to have children, grandchildren and even great-grandchildren.

Although Greeson never knew any of the people he saved, and they never knew him, a scripture was read from the Gospel of John: "Greater love hath no man than this, that a man lay down his life for his friends."

Julie and Jackie grew up in the same small east Texas town of Hawkins. They were married on May 10, 1950. Greeson received his pilot's wings two days later.

He was assigned to Turner Air Force Base in Albany.

They had only been married 11 weeks when he died.

He never knew he was going to be a father.

His son, James Robert "Rob" Greeson Jr., was named after him. Julie Greeson remarried on Dec. 26, 1951, when Rob was 9 months old. Her husband, Weldon Wells, later adopted Rob, who took his stepfather's last name.

Family members said Rob got his dad's outgoing personality and good looks, right down to the red hair. He has been able to construct memories of his father only by asking others.

"I miss the fact that I didn't have a life with him," he said. "But I'm proud of what he did. It was a selfless act of heroism."

Rob Wells is now a dentist in Henderson, Texas. About a month ago, he rode his motorcycle to Hawkins, and visited his father's grave.

Sunday, his eyes stretched across the south Georgia field where his father's life ended. A trumpet played taps, and a wreath was placed at a newly dedicated memorial marker.

"This brings some closure," he said. "I learned more about my father, what happened and the lives he touched."

Gratitude comes with wooden nickels

November 9, 2005

WARNER ROBINS — For Donnie Powell, every day is Veterans Day.

Friday may be the designated time on the calendar when we pay tribute to those who served our country.

But Donnie is mindful of their sacrifices the other 364 days of the year, too.

He rarely leaves his house without a handful of wooden nickels stuffed in his pockets. He has had some 2,000 of them special-made by a company in San Antonio.

On one side is an emblem of the American flag with the words: "Dear Vets. Thank You!" The other reads: "Vets accept a sacred trust to preserve the USA."

When he sees someone in the bread aisle at the grocery store or pumping gas over at Bob's Chevron on North Houston Road, he might stop and ask if they are a veteran.

He then reaches into his pocket and produces the wooden nickel.

"The men and women of the military are truly remarkable," he said. "This is one way I try to honor them."

He is in good company. This town is full of them.

He has listened to many of their stories about helicopter missions and fighting in the Battle of the Bulge.

Some still carry the battle scars, the limps, the shell-shock.

Once, when he noticed a car in a parking lot with a "Vietnam Veteran" license plate, he left a plastic bag full of the wooden nickels on the windshield.

Time, circumstance and an asthma condition kept Donnie out of the military. But he is a retired civil service worker, so he passed through those gates at Robins Air Force Base most every day for more than 30 years.

He has had family members and in-laws proudly wear a military uniform. He has known many reservists, poised and ready to defend our country at a moment's notice.

He got the idea for the wooden nickels at the annual Christmas parade in Warner Robins a few years ago. A local church was passing them out to promote a play. He wrote the company that makes the wooden nickels and ordered a shipment of 1,000.

"I have handed them out to veterans at the mall, at Sam's, in restaurants and stores. They (the vets) have always been appreciative," he said. "One day there were two vets of World War II in the same store. One had killed 47 Germans and had been shot, which required about 40 operations. Another was on D-Day all the way to Germany, and then on to Okinawa."

A friend, who was a helicopter pilot in Vietnam, invited him to a reunion. Donnie did not attend, but he had some wooden nickels delivered to the hotel in Texas where the Vietnam veterans were staying.

He laughs about meeting a motorcycle rider. He gave him an ample supply of wooden nickels to distribute to his fellow vets.

"It's not every day I approach a biker in black leather," he said.

He often gives the wooden nickels to current military personnel because, he said, "they will be vets some day."

He also takes the time to thank those in law enforcement and public safety, too.

He had one police officer in Centerville tell him: "We don't hear a lot of that."

And that's a shame. Are we becoming a nation incapable of showing gratitude to those who defend and protect us?

Every day should be Veteran's Day.

You don't need a wooden nickel to say thank you.

Great is thy faithfulness

Where they care enough to ask

March 24, 2005

It has been said Macon has more churches per capita than any city in the country.

Of course, the same claim is made by almost a dozen other cities, including Dallas, New Orleans, Nashville, Tenn., Charlotte, N.C., Tulsa, Okla., Lynchburg, Va., Pensacola, Fla., New Haven, Conn., and Las Vegas.

New Orleans? Doesn't it have the most bars?

Las Vegas? Must be counting the Elvis Wedding Chapel down on the strip.

I would say let's challenge them all to a fight, but that would probably be breaking a commandment. Or two.

From historic sanctuaries to worship centers the size of Super Wal-Marts, there are more than 400 churches listed in Macon's yellow pages.

That's one church for every 238 people. That's more than three times the average in the deeply religious South, where there is one church steeple for every 650 folks.

I don't think that makes us any holier than, say, Wheaton, Ill., which is No. 1 according to the board game "Trivial Pursuit."

But it does mean we are a people of great faith. And, with Passover and Easter this week, this is an appropriate time to point it out.

It's something I certainly do when I give tours every spring as part of the Cherry Blossom Festival. Especially with groups like the one I had Wednesday — about 20 seniors from the McDonough Presbyterian Church.

They were impressed with our bounty of churches. For example, there is a section of Vineville Avenue where Vineville United Methodist, Bethlehem Primitive Baptist and Vineville Presbyterian occupy a two-block stretch.

Of even greater density is the downtown area from the base of Cherry Street, bounded by Washington Avenue, Orange Street, New Street and Forsyth Street.

In this space, there are three Baptist churches, a Catholic church, a Jewish synagogue, an AME church, a CME church, a Presbyterian church and a Unitarian Universalist church.

That's nine churches in an area only slightly larger than three city blocks. Does that make us the buckle of the Bible Belt? We could probably make a strong case.

The festival should be commended for recognizing the significance of churches in our community.

This year's Cherry Blossom print, by Atlanta artist Annie Moller, is titled "Macon Houses of Worship." It features the historic downtown churches Mulberry Methodist, First Baptist, Christ Church, First Presbyterian, St. Joseph Catholic and Temple Beth Israel.

I often recite the famous passage from the book *Midnight in the Garden of Good and Evil* to my tour groups. Author John Berendt wrote that, in Augusta, people want to know your grandmother's maiden name. In Savannah, they want to know what you like to drink.

"If you go to Atlanta, the first question people ask you is, 'What's your business?'" wrote Berendt. "If you go to Macon, they ask, 'Where do you go to church?'"

I'm proud to live in a place where they care enough to ask.

Cleanliness and godliness

February 19, 2006

The phone rang one night, and Robert Hubbard was there to answer, ready to reach out and touch someone's life again.

"You're out to save the world," his wife, Evelyn, told him.

"I'm almost there," he said.

He works at Christ Church, the oldest church in Macon. It was founded in 1825 and has a history and tradition as steeped as its beautiful spires.

Robert is the church sexton. He wasn't quite sure what a sexton was — or exactly what a sexton did — when he applied for the job 10 years ago.

"I had to look it up in the dictionary," he said.

His consultation with Noah Webster offered this broad definition: "A church custodian charged with keeping the church and parish buildings prepared for meetings, caring for church equipment and performing minor related duties."

He took the job.

Every day he redefines it.

"I've never met anyone like him in my life," said Stella Patterson, a parishioner at Christ Church. "He's a guardian angel. He's a saint. If we could ordain him, we would."

There's a lot more to Robert's rules of order than sweeping the floor and polishing the door knobs.

The 48-year-old Macon man routinely feeds the homeless, cares for the elderly and visits the church nursery on Sunday mornings so he can learn all the babies' names.

After all, the children at Christ Church grow up knowing Robert. And they adore him.

Patterson's daughter, Elizabeth, once wrote him every day from summer camp to tell him how much she missed him.

"So often, he is that first face people see when they come to our church," said Connie Menendez, a longtime parishioner. "And what a wonderful, smiling, caring face to see. Everybody downtown knows Robert. I've seen him wave to lawyers on their way to the courthouse. I've seen him greet homeless people on the street."

Robert used to find a homeless man named "Ricky" sleeping in the breezeway between the sanctuary and the parish house. But rather than sending the man away, he befriended him. He provided him with food, money and clothes. He encouraged him to make a better life for himself.

Now "Ricky" has turned things around. He lives with his daughter and drops by to thank Robert. He tells Robert how much he loves him.

"I've never heard an unkind word come from Robert's lips," Patterson said. "He truly exemplifies the Christian life."

Robert never knew his parents while growing up in Macon. He was placed in three different foster homes. He credits each of those families for giving him love, care and support.

After graduating from Southwest High School in 1976, he went to work as a custodian at Duresville Elementary. He later held jobs at several other schools and as a mail courier at a local bank.

He found his birth mother while reading the obituaries one morning.

"I usually don't read the obits, but I saw them that day," he said. "My mother's sister had died, and I recognized my mother's name from my birth certificate."

He connected with his mother and now enjoys a close relationship with her.

When the church's former sexton, Oscar L. Jackson, died in May 1996, Robert was recommended by Peggy Puryear, a parishioner who was a teacher at Duresville when he worked there.

Now, Robert welcomes his job each day with his arms and heart wide open. Four days each week, he coordinates the church's Meals on Wheels program. Before the church underwent its renovation, he would lead the children up to the bell tower Sunday mornings to ring the bell.

"They followed him up there like the pied piper," Menendez said.

There's probably not a task at the church Robert has not handled or could not handle. Last week, he even called bingo for a group of church ladies.

"Some people have come here to church thinking I was the priest," he said, laughing.

When his church duties are finished each day, the work is far from finished. He and his family operate a janitorial service that cleans the offices of Cox Communications and two local dentist offices.

I asked Robert if he had finally figured out the definition of a sexton.

"Clean up, take care of people and keep everyone happy," he said.

He may never get to preach a sermon from the pulpit, but that's quite all right.

I've said many times I would rather see a sermon than hear one any day.

Joining the congregation of the curious

August 9, 2006

SOUTH NEWPORT — The sign at Christ's Chapel claims it is the "Smallest Church in America."

A few others have challenged that distinction over the past 57 years. But, in the confines of a sanctuary that's 10 feet wide and 15 feet deep, it's easy to brush elbows as you fold your hands to pray.

The church's former pastor, the late Rev. G.W. Ward, used to chuckle and say there was room for 13 worshippers — if everyone held their breath.

There are no longer worship services in the tiny chapel that rests in the shade of water oaks on a clump of land known as Memory Park.

Church starts whenever you want it to begin. Open 24 hours a day, seven days a week. Just like Wal-Mart.

You're always early, late or right on time. Just remember to close the door when you leave. The lights are programmed with the opening and closing of the chapel door. Last month's electric bill was $34.77, so donations are welcome.

A few weeks ago, I joined the congregation of the curious. (I have also visited the "World's Smallest Police Station" — a phone booth on U.S. 98 in Carrabelle, Fla.)

The chapel is about a mile off Interstate 95 at Exit 67 between Brunswick and Savannah. South Newport is a dip in the road along Ga. 17, one of the many coastal communities scattered along the marshes and fishing villages.

Agnes Harper, a widow who ran a rural grocery store, opened this nondenominational church in 1949. She had a bit of a squabble with her local house of worship, so she went out and built her own.

She acquired the land from her son-in-law and deeded the property to Jesus. There are 13 seats inside, representing Christ and his disciples.

"Whenever I'm upset, I go in there and pray," said Effie Young, who lives six miles down the road. "All my troubles go away."

Miss Effie became the church's caretaker after her husband, Otis, died in 1993. She checks on the "dollhouse" every morning and afternoon.

Visitors from as far away as Michigan and New York routinely sign the guest book. Some are inspired to record their own thoughts and meditations in a notebook next to the pint-sized pulpit.

Although services are no longer held, Miss Effie is called at least a half-dozen times a year by couples wanting to get married. One man told her he was a senator from Ohio, but politely refused to give his name.

On cleaning days, she sweeps, dusts and wipes the smudges from the stained-glass windows. Usually, there are a couple of dollars in the donation box.

Sometimes the money goes for repairs. Vandals struck so many times one holiday season, the locks had to be replaced five times. Another time, she and her husband arrived to find all the chairs had been taken outside and broken.

She grew weary of people abandoning animals at the church, so she posted a sign. She once found a dead dog in a bag. "He must have died in the car, and they just pulled over and left him here," she said. "It smelled so bad. My grandson got a shovel, and we buried it."

Miss Effie will turn 70 on Saturday. Caretakers have birthday parties, not retirement parties. "I reckon I'll keep looking after the little church until I die," she said.

She recalled one afternoon, after a terrible storm, she and her husband went expecting the worst.

"I was worried to death," she said. "A tree had fallen across the top of the church, but it never touched. It was the most amazing thing."

She has seen gigantic miracles, even in the smallest church in the kingdom.

The apostle of Walnut Street

June 22, 2008

The box fan on the chair inside the gas station has three speeds to stir the air.

The three Bibles on the desk are there to stir the soul.

Lee Hencely's eyes and heart have made the 1,406-page journey from Genesis to Revelation, and he is reading the Bible again. He has dog-eared pages in the Old Testament, underlined verses and made notes to himself in the Gospels.

There's the wisdom of an "Archie" comic book on the desk, too, for good measure.

Lee works at the Saf-T Oil at the corner of Walnut Street and Martin Luther King Jr. Boulevard. It's a tiny building, just a few bricks wide and deep, a throwback to the days of concrete floors and rear restrooms. I'm convinced it's one of the few remaining full-service gas stations in civilization.

It's obvious Lee loves his job. He will pump your gas, check your oil and put air in your tires. He moves around with a cheerfulness he refers to as "pep in my step." Service with a smile. You sure don't see that much any more.

He has lost count of the number of times he has had to push stalled cars out of the busy intersection. He's been the extra mile, too. He once drove a stranded woman to her house to Warner Robins.

A few years back, a man from Indiana hobbled in with a broken car and no money in his pocket. Lee bought him breakfast, filled his tank, put on a new fan belt and sent him on his way at no charge.

When the man got back on his feet, he sent Lee a $100 bill.

Lee works alone, but he is never lonely. There are always folks hanging around. Loyal customers come by to shake his hand and bend his ear. There is rarely a dull moment on one of downtown's busiest corners.

Sometimes, a few homeless men will wander up from the river. They drop by to get a drink of water or use the telephone. They share their life stories and heartaches with Lee. They talk because they know he will listen.

He has been there.

He has walked in their moccasins.

The man who once ran this same gas station threw Lee a life preserver 43 years ago.

It took Lee a long time to soak up the lessons of all those life experiences, but they are now mounted on his running board.

Six months ago, he started an urban ministry called "Taking It Back to the Streets." He writes his sermons on yellow legal pads and is engaged in reaching and preaching to the homeless and less fortunate.

He holds non-denominational services once a month at Central City Park. Jesus fed the multitudes with loaves and fishes. Last month, Lee served hot dogs from Nu-Way Weiners and collards, black-eyed peas, corn bread and cabbage from the Cox Cafe on Lower Poplar Street.

"God tells us to help our neighbor," he said. "Our neighbor is whoever is standing next to us."

No, Lee is not your typical gas-pumping, Bible-thumping preacher. He is not ordained. He never attended seminary.

He has never worn a coat and tie for one minute of his life. He keeps his long hair pulled back in a ponytail. He has been married five times. He used to drink a case of beer every day. He has a tatoo on his right arm of a Cherokee Indian woman. It is there to remind him of his mother.

He does not run from his past. He doesn't try to hide his flaws, his warts, his human frailties.

His wife, Charlene, is black, and Lee is the only white member on the rolls at Union Baptist Church in Fort Hill. There was a time in his life when he didn't care much about religion. Now, he can't get enough of it.

"I'm an example," he said. "God can take a nobody and make something out of him. I can talk to people honestly."

He used to shoo away the homeless, like flies at a picnic. It made him angry when they would trespass or loiter, cut through his parking lot and trash his stoop.

"I had a hard heart," he said. "I used to argue with them. I was combative and mean. I tried to take out on others what had happened to me."

Lee ran away from his home in Forsyth in 1965, when he was 10 years old. His family life was troubled, and often abusive, so he had to get away.

He landed barefoot on the streets of Macon. He wore overalls, slept in abandoned buildings, and found food in trash cans and dumpsters.

One day, Bob Mullis noticed the youngster walking along Walnut Street and took him under his wing.

Mullis was the owner of Saf-T Oil. He pumped the first gallon of gas there when the station opened in 1935. He gave Lee a room above the garage, taught him to read and write, and put him to work pumping gas for 50 cents an hour.

Lee has never forgotten it.

He is not afraid of hard work. For years, he found work in the spinning department at Bibb Mills. He also worked at the Macon Regional Youth Detention Center.

Today, he labors almost as many hours as there are in the day. He moonlights as a security guard at John-Wesley Villas, does janitorial work at Tabernacle Baptist Church, and cleans a half-dozen parking lots and a car wash.

But most of his time is spent at the gas station, where he's just as weary of raising the prices as people are of watching the high numbers keep going up.

There is still "pep in his step," though.

Jerry Carter is one of the homeless men he befriended a few years ago. Jerry sometimes refers to himself as Lee's "secretary." He hangs out and answers the phone when Lee is busy. He lives in a tent down by the river and roams the streets almost every day looking for work.

Two weeks ago, he earned $20. What did he do with it?

He bought Lee a shirt and gave it to him.

For Father's Day.

The greatest blessing of every week

April 16, 2006

In the checkout line at the grocery store last week, the cashier asked if my family had any plans for Easter.

I thought for a moment, sorting through the pages of my mental calendar. Although it is a special day, we have no special plans.

"Not really," I said. "Probably the same thing we do every Sunday. We will go to church."

It was not intended as a holier-than-thou answer. I'm not someone who wears religion on his sleeve. I don't try to convert sinners, beat people over the head with sanctimony or thumb my nose at those who don't share the same religious beliefs.

Over the years, I've been called to preach a few sermons and lead a few prayers. For the most part, though, my spiritual life is very private.

So, don't worry. I'm not going to try to baptize you this morning. Or turn you into a nun.

Still, if there is one constant in my life, it is Sunday mornings. I have made a permanent reservation. I was brought up in the church. I have tried to instill those same values in my own children.

Trust me, I will never win a perfect attendance pin. That won't bother me. I have no real desire to collect a prize or earn a badge.

I simply place certain expectations on myself, and the routine of attending church every Sunday is one of them. I believe it is the foundation of my spiritual discipline. At our church, we call it the "spirit of presence."

When I was 14, I was given the words to a Paul Anka song called "The Teen Commandments." The one commandment I committed to memory was: "Go to church faithfully. The Creator gives you the week; give Him back an hour."

I am no longer a teenager, but that's still practical advice. There is no other institution that can help steady the rhythm and calm the pace of this crazy world.

For me, church is not a fashion statement. It is not a contest to see whose name will be entered in the book of good deeds.

It is a community of faith where I can learn, draw strength and recharge my batteries.

Today is Easter Sunday. Of course, there will be the usual "CEO" sightings in every congregation. That's the "Christmas and Easter Only" crowd.

Parking lots will be full, pews will be packed and ushers will scramble for folding chairs to seat the overflow in some churches.

And that's OK. It's better to attend church twice a year than never at all.

I know plenty of people who have fallen out of favor with church life. They have simply stopped going. They're disappointed or disgusted with organized religion.

They would rather chill out Sunday mornings. Sleep late. Read the newspaper. They claim they don't require a building for worship. Their sanctuary is the golf course. Or some quiet fishing hole at the lake.

Que sera, sera. I just know that making the effort to walk through those church doors is the greatest blessing I receive each week.

I may not remember a word of the sermon. By Monday morning, I usually have forgotten what scripture was read or hymns were sung.

Some Sundays, my mind wanders under a bridge and I lose the signal.

So I sit there and marvel at how the sunlight shines through those beautiful stained glass windows, splashing colors against walls built more than a century ago.

I believe there is something very spiritual in that.

It is a sacred moment when I understand why I am there.

School days

An open letter to all students

August 5, 2009

Welcome to the first day of school. Summer is officially over, so it's time to wake up. No more snoozing until lunch. Time to wipe off the dust and rust.

I hope you're looking forward to an exciting year. I see where you bought a new backpack during the tax-free weekend. Looks like you've got some other cool stuff, too. I like those new shoes. Your pencils are so fresh, they don't even have teeth marks.

No, I am not your self-appointed teacher. I'm more like a surrogate professor or coach. I'm someone who has been brought in to give you a pep talk at the beginning of the academic year.

This message is for first-graders at Quail Run Elementary in Warner Robins, seniors at First Presbyterian Day School in Macon, and every grade and school in between.

Others may read over your shoulder, but I've saved this space especially for you. And it has nothing to do with geometry or sentence diagramming.

Follow these principles and you will have the best school year of your life. So listen up.

Respect your teachers. They are your friend, not your enemy. They have to wear a lot of different hats. It's a thankless job that doesn't pay nearly enough money. Teachers often have to dig into their own pockets to keep things going. And a million trees have to die to keep up with all the paperwork. Don't make their jobs any more difficult. One day, you may be asked to name the three people who have had the most influence on your life. No doubt a teacher will be one of them.

Learn something new every day. And not just what you're assigned to learn. Be curious about the world. Fill yourself with wonder.

Don't be cruel. Never make fun of the way someone looks, talks or dresses, especially if they cannot help it. My family moved around a lot when I was growing up, so I was always the "new kid" at school. I had a difficult time fitting in and was the victim of a lot of insensitivity. So I know how it is to have your feelings hurt. Maybe you do, too. Channel your energy into something constructive.

Look people in the eye when you talk to them. That's the best piece of advice anyone ever gave me. We live in a world of disconnect, so never underestimate the value of eye contact when you communicate. It's like holding hands with someone's face. You might be surprised at how much more you actually listen, too.

Move your body. Don't be a couch potato chip. Life is not a spectator sport. Exercise something besides your thumbs in front of a video game.

Vaccinate yourself against the whine flu. So what if you don't like the food in the cafeteria? Be thankful you have something to eat. Some people in the world don't.

Be well-rounded. Nobody likes a square. You won't learn about life by always burying your head in a book. Join a club. Start an adventure. Get involved in community work. There's a lot more to it than your grades. Experience is the best teacher you'll ever have.

Have fun. Be good. This is some wisdom my local preacher friend always dispenses to his daughters. It's about balance. Moderation. Have fun — but not so much fun that you can't be good. And be good — but not so good that you can't have fun.

I'll see you at graduation.

Always there for roll call

May 2, 2010

MCRAE — The world brings its share of certainty. Death and taxes. High prices at the gas pumps. The Braves needing more power in the middle of their lineup.

There is a given in Telfair County, too. It's as reliable as the sun reflecting off the tracks along Railroad Street every afternoon in McRae as you head west toward Helena.

The Kahrmann family never misses a day of school.

Headaches, scratchy throats and broken bones don't stop the Kahrmanns. Rainy days and runny noses don't even slow them down.

When Matt Kahrmann graduates May 21 from Telfair County High School, where he ranks third in a class of 99, he will carry the distinction of never having missed a day of school.

Every time the roll has been called, he has been there.

It's not just a perfect attendance award. It has become a family tradition. A badge of education dedication. A blessing of good health.

His older brother, Nick, graduated from Telfair last year, ranked third in a class of 107, and never missed a school bell, either. He has continued that streak this year as a freshman at Middle Georgia College in Cochran.

His mother, Carol, was valedictorian of Telfair County High in 1979 and started the no-miss legacy. Her brother, Jimmy Ray, graduated from Telfair High 10 years later without being absent. That accomplishment has carried over into his adult life. He has a 33-year string of perfect Sunday School attendance at the McRae United Methodist Church.

Matt's younger brother, A.J., still has a way to go. He has maintained a perfect mark, too, through the fourth grade.

He knows the Kahrmann family policy. Earache? Bellyache? Sometimes you gotta play hurt.

A.J. has learned reporting for school every day "isn't going to kill you."

Yes, it's all karma to the Kahrmanns.

"My mother passed this down to us," said Carol. "It's part of our everyday life. Not being there is never even discussed."

Carol and her husband, Randy, are both teachers at Telfair Middle School. It was important to her mother, the late Erma Ray, that Carol never miss a day of school. Carol's older sister, Debbie, had lupus and was absent from school most of her life because of illness.

So Erma made sure Carol was there — no matter what. When Carol broke both arms jumping on a trampoline, her mama still took her to school every day. When Carol broke her leg in another accident on the playground, Erma carried her up the steps in the old two-story schoolhouse. (Erma was even pregnant with Jimmy at the time.)

"My mother believed school prepares you for life," said Carol. "She insisted if you were not seriously sick or dead, you should be at school and learn as much as you were capable of learning. This was non-negotiable."

Her mother insisted she be at the school every time the doors opened.

"It took a lot of effort, because we made a lot of trips to Augusta when my sister was in the hospital," Carol said. "It wasn't like I went to school sick. It was always more my mother's dream than mine. When I was living it, I didn't see it."

After Carol married and had children of her own, she began to understand how important school attendance was to her mother. Erma worked at the family's Ford automobile dealership and never missed a day of work.

"She asked one thing of me, to make sure my three sons went to school to learn, and this meant every day," Carol said.

Nick, the oldest, even delayed getting braces until after he graduated. He was concerned that missing any part of the school day might cause his teachers to mark him "absent."

Nick played sports at Telfair and never missed a practice or game. While the school building was being remodeled, school officials asked some students not to report to class. With the displaced classrooms and cramped conditions, there was no place to put everybody.

But Nick didn't volunteer to stay home. He kept getting up every morning and returning to homeroom like a boomerang.

He teases Matt about his perfect attendance mark, claiming his younger brother didn't have to work nearly as hard at it. Matt is only 16 and is graduating more than a year ahead of schedule.

Matt has always been a math prodigy and scored a perfect 800 on the math portion of his SAT. There have been times in his educational life when, his mother says, he "could not learn enough or fast enough."

When he was 4 years old, Matt could add, subtract, multiply and divide. Instead of bedtime stories, he would ask for word problems.

"People would see us at McDonald's and ask Matt what was 26 times 27, and he would rattle off the number," said Carol. "When he was in the first grade, he was doing math on a fourth-grade level. A bus would pick him up at the primary school every morning and take him to the fourth-grade class at the elementary school.

"His feet didn't even touch the floor when he sat in the desks, and he couldn't read some of the words in the problems. But he could do the math and finished with the highest average in the class."

At no time was the Kahrmann family's dedication more evident than when A.J. was born three-and-a-half months premature in February 2000. A.J. spent the first 31 days of his life at Coliseum Hospital in Macon, and the family made the 163-mile round trip almost every day to visit the newest member of the family.

Erma wanted to make sure her attendance legacy would continue. She died of congestive heart failure four days after Thanksgiving in 2007.

When the Kahrmann boys learned the funeral at the Methodist church had been scheduled for 10 a.m., they made a request.

Could the time of the service be changed until after 3 p.m., so they would not have to miss school?

They wanted to honor their grandmother.

And they did.

To our grads: 'Dwell in possibility'

May 29, 2009

Excuse me. Yes, you.

Third row from the back. Grin on your face. Praying that you don't trip when you walk across the stage to receive your diploma.

You have been waiting for this day. Now you must sit through baccalaureate, valedictorians, salutatorians and at least three other words that require a spell check.

At the appointed time, you will move your tassel from right to left.

Now what?

Some of you are smarter than I will ever be. I am remedial when it comes to trigonometry. I would need to brush up on social studies and British literature to keep pace with you.

My advantage is my wealth of experiences. I have been gathering slices of life for longer than you have been alive.

I have looked at this world through different prisms. I have worn more than one pair of boots.

So a little advice is the best graduation gift I can offer you. You must do the rest.

Never trust a blinker.

Life is more circumstance than pomp. Get used to it.

Look people in the eye when you speak to them.

Grow where you're planted.

Remember the little things. They add up.

Loyalty is a virtue. Don't let it disappear from your screen.

Never make fun of the way people look. Or where they live.

You will not make better time — but you will have a better time — if you take the back roads instead of the interstate.

"All great change in America begins at the dinner table." (That one belonged to former President Ronald Reagan.)

Do something nice for somebody every day. Then do something nice for yourself.

If you tell the truth, you won't have to remember what you said.

Keep a song in your heart. The words and tune may change, but the song should always stay there.

Don't forget the boys on the back row.

If you laugh, you will live longer.

Eat your vegetables. (I will give you a pass on the beets.)

You don't always have to catch fish to have fun while you're fishing. But it helps.

Faith and responsibility are wonderful words to know. And practice.

Your mama was right about the jacket and umbrella. It's better to have it and not need it than to need it and not have it.

Don't forget the thank-you notes.

We would all be better off without fine print.

You usually get what you pay for.

Duct tape holds the world together.

Read to your children.

Do your heavy lifting in the morning.

Give back.

Three words from poet Emily Dickinson: "Dwell in possibility."

Enjoy the rhythm of life. Don't be in such a hurry that you neglect to enjoy the journey. Sometimes the reward is in going, not getting there.

Invest in people.

Folks will help you along the way. Never forget them. But remember the best helping hand can be found at the end of your arm.

Let your childhood buddy, Dr. Seuss, keep on teaching you. "Don't cry because it's over," he once said. "Smile because it happened."

Good sports

Thanks for the memories, Mr. Munson

September 23, 2008

We never really listened to Larry Munson. We listened with him.

Two hundred miles away in our living rooms, we huddled with him between the hedges. He glued us to the seat next to him in the press box at Sanford Stadium.

We rode tandem on warm Saturday afternoons in September. He could make us see his breath when the November chill set in.

Get the picture. The Dawgs are dressed in their red jerseys and silver britches.

We heard his emotions crackling from transistor radios in Tifton. His play-by-play was strapped to the left end of the AM dial in places like Hawkinsville. And split wide right on the knob in Sandersville.

We didn't have to find him. He had a way of finding us.

His unmistakable voice rushed down from places like Rocky Top and Death Valley. His words stretched across the plains of Auburn and along the banks of the St. Johns River in Jacksonville.

Oh, look at the Sugar falling out of the sky.

Gator Bowl rocking. Stunned. The girders are bending.

My Godawmighty! He ran right through two men.

We just stepped on their face with a hobnail boot and broke their nose! We just crushed their face!

For more than 40 years — Georgia fans believe there must be something biblical about that — his rough, knobbly voice made us watch the radio to see every blade of grass on the field.

Turn down the sound on the television. We're listening to Munson.

Whatcha got, Loran?

I cannot remember the first time I heard Munson come charging like a linebacker through my antenna. He just always seemed to be there. Back in the days when only a handful of games were on TV every season, he was every fan's eyes, ears, nose and throat.

Heart, too.

He could raise your blood pressure like a wobbly field goal hitting the upright under the lights in Lexington. He could make your heart skip like a scratchy 33 rpm record playing in Bear Bryant's den.

Yeah! Yeah! Yeah!

Hunker down, you guys! ... I know I'm asking a lot, but hunker down one more time.

Run Lindsay! ... Lindsay Scott! Lindsay Scott! Lindsay Scott! I broke my chair.

During my sportswriting career, I had the opportunity to be a guest three times on the Georgia pregame show with Munson. What an honor. What a thrill.

I sat so close to the man, I could hear him clear his throat through my headset. He was a student of the pre-game warm-ups. His palms would sweat. He would get himself worked up over the size of the Ole Miss line or Vandy's kickoff coverage team. Nobody could ever accuse Larry Munson of overlooking an opponent. He was such a worry wart, he made Vince Dooley look like an optimist.

I'm sure Monday's sudden retirement announcement stunned the Bulldog Nation. After all, Munson had battled back from his off-season health issues. He was enthused about another season. With Georgia in the hunt for a national title, there were hopes he might ride off the field on their shoulders.

In four days, Georgia will play Alabama in its biggest home game in 25 years. It will come in front of another "blackout" crowd at Sanford Stadium and a national television audience. So Munson's timing appears a bit awkward.

But many fans who listened to him call the season opener against Georgia Southern noticed the tell-tale signs. He strained, struggled and seemed to wilt toward the end of the game.

It did not sway their admiration, though. Munson was still the best sports broadcaster in the business, even with both hands tied behind his back.

Maybe it was time, though. After all, the man will be 86 on Sunday. I'm sure he didn't want to be like the old boxer who tries to go one round too many.

Bulldog fans will forever be endeared to his contributions to the program. Players and coaches come and go. Mascots die. Fields are striped and re-sodded.

Munson threaded a loop through every pair of silver britches from Jake Scott to Moon Pie Wilson to Ben Zambiasi to Herschel Walker to Champ Bailey to Knowshon Moreno.

The legend can be measured by the intense devotion of his audience. Just walk through campus before any home game. From the footballs being tossed through parking lots on north campus to the smell of fried chicken on the tailgates behind Clark Howell Hall, you can hear the ghosts of Munsons past.

They replay those moments on the pre-game radio show, but fans already have the archives cued on their CDs.

They relive them before every kickoff. They listen to Munson's classic calls from games before some of them were born. Makes no difference. They have memorized every inflection in his voice.

It's not living in the past. It's history. It's goosebumps. It's reverence.

It's Run Lindsay against Florida in 1980.

It's the hobnail boot against Tennessee in 2001.

It's flying down the field against Georgia Tech in the closing seconds on Thanksgiving night in 1971.

Thanks for the memories, Mr. Munson.

To the mountain and back again

February 12, 2006

Every now and then, a cold wind will catch him on the face, and Chip Minton will close his eyes and remember.

The chill of a February day lifts him back to mountaintops in Lake Placid, N.Y., and Calgary, Alberta. Then the wind shifts, and he is dressed in red, white and blue, marching with the U.S. Olympic team in the opening ceremonies at Lillehammer, Norway, and Nagano, Japan.

His eyes still closed, he is tucked inside the bobsled again. He is breathing hard between the fiberglass, his body pressed against his teammates. They are racing down the icy hill, at the mercy of gravity and athleticism, through the curves and straightaways.

Was he really there?

"Sometimes I ask myself: 'Did I really do that?'" he said. "I look at the photographs and read the newspaper articles to see that I really did."

Macon isn't exactly famous for producing Winter Olympians. We have sent young men to play football between the hedges and shag fly balls against the ivy-covered walls of Wrigley Field.

But Minton is the only bobsledder in history to grow up in Bloomfield.

He came out of nowhere to make the U.S. team in 1994 and again in 1998. He became a household name from Dry Branch to Sandy Run. His hometown honored him by selecting him to carry the Olympic flame as it passed through in the summer of 1996.

"He was the toast of the town," said his mother, Barbara.

Then Minton fell off the mountain.

A disappointing career as a professional wrestler and a failed business venture nearly pushed him over the edge.

He turned to a life of self-destruction. Drugs. Alcohol. His marriage crumbled. He moved out of his house in Lizella.

A series of overdoses put him in the hospital. Once, he found himself in handcuffs. He spent a night in jail. He was sent three times to a detox center to dry out. He lived for a month in a $26-a-night motel, the curtains drawn, trying to drink himself into oblivion.

One night, as he sideswiped death, the foot of his hospital bed might as well have been equipped with an epitaph.

"Look at the angels," he said. He was hallucinating.

His wife, Dannah, broke down and cried.

For months, Barbara Minton was convinced her son was going to die.

"I could look in his eyes and see the life going out of him," she said. "There was no joy. I was afraid he was going to hurt himself or somebody else."

He moved into the Massee Apartments on College Street. He would wake up crying in the mornings.

"I hated myself," he said. "I was a former Olympian, and I had no self-esteem. I couldn't even look in the mirror."

Thoughts of suicide raced through his head.

"I had an insurance policy," he said. "I thought about getting in my truck and crashing it into a telephone pole."

Then, on the morning of June 27, 2003, two weeks after his 34th birthday, Barbara Minton's phone rang at 5:15 a.m.

It was Chip.

He was sitting in his truck.

In her driveway.

Could he come inside?

He sat at the kitchen table and sobbed.

"I had never really seen him cry like that," she said. "It tore my heart out. He said he couldn't go on like this. He said he wasn't going to make it."

The heartache. The pain. The regret. It all spilled out in those quiet moments before dawn.

Then hope clawed its way out of the rubble of a young man's life.

"It was the worst of mornings, and the best of mornings," said Barbara.

The next day, Chip Minton checked into a rehabilitation program and started climbing the highest mountain of them all.

It is impossible for me to emotionally detach myself from Chip's story. I have followed it almost from the beginning.

In May 1992, my friend Skeebo Knight invited several athletes from his gym, Conditioning Unlimited, to participate in a regional tryout for the U.S. Olympic bobsled team.

Skeebo was afraid nobody would show up at the Tattnall Square Academy track. Folks looked at him like he was crazy. About the closest anyone around here had ever come to a bobsled was having a friend named Bob who owned a sled.

But Minton, a 24-year-old corrections officer, was a marvelous athlete. He had played football at Southwest High School and was an avid body builder. He weighed 245 pounds, had a 38-inch vertical leap and could run the 100 meters in 10.5 seconds.

Dannah sat in the bleachers that day, pregnant with their daughter, Taylor.

Thus began one of the most improbable stories I have ever had the privilege to cover.

A bobsledder from Macon? Hollywood should have been right there, making a movie.

He trained by pushing his truck up a hill. He borrowed a 16-pound bowling ball from Gold Cup and tossed it like a shot put to work his arm and chest muscles.

Dannah, now an art teacher at Westside High School, became the family's primary bread winner. She made incredible sacrifices while her husband traveled the world to train and compete.

But she never complained.

"It was exciting, like winning the lottery," she said. "He was my husband, and I was going to do whatever it took to help him realize that dream."

The U.S. bobsled team finished 14th at Lillehammer, and Minton quickly seized on his celebrity when he returned home. He brushed elbows with skier Picabo Street, met the Clintons at the White House and dined with MTV's "Downtown" Julie Brown.

He also launched his professional wrestling career, competing in World Championship Wrestling as "Mr. World Class."

As if to prove his first Olympic experience was no fluke, he made the team again in 1998, when the U.S. four-man bobsled team missed winning its first medal in 42 years by 0.02 seconds.

Afterward, a teammate blamed Minton for lifting his head at the start, costing the team critical time. Television replays later showed Minton was not at fault, but not before the comment had already been printed in USA Today.

"He took those comments hard," Dannah said.

In 2002, Minton failed to make the team. His disappointment was compounded when the U.S. team went on to win a silver medal at Salt Lake City.

When he was born, Minton weighed 8 pounds, 10 ounces. His bald baby head prompted the nickname "Mr. Clean," after the famous cleaning product character.

Mr. Clean? The irony has not been lost on anyone.

Minton admitted he was a social drinker in high school. During his training for the Olympics, he would often reward himself with a six-pack of beer after a long, hard day. Gradually, his reward system grew more generous. In 1998, he began mixing alcohol with painkillers and other prescription drugs. He began using hard drugs, such as meth, cocaine and GHB. His life began unraveling.

"It began taking control of me," he said. "Everything started falling apart, and I was blaming everybody but myself. Dannah begged me to stop. I would blame her, and we would start fighting."

Dannah said, "He was very good at hiding it. He would drink, but he wouldn't stumble around. I would come home, and he would have been on the couch all day. I would say: 'Look at what you're doing to yourself!' But he never came off that couch."

After his professional wrestling contract was not renewed, he opened a business he called Chip Minton Supplement Sports in a cluster of small shops near the intersection of Mercer University Drive and Columbus Road. He sold vitamins, protein supplements and weight training merchandise.

"He knew nothing about running a business, but he wanted to prove himself," Dannah said. "He wanted to be somebody. He wanted to have a business card."

His substance abuse had escalated to the point where he overdosed several times while working at the store. Twice, he was found by customers who called 911.

He describes those days, many so hazy he now can't remember them, as "unorganized chaos."

"I was comfortable being uncomfortable," he said.

His family tried to reach out to him. His younger brother, Chris, is the pastor at Musella Baptist Church.

But family members wondered if Chip had reached the point of no return.

"It was a bad ending to such a big dream," said Dannah. "I had wanted so badly for him to do all this, then it turned out completely different from the way it was supposed to. It was a horrible time for all of us. It was almost worse than someone dying."

Barbara Minton said she and her husband, Nathan, prayed for their son every day.

"One day, we were on the couch, and I told my husband we needed to pray for Chip," she said. "We had never really prayed together, but that day I told Nathan maybe that's what God wanted us to do. Get down on our knees and pray together."

The day Chip made the decision to enter rehabilitation, he called the human resources department at Graphic Packaging, where he works in the lab. The company gave him its full support.

His family and friends rallied to his side. He remains separated from Dannah and Taylor, but tells them every day how much he loves them, misses them and how sorry he is that he hurt them so deeply.

He joined a 12-step recovery program, which he faithfully attends six nights a week. He keeps the recovery manual on the dashboard of his truck. It even looks like a Bible.

"How do you know when you've hit bottom?" someone asked him.

"When you stop digging," Chip said.

On a recent morning, he was watching TV and saw former figure skater Tonya Harding, who was a fellow Olympian in 1994.

"She has really changed," he said.

So has Minton.

"He's wonderful now," said Dannah. "It's a complete turnaround. I know he has to struggle with this every day."

Barbara calls it a "detour" in her son's life.

"I can honestly say I'm more proud of the way he has turned his life around than anything he ever did in the Olympics," she said. "It couldn't have been easy."

The 'miracle' of the Miracle League

May 11, 2009

LIZELLA — It was the shot heard around the world. Or at least around West Macon Park.

It happened two weeks ago, and it is still resounding.

Benjamin Marsh can't stop talking about it.

He has told everybody at his school. He has told everybody at his church. He has told the dog.

Nobody is tired of hearing about it.

It's a good thing Ben's favorite subject in school is history. Saturday morning, April 25, he made history.

Big Ben — that's what his family, friends and teammates call him — smacked the first over-the-fence home run in the five-year history of the Miracle League, a baseball program for children with physical and mental disabilities.

Dan Morton, co-founder of Macon's Miracle League, was in the first-base dugout when Big Ben's blast easily cleared the fence in left-center field and rattled a couple of cars in the parking lot.

It was a tape-measure home run (150 feet) that keeps getting longer with each replay.

Ben's proud parents, Alan and Gina Marsh, laughed and said by next week, it may have broken a window over at the Harley-Davidson dealership. By late May, folks may be hearing about how it landed in the median over on I-475.

It should be considered somewhat of a miracle that Big Ben was able to circle the bases without tripping over his Big Grin.

Or that his home-run trot was so smooth, given all the goose bumps he had to hop over.

Ben is 19 years old, a junior at Rutland High School and one of the nicest young men I have ever met. Let me repeat that: EVER.

He has cerebral palsy. When he was born three months premature in March 1990, doctors gave him a 5 to 10 percent chance of surviving. He weighed 1 pound, 8 ounces. He spent 20 weeks in the neonatal intensive care.

When he finally did leave the hospital, there was a front-page story and photograph in the *Telegraph.*

The headline read: "The Little Fighter: Emotions run high as miracle baby goes home."

Now, the "miracle baby" has become a legend in the Miracle League.

"He's the heart and soul of it," Morton said. "He has been with us since the beginning, one of the pioneers. Everybody loves him. Everybody pulls for him. His personality is contagious. Hitting the first home run couldn't have happened to a more deserving kid."

Ben is a manager for Rutland High's football and soccer teams. He is a member of his high school drama team and is involved with his church, Lizella Baptist.

Had it not been for the Miracle League, however, Ben never would have had a chance to play organized sports. He has been a baseball fan since he was 2 years old, when he started doing the Braves' tomahawk chop from his hospital bed after surgery.

At the first Miracle League game this season, members of Stratford's baseball team volunteered to serve as "buddies" and assist the special-needs players. In the Miracle League, every kid on the field is on the "disabled" list.

Stratford coach (and former Atlanta Braves infielder) Jeff Treadway was so impressed with Ben, he invited him to throw out the honorary first pitch at Stratford's next home game. A few weeks later, Ben was asked to throw out the ceremonial opening pitch for Mary Persons High in Forsyth.

Ben, who plays for the Yankees, has been flirting with a home run for several seasons. He has smacked two long hits that bounced over the fence. Another time, he hit the fence on the fly. He blames a gust of wind for "robbing" him of a round-tripper a few weeks back.

There was no doubt about this one, though. As he stepped to the plate, he heard some fans cheering for him to point to where he was going to hit it out of the ballpark.

With a little showmanship, Ben did his best Babe Ruth impersonation. He turned and pointed in the direction of center field.

"I was just joking around," he said. "But the rest, they say ... is history."

He said the pitch was a curve ball. (I had to chuckle about that.) Members of Tattnall Square's baseball team, who were helping out as "buddies," dropped their jaws in awe.

"I knew it was gone when I hit it," he said. "I screamed: 'That baby is out of here!' When I was running the bases, I heard somebody say, 'Hey, dude! You hit a car!'"

Ben wants to be a sports broadcaster one day. For now, he's getting plenty of practice re-creating the crack of the bat, the roar of the crowd and the thrill of watching the ball disappear over the fence.

They don't keep score at the Miracle League.

They don't even have a scoreboard.

Somebody won that day, though.

I'm pretty sure it was everybody.

Holes in the floor of heaven

June 18, 2006

In the photograph, Molly Muse is as tall as her father, but only because she is standing on top of a television console.

She has on a red plaid outfit. Her father is wearing red plaid pants.

People have always said the two of them were cut from the same cloth.

Molly keeps the Polaroid pressed between the pages of a photo album. There is also a snapshot of her with her mother taken on that same day in December 1969, when she was 2 years old.

Murrill and Helen Ralsten are smiling in the pictures. Those smiles, along with the stories Molly has been told, are her only means of constructing memories of her parents.

Those who knew them tell her she is pretty like her mama and personable like her dad. She paints her own portrait of them using the recollections and words of others. She remembers very little herself. Only those who are older can fill in the blanks.

"I can't even remember the sound of their voices," said Molly, now a Realtor with Sheridan Solomon & Associates in Macon.

Her father was 38 when he died, the same age she is now. Molly has two children, just as her mom did when she died at age 32.

Eleven months after those photographs were taken, Murrill and Helen Ralsten were killed in a famous plane crash. It claimed the lives of 75 people returning from a Marshall football game against East Carolina University on Nov. 14, 1970.

Thirty-six players on Marshall's football team, along with members of the coaching staff, faculty and booster club, died in what was the worst tragedy involving a sports team in U.S. history.

The school's efforts to rebuild the program the following season have served as the inspiration for an upcoming Warner Brothers movie, "We Are Marshall," starring Matthew McConaughey and Matthew Fox. Many of the scenes were filmed in Athens and Atlanta. Gov. Sonny Perdue has a role as the East Carolina football coach.

Molly has her own part in the film. At the end, she is gathered around the memorial fountain on the campus in Huntington, W.Va., with others who lost family members.

Molly and her brother, Matt, are two of more than 70 children who were orphaned when the Southern Airways DC-9 was returning from Greenville, N.C., following Marshall's heartbreaking 17-14 loss to East Carolina.

The pilot was attempting to land in cold rain and fog at the Tri-State Airport in Kenova, W.Va., when the plane hit the tops of the trees above a ridge and crashed into a thick, wooded hollow with almost a full tank of fuel.

She and her brother were adopted and raised by her uncle and aunt, John and Catherine "Carol" Ralsten.

Father's Day is a different kind of Sunday for those who were so young when their fathers died that they cannot recall climbing into their laps or hugging their necks.

Molly was only 3 years old when her world changed. She was too young to understand. The grieving would come later.

"I don't remember anything about the plane crash," she said. "I don't remember the news, or how I took it. My brother was 5 years old, so he does remember. He sat by the window, waiting for them to come home."

Murrill Ralsten owned a men's clothes store in Huntington and was a city councilman. He was friendly and popular, and folks said he might well have been elected the city's next mayor.

He grew up in Beckley, W.Va., and the Beckley family name ran deep on his family tree. It is why Molly and her husband, Ed, named their oldest son "Beck."

He met Helen Banda at Marshall, where they were both students. She was from the steel town of Weirton, W.Va., the first in her family to go to college. She was tall and athletic. Her nickname was "Flip."

They were invited to make the trip with several other Marshall boosters. It might not have been a big deal to larger colleges with high-profile athletic programs, but it was an impressive road trip for Marshall. It was the first time the school had ever traveled by plane to a road game.

For some of the players, it was their first experience on an airplane. A few parents were superstitious and raised objections about flying to North Carolina on Friday because it was a Friday the 13th.

At the time of the crash on the night of Nov. 14, Molly's Aunt Carol already had two children and was pregnant with her third child. She moved to Huntington to stay with Molly and her brother.

When the baby was born, they moved back to Washington, D.C., where John Ralsten was finishing his residency at Walter Reed Army Hospital. Later, the Ralstens and all five children moved to Vienna, W.Va.

"I have literally been in places all over the world where I have met people who had some connection with my parents," said Molly. "It has happened my whole life, and it hasn't been a sad thing. It has helped me learn more about them."

She still calls her Aunt Carol and Uncle John her mother and father. She considers herself blessed they adopted her and raised her with the same love and understanding her parents would have shown.

She met Ed at the University of Georgia, and they were married a few weeks after the Great Flood of 1994 at Christ Church in Macon.

It was an emotional moment when her Uncle John walked her down the aisle to give her away. It was emotional for her. It was emotional for him. After all, Murrill was his big brother.

People ask her all the time if she is afraid of flying. The answer is no. After she received a casting call from Warner Brothers one Thursday in April, she was on a plane to Huntington the next Monday.

Life carries its reminders. She has her mother's charm bracelet. She has some of her dad's furniture. Her brother gave her a painting of the old family house in Huntington.

On days like today, Father's Day, she reflects. It is the same with Mother's Day. And Nov. 14, the anniversary of the crash. These are the holidays, the anniversaries, that are the toughest.

For the longest time, she put off telling her children, Beck and Matt. Then, one day Beck saw an old photograph of Molly's mother holding Molly's brother.

He was convinced it was Molly holding him.

She believes her parents are looking down through those holes in the floor of heaven.

They have watched her grow up, get married and have a family. They will be watching when she celebrates her 39th birthday in a few weeks.

"They haven't missed anything," Molly said. "I know they are proud of me. I know they can see how happy I am."

Devotion is a Trojan 'hoarse'

October 9, 2009

FORT VALLEY — By the time the sun rises over the peach orchards this morning, and flags have run up every flagpole in Fort Valley, Tim Wilson will already have on his game face.

He will be a clock-watcher all day, counting down the minutes to tonight's kickoff. He will be feeling the butterflies because, yes, he still gets nervous, even after all these years.

When Tim leaves his job at Kay's Community Service Center, where he works with developmentally disabled adults, he will wander downtown to catch the pregame buzz. Football is what everybody talks about on Fridays such as this one, especially those motor mouths over at Wilder's Garage.

Tim will allow himself plenty of time to go home, fetch supper and put on the black T-shirt with all those battle-tested spirit pins.

Tonight, the second-ranked Peach County Trojans are hosting defending state champion Cairo, a team with a nickname — the Syrupmakers — that tends to stick with you.

Tim will follow his own hallowed tradition of parking in the same space at the stadium — the sixth spot on the right, near the drain pipe. He will take his place in seat K-22 in the bleachers, next to friend Grady Walton.

He is not a chair-weather fan. He doesn't even really need a seat, just a place to stand and holler longer and louder than anyone else between the goalposts.

He'll try to spare enough of his voice to lead the singing Sunday morning at Chamlee Memorial Baptist, where he is the minister of music. He pushes his vocal chords every football season with the true definition of a Trojan "hoarse."

Fort Valley, the land of those yellow Bluebird school buses, is also home to a 47-year-old man who just might be the most devoted high school football fan in America.

Tim Wilson hasn't missed a Trojan football game — home or away — in 35 years. Tonight will mark another milestone, his 400th consecutive game.

Forget death and taxes. The "streak" is as sure as it gets. Tim and his wife, Alicia, changed their wedding date 17 years ago, then rushed back from their honeymoon in Pigeon Forge, Tenn., so he wouldn't miss Peach County's season opener against Perry. Even when his father, Merrill, was in a coma a few years back, Tim managed to keep both the streak and his dad alive.

"When he came out of the coma, I told him I had been to a game," Tim said. "He said that's what I should have done. He didn't want me to miss one on account of him."

The streak was born when Tim was 12 years old. The Trojans have won 275 of those 399 games, including 10 region championships between 1992-2006 and back-to-back state titles in 2005-06.

"I am there to support the school and these young people," he said. "I don't have any children of my own. I like to think I'm there to represent all the parents who aren't able to attend."

He graduated from Peach County in 1981. He never played sports but holds the distinction of being the school's first male cheerleader. In 1996, he was issued his own letter jacket in appreciation of his dedication and support.

"Sometimes, I think I must be crazy," he said. "But I love it."

It has its way of loving him back.

Batboy comes home to say goodbye

April 23, 2008

FITZGERALD — Charley Ridgeway was buried on a perfect baseball day. There was a breeze blowing out to center field.

As eulogies were being delivered and last respects being paid in the chapel at Paulk Funeral Home, the local high school baseball team practiced a few miles away on the field named in Ridgeway's honor.

He devoted 60 of his 84 years to this town — first as a minor-league baseball player and coach, then as the voice of the Fitzgerald Purple Hurricanes and Irwin County Indians. He broadcast games on WBHB-AM, his voice carrying over the tops of pine trees to radios from Waterloo to Bowen's Mill.

He did play-by-play in cramped press boxes and crowded gyms. He often broadcast baseball games, track meets and wrestling matches from the bleachers.

"You never forgot the day he mentioned your name on the radio," said Fitzgerald Mayor Gerald Thompson.

Among the mourners at the chapel was a distinguished gentleman with white hair and a dark blue baseball tie.

"He was like a daddy to me," said Joe Louis Reliford. "I have lost a dear friend."

Charley once called Joe's name, too, but not on the radio. It was from the dugout of baseball immortality. As improbable as it might have seemed, their lives became entwined.

Charley was a white, Northern transplant who settled in Fitzgerald in the late 1940s. Joe, a 68-year-old black man, was born and raised in Ben Hill County. (He is now retired after 25 years in law enforcement in Douglas.)

They were both fighters, with a bit of scrap in them. Charley had been a P-51 Mustang fighter pilot during World War II. Joe, one of nine children, was born a heavyweight. When he weighed in at 12 pounds, they named him after the famous boxer.

On the night of July 19, 1952, the Class D Fitzgerald Pioneers were playing in Statesboro. Charley had been named manager midway through the season. Joe was the team's 12-year-old batboy.

Statesboro was winning 13-0 in the eighth inning, when the fans started hollering to "put in the batboy."

"If they want a show, we'll give 'em a show," said Charley. He pulled his top hitter, Ray Nichting, out of the game and sent 4-foot-11, 68-pound Joe to the plate to pinch hit.

Joe grounded out to third base. He played right field in the bottom of the inning. Adoring fans mobbed him after the game. The Georgia State League frowned on the publicity stunt, fined Charley $50 and imposed a five-game suspension.

Joe has stretched his 15 minutes of fame into 56 years. A record of his achievement is on display at the Baseball Hall of Fame in Cooperstown, N.Y. He has been listed in the "Guinness Book of World Records" and Ripley's "Believe It Or Not" as the youngest (12 years, 234 days old) person ever to play in a professional baseball game.

He has been featured in magazines and newspapers and recognized by the state legislature. He has been approached about turning his life story into a movie.

Charley spent his last days in declining health in a nursing home. Joe went to see his old friend three times in the past month.

"The first time, he acted like he recognized me," he said. "But he couldn't talk. That bothered me, because we're both talkers. When I went to see him last Thursday, he was asleep."

Then on a Monday when the baseball gods bowed their heads in reverence, the batboy came home to say goodbye.

The hills are alive

February 14, 2010

In many ways, Ernie Johnson Jr. started at the top.

It was the top of the hill on Gray Highway where he was hired by WMAZ for his first job in television in 1979.

Even after graduating from one of the nation's top journalism schools at the University of Georgia, he quickly realized he had even higher hills to climb.

It didn't matter that he was the son and namesake of well-known sports broadcaster, Ernie Johnson Sr.

He still had to push the right buttons on the camera, rush off to cover a fire, balance a cheeseburger on his leg while driving back to the studio, edit film on deadline and have enough breath left to tell about it on the 11 o'clock news.

"It was the foundation for everything," he said. "I learned from watching dedicated and hard-working folks like George Jobin cover sports and Ron Wildman report the news."

There was another side to this TV life, too, something they never prepared him for in journalism school.

"I had to do commercials," he said. "I still remember the one I did for Tommy's Recaps: 'They'll save you dollars ... and that makes sense!'"

He managed to save a few dollars himself, at least what he could on a beginning broadcaster's salary. And every payday he would drive a block down Gray Highway toward the city — there's that hill again — to the C&S Bank.

Not a Valentine's Day goes by that Cheryl and Ernie Johnson Jr. don't reminisce about those trips to the bank, because Cupid must have been riding shotgun with Ernie in the front seat.

Cheryl was working her way through school as a student at Mercer University and had a job as a teller. Their eyes would meet over the tops of his deposit slips. Ernie always went out of his way to get in line at Cheryl's window.

They talked a few times. If he thought he could impress her as a local TV celebrity, he was wrong.

"She didn't have a clue who I was," he said. "She was working two jobs and going to school, so she didn't have time to watch TV. She just noticed my check and asked me what I did at WMAZ. I told her I was a news anchor."

They went to dinner at Beall's 1860 on College Street. She accompanied him to a talent show sponsored by WMAZ where singers James Brown and Larry G. Hudson were in attendance.

In 1981, after a year and a half working at WMAZ, Ernie was hired at WSPA-TV in Spartanburg, S.C. Even though the relationship cooled across the miles, he still thought of her.

"My mom and dad would ask me about it, and I would tell them I thought I had really blown it with that girl at the bank in Macon," Ernie said. "They had never met her. They just knew her as 'the girl at the bank.' "

When they got back together, Ernie eventually asked for her hand in marriage. In August, they will celebrate their 28th wedding anniversary.

They have come a long way from the top of that hill.

I have known Ernie since we were freshmen at UGA and lived in the same dormitory. We had several journalism classes together. We have kept up over the years. I really admire the guy.

Today, on this Valentine's Day, he is in Dallas, Texas, reporting on the NBA All-Star Game for TNT.

I could try to amaze you with his résumé. After all, he has won two Emmys and has become one of the nation's top sports broadcasters. He has covered everything from NBA basketball to Major League Baseball to pro football, the PGA Tour, Wimbledon and the Olympics.

However, if you ask him what is most meaningful in his life, be prepared for a completely different list.

He and Cheryl have four children. Son Eric is 25 and daughter Maggie is 22. In 1991, they adopted their son Michael, 21, from an orphanage in Romania. Michael has muscular dystrophy and has been a true inspiration to the family. The Johnsons adopted daughter Carmen from Paraguay. She is now a junior in high school.

Ernie became a Christian in 1997, which led to his involvement with such organizations as the Fellowship of Christian Athletes and Samaritan's Feet. In 2007, he was presented with the first-ever "John Wooden Keys to Life Award."

It is an honor given to individuals who exemplify the former UCLA basketball coach's seven key principles.

Be true to yourself. Make each day your masterpiece. Help others. Drink deeply from good books, especially the Bible. Make friendship a fine art. Build a shelter against a rainy day. Pray for guidance and give thanks for your blessings every day.

In 2003, Ernie was diagnosed with non-Hodgkin's lymphoma. He underwent chemotherapy in 2006 and is now in remission.

"There is no way I could have gotten through that without my family and my faith," he said. "I love living the unscripted life and seeing what God has in store for me next."

On deck — after he returns from all the snow and basketball in Dallas — is a trip to Macon on Saturday night. He will serve as master of ceremonies for the 2010 Georgia Sports Hall of Fame Induction Ceremony at the City Auditorium.

His 85-year-old father, Ernie Sr., a former major league pitcher and long-time Atlanta Braves broadcaster, is one of the seven inductees.

Ernie Jr. was born in Milwaukee in 1956. The next year, his dad helped pitch the Milwaukee Braves to a World Series championship. As a broadcaster, he has followed in his father's footsteps.

"He has been a huge influence in my life," he said. "When I was growing up, I would tag along with him to the ballpark. I learned so much by just watching him interact with people. The best advice he ever gave me was: Be yourself. So, when you show up for work every day, you don't have to be this 'other' person. The same Ernie Johnson you would hear on the air every night when the Braves were playing was the same Ernie Johnson you might bump into down at the drug store."

He considers it an honor to have been asked to emcee on the night his father will be inducted. His family will be there. He expects he might get more than a little choked up.

"I'm an emotional guy anyway," he said. "I cry at movies. 'It's a Wonderful Life.' 'Field of Dreams.' 'Hoosiers.' I just saw 'The Blind Side.' I was fighting it the whole time."

And he will return to the city where so many chapters of his life started 30 years ago.

It was on top of a hill. Faith moves mountains.

Where home plate began

August 19, 2009

WARNER ROBINS — When Claude Lewis arrived as the city's recreation director 52 years ago, he found the local youth center with a padlock on the door.

There had been a skirmish between local high school students and a few young airmen stationed at Robins Air Force Base. Parents pleaded for him to do something to help keep those rough-and-tumble kids off the street.

Of course, there weren't all that many streets in Warner Robins at the time. The population was only about 14,000. Watson Boulevard — the community's main drag running straight through town — had just been paved.

Claude soon found plenty for the young people to do with all that youthful energy.

He organized and coached the city's first girls softball team.

He also took a batting tee and made history.

Claude has been recognized nationally as the "Father of T-Ball," an instructional game for younger players using a batting tee.

He celebrated his 83rd birthday this past Friday, so he is now more like the "Great-Grandfather of T-Ball." (Mary, his wife of 55 years, died in 2001. He still works four days a week as a bailiff at the courthouse.)

There's not a person who has ever swung a bat or thumped a mitt in this town who does not owe a debt of gratitude to Claude Lewis.

From here, it's a 697-mile drive to right field from Warner Robins to Williamsport, Pa., where the boys Little League World Series opens play Friday.

It's a 2,252-mile shot to deep left field in Portland, Ore., where the Little League Softball World Series is being played.

For Claude, it's all so close to home plate.

The Warner Robins American Little League boys will be trying to win their second title in three years.

The girls softball all-stars are in Oregon, trying to beat the odds of teams from the same league winning both titles.

Claude knows these kids. He knows their families. He has seen many of them grow up on the diamonds.

Their success is also a direct reflection on the man who made Warner Robins one of the top recreation departments in the state in his 30 years as director (1957-87).

When WRALL named one of its fields after Claude three years ago, he called it "one of the happiest" days of his life.

There have been plenty of others. The first came on a Sunday morning on Rembert Avenue in Macon when he was 9 years old. He was delivering *The Macon Telegraph* on his paper route. But not on a bicycle. He used a wagon pulled by a billy goat named Bill.

He stopped to deliver a paper to Mrs. Wilma Beggs, a widow who was director of the city's recreation department. She asked if he was hungry. She knew he had a difficult home life. She took him in and fed him breakfast.

She also started taking him to Sunday School at Tattnall Square Baptist. At age 15, she put him in charge of the city's sandlot program.

"She saved my life," he said.

At Warner Robins, he organized a baseball league for youngsters too young to participate in Little League, which began at age 9.

He borrowed a page from the playbook of his baseball coach at Lanier High in Macon.

Coach H.P. "Hot Papa" Bell had used batting tees as a teaching tool. Some major-league players, most notably Ted Williams, had used a tee as far back as the 1940s.

Claude found a local businessman in Warner Robins to make iron pegs. Then he went to a junkyard and found several radiator hoses. He attached the rubber hoses so they would slide up and down the pegs to adjust to the height of a young batter's swing.

He substituted tennis balls for baseballs and fashioned a loose set of rules — every player bats and teams don't keep score. Word of the new game spread as far as Europe, and he traveled to Germany, France and Spain to help organize leagues. He received a personal letter from Israeli Prime Minister Golda Meir, who summoned him to Israel for eight days to start a T-ball program in her country.

Mexico sent a delegation to Warner Robins. And recreation officials from all over Georgia patterned their own programs after the one Lewis created.

Last year, Claude was invited to the White House, where 50 young T-ballers played a game on the South Lawn. He was introduced to then-President George W. Bush, who showed him a baseball card of himself when he was a 6-year-old playing T-ball.

It's a good thing Claude had the key to open that padlock 52 years ago.

It certainly has opened a lot of doors.

The Warner Robins American Girls Softball All-Stars won the World Series in 2009 and 2010.

If you can't play a sport, be one

April 16, 2008

I don't have any career tackles. I can barely hold serve on the tennis court. I played my entire church basketball career below the rim. (I "retired" when my body told me to start taking two Advil *before* every game.)

I have never had my number retired or played on a championship team. I did walk four times in a Little League baseball game. And I bore my children to tears when I brag about being the second-fastest boy in the fifth grade.

Once upon a time I won a "closest to the pin" contest during a company golf tournament. Yep, I took out a 7-iron and lofted that Top Flite X-Out in the shadow of the pin on No. 4 at Bowden.

Then my partner had to ruin it by telling everybody what really happened. I duck-hooked my tee shot into a tree, where it ricochetted at a sharp trajectory and bounced onto the green.

Lucky shot.

That's how I expect to feel Thursday night when I am inducted into the Macon Sports Hall of Fame as a "contributor" to the local sports scene.

Lucky shot.

Maybe fortunate is a better word. Blessed is even better. Mark it down as one of my "Forrest Gump" moments.

My athletic feats never could have carried me to this place, with my own plaque on the wall at the Coliseum.

The desire was always there, even if the talent was not. A young man's dreams of playing in the World Series never made it out of the back yard.

I used to fancy myself on the mound for Game 7. One day, I had the notion to gather gravel in the driveway and take aim at an imaginary plate — the license plate on my mother's station wagon.

I was a bit high with my fastball, and the sound of the back windshield shattering could be heard above the roar of the imaginary crowd. That cost me a bunch of allowance.

Then, somewhere along the way, I learned:

If you can't play a sport, be one.

Writing was my real love, so I wrote about sports in high school and college. I cut my teeth in frigid press boxes and sweaty locker rooms and loved every minute of it. I spent 18 years in the sports department at *The Telegraph*.

I would not trade those years for anything. I got to travel, meet people, sharpen my saw and learn the craft. It was a marvelous training ground, and I could have been happy doing it for the rest of my career.

I still maintain the most creative and hardest-working journalists at any newspaper wear the badge of sports writers. Their productivity, energy level and enthusiasm are unmatched.

The job is often thankless, but that's OK. The rewards are there because people go to sporting events to have fun. They read the sports pages to have fun again.

Those who follow sports are passionate. At times a little too passionate, as I remember from some of those 3 a.m. phone calls I used to get from the local watering holes.

Oh, I ruffled a few jerseys during my sports writing days. But my heart was usually in the right place. I led crusades. I challenged Macon to become a better sports town and rolled up my sleeves to help out. I tried to give back by coaching youth sports teams and serving on countless committees.

I look at the list of 11 other inductees, and I am humbled. Athletes. Coaches. Olympians. They are exceptional men and women I admire and respect.

I believe there are so many other "contributors" who are far more deserving than I am. I should be trading places with many of you.

More than 400 people are expected for the banquet Thursday night. Thanks to everyone who helped me get there. I am honored.

I stand on your shoulders.

Rest stops

The journey I make every day

March 24, 2008

LAGRANGE — The house is just as I remember it, only older and smaller. When I was 7 years old, it seemed larger than life. Time has a way of cutting our memories down to size.

My mother said I probably wouldn't remember much about the town where I took my first steps, learned to spell my first word and opened my first lemonade stand.

I told Mama she was wrong.

On a recent afternoon, I reaffirmed just how much of this place has stayed with me, forever stamped on my heart. We lived here for nine wonderful years. The tapestry has not faded.

Funny how I sometimes can't recall what I had for lunch yesterday. Names disappear inside my head like ships in the Bermuda Triangle. I have to write reminders to find my reminders.

But LaGrange remains much the way I left it. The sidewalk that carried my feet to school every day. The church on the corner where I was baptized. The city pool where I learned to swim.

I rode by the creek where I used to catch salamanders. I went to the public library where I would check out as many books as I could carry. The building was just like yesterday, even though everything was moved to a new location a few years ago.

Time has not erased the memory of the morning my father and mother appeared in the doorway to tell me my elementary school had burned down during the night. That was every kid's dream, although it is so sad to me now.

With all due respect to Thomas Wolfe, you can go home again. I can remember the lay of the land without a map. I have dialed up so many of these images, how could I ever forget them?

I will be reading a book or listening to a story, and my imagination is transported back to my childhood in LaGrange. I have more mental snapshots of this place than I have gigabytes to store them.

A huge oak tree still guards the house on Sylvan Drive. Dozens of rings have been added since we lived there. On a black-and-white TV in the front room, I once watched Popeye open a can of spinach and yank a tree out of the ground.

I ate all my vegetables that night, excused myself from the supper table, then went out and wrapped my little arms around the trunk of that mighty oak. It wouldn't budge.

Four years later and six blocks away, I summoned the courage to tell a lovely young lady in the third grade how much I loved her. I can still feel the lump in my throat.

She assured me that she loved me, too. She then recited the names of three other boys she loved, so I figured my heart had better take a number and get in line.

These recollections of a simpler time are like leaves pressed between the pages of an old book. Brittle, but still there.

The room where we played hammerhead sharks on the floor of Mrs. Greene's kindergarten class. The hospital where my father worked so many long hours. The tree house in the backyard. The gas station where Mr. Bill once gave me a baseball cap. The chair where I pulled my first tooth.

It is 112 miles from my doorstep in Macon to the threshold of the three houses we called home in LaGrange.

I don't have to travel to go back there.

It's a journey I make every day.

Allentown is a four-way stop

March 16, 2008

ALLENTOWN — I really should have been tired the other day.

Tongue hanging out. Sore leg muscles. Asleep before my head hit the pillow. After all, I jogged through four counties.

I started out on a beautiful spring afternoon in Wilkinson County. I trotted over to Twiggs County, then planted my size 10s in Bleckley County and sprinted into Laurens County without breaking a sweat.

Just for good measure, I backtracked to Bleckley, made a beeline to Twiggs and returned to Wilkinson before the sun had time to move another inch in the sky.

And I wasn't even winded.

I have a witness, too. His name is Cloyce Pittman Sr., and he is the mayor of Allentown.

OK, I must confess. There is a spot in this tiny little town of 287 folks where all four of those counties come together. You can hop from Bleckley to Wilkinson in 1.3 seconds. You can dance a jig in Twiggs and leap into Laurens in the blink of an eye.

They claim you can see seven states from Rock City atop Lookout Mountain near Chattanooga, Tenn. But, to my knowledge, you can't have parts of your nose, elbow, big toe and back belt loop in four counties at the same time.

Allentown is the only town in Georgia with such a distinction. Braselton, in northeast Georgia, has attempted to make such a claim. But the junction of Hall, Gwinnett, Barrow and Jackson counties falls west of the city limits.

There is a granite marker in Allentown that stakes the spot. It is not exactly a tourist attraction. In fact, you have to go off-road to get there. Surrounded by tall pines, it is Allentown's own "Back Four-ty."

On each of the marker's sides is a letter — "W" for Wilkinson, "T" for Twiggs, "L" for Laurens. The "P" for Pulaski has not been changed. Bleckley County was formed in 1912 from portions of Pulaski and Laurens, so the marker is at least that old.

It doesn't take sides, either, although time and gravity have caused it to lean slightly in the direction of Bleckley. If anything, it should throw most of its weight toward Wilkinson, where all but about 50 of the town's residents live. The rest are in Twiggs. (None of the population is in either Laurens or Bleckley.)

The town trumpets its uniqueness on the city limit signs. There also is a Four County Bank and Four County Exchange Club.

If there is one thing we have an abundance of in Georgia, it is counties. There are 159 of them. Only Texas has more (254).

Life is pretty simple in Allentown. There are no city taxes. The town doesn't have a police department but does boast a brand new fire truck. Every morning, a group of locals who call themselves the "Liar's Club" gather for coffee at the A&A Restaurant on U.S. 80.

It can be a bit complicated, though. When Pittman went to the state legislature on some business two weeks ago, he must have felt like he was running laps around the four-county marker.

Allentown is represented by five different state legislators — Allen Freeman, DuBose Porter, Ross Tolleson, Robert Brown and Jimmy Pruett.

From the center of the railroad tracks that cross Ga. 112, the city forms a 1-mile circumference. For now, anyway. A move is under way to annex portions of land down toward Interstate 16. Petitions are being signed. So far, there has been no opposition.

Pittman moved to the area from Macon in 1976. He is in his second term as mayor.

"I couldn't find anybody to run against me," he said, laughing.

There are no plans for a "Four-County Festival," although there is an annual Fourth of July celebration.

Good things come in fours.

Pay no attention to the calendar

October 23, 2005

At Jarrell's Grocery, the clock always operates on EST.

That stands for Estelle Standard Time, which means the doors open about 9 a.m. Or thereabouts.

Estelle Jarrell looks out her kitchen window every morning. If someone is already in the parking lot next door, she will fetch the key.

At quitting time, Miss Essie doesn't need a watch to tell her it's time to turn out the lights and go home to start supper.

Jarrell's is open five days a week. Essie closes on Sundays, because it's the Lord's Day. She also takes off on Thursdays, the day she goes to Butler to get her hair fixed up at Benns Beauty Shoppe.

I wish the pace of life could be like it is in northwest Taylor County. Who needs a Super Wal-Mart when you can buy hoop cheese at Jarrell's? Better yet, you can wash down the sharp cheddar with crackers and a cold Coca-Cola from the bottle — the way the Good Lord intended it to fizz on your lips.

Either way, you won't go thirsty. Folks claim Miss Essie can find water with a divining rod.

Jarrell's Grocery is celebrating its 100th birthday this weekend. Old-fashioned? About the only web site you'll find at Jarrell's is a few cobwebs under the front porch. It's best to have an appreciation of cracker barrels before there was a Cracker Barrel.

The sign out front reads: "Est. 1905." Miss Essie is 90, so she can remember most of those years. She has worked at the store since she was 20. She used to visit the store as a child, then started getting the family discount after she married Fred Jarrell Sr. in 1934.

Her father in-law, Floyd Jarrell, opened a dry goods and hardware store in the back of his house a century ago. He eventually built the store across the road, selling much more than groceries.

Fred ran the dairy farm until his dad died, then took over the store. He passed away 18 years ago, and sons Fred Jr. and John now do their best to help Mama with the business.

Granddaddy's walking cane still hangs on a wall in the back, and people come from miles around just to see the wooden meat box in the corner. The antique cash register is as old as dirt, but Miss Essie writes up all her sales receipts by hand anyway. She accepts food stamps but doesn't take credit cards. She keeps careful track of those who buy on credit. Don't even think about not paying or she'll have one of the boys come knocking on your door.

You can find Jarrell's on Ga. 208, just a few miles west of U.S. 19. Route 208 is a history lesson in itself. The locals still refer to it as the "Old Wire Road."

The telegraph wire from Richmond, Va., to New Orleans once ran along 208. In the Jarrell community, the dirt road detoured in both directions around a large oak tree, giving new meaning to "divided" highway.

It's not unusual for curious travelers to pull over and take pictures. Once a church bus stopped. Soon, everyone was walking back in time across the plywood floors. In the rear of Jarrell's is a circle of chairs by the space heater. Seats are available during visiting hours, which is just about any time neighbors like Eloise and Bill Doty stop by.

I had the good fortune to pull up a chair and sit a spell last week. Of course, they wouldn't let me go home without some hoop cheese.

You can go home again

March 22, 2009

The Chevy Bel Air was turquoise green, and it was so bright folks could see him coming long before they could hear him shifting gears.

Durwood Fincher would holler out his back door for Pearl Whitlock to hurry up and powder her nose. He was coming to get her. She lived in the next block, in the last white house on Brigham Street in the Payne City mill village.

She would slide into the seat next to him, and Durwood would drive slowly. Not only was the posted speed limit 15 mph, but he had to be careful not to stir the dust along the narrow streets.

No need for blinkers. Everybody already knew where he was going.

"It was like he was always on parade," Pearl said.

Sometimes, his friends would pile into his big Bel Air and head downtown to cruise Cherry Street. It was what teenagers did in Macon in the early 1960s, like something out of "American Graffiti."

Some people can travel the world and never notice a thing. Durwood could road trip past Woolworth's and the Ritz Theatre and see the whole world.

Still, never in his wildest dreams could he ever have imagined making that same journey this afternoon as grand marshal of the Cherry Blossom Festival parade in his hometown.

Imagine that. A lint head from the village wearing a size-44 pink sports coat. Imagine that. A boy from the "other side of the tracks" riding in a fancy convertible on a street with a pink line down the center and cherry blossoms painted on the pavement at every corner.

Imagine him being given the key to the city by Mayor Robert Reichert at the ball Friday night. And taking center stage tonight as part of the Kaleidoscope of Cultures at Wesleyan College's Porter Auditorium.

There will be several languages spoken during the international-themed program, including his own. It's not far from the old auditorium stage in the mill village, where he wrote, directed and starred in his own childhood productions.

For the past two years I have been writing a biography of Durwood Fincher, better known as "Mr. Doubletalk," a name given him by Allen Funt of "Candid Camera." The book, and accompanying DVD, are called "Once You Step in Elephant Manure You're in the Circus Forever."

One of the most gratifying experiences that has been a direct result of telling his amazing life story has been watching Durwood reconnect with his hometown.

Like others who first blossomed here, then found fame and fortune elsewhere, he never realized there were so many reasons to look back. He now lives in a 14th-floor condominium above Piedmont Park in Atlanta. You would have to stack at least a dozen of those tiny houses from the village to get that high off the ground.

Over these past months I have watched him reunite with old friends and make new ones. Folks from the village. Classmates from Bellevue Elementary and Lanier High. Folks who watched him never miss Sunday School in 13 years at Bellevue Baptist. Or who knew his mama, the late, great Ella Mae Fincher, and tell him he reminds them of her — how she loved and embraced life.

He has laughed and told me he has spent more time in Macon these past two years than he did in the 18 years he lived here.

It has been a joyful journey to now see him honored in the place that nurtured him. Sure, it's neat to invent something call "Toe Floss," doubletalk the world and appear on camera in front of millions of viewers on Regis and "The Today Show."

But it will be just as special to ride and wave and blow kisses along Cherry Street.

He promises if he ever finds Thomas Wolfe, he's going to tell him he was wrong.

You can go home again.

Where the mockingbird still sings

June 16, 2004

MONROEVILLE, Ala. — When she was growing up in the 1950s, Jane Ellen Clark's family would drive to Monroeville from Pensacola, Fla.

This was her mother's hometown, and Clark remembers the familiar bend in the road where Highway 21 became South Alabama Avenue, just a block from the courthouse on the town square.

On the left, her mother would point out where "Nelle" once lived. They had been classmates. Nelle's daddy was a lawyer.

Of course, Nelle would be introduced to the rest of the world after she painted her masterpiece. Her name was Nelle Harper Lee, and the only book she ever wrote — "To Kill a Mockingbird" — was one of the 20th century's most influential novels.

There's not another neighborhood on the planet that can match the literary legacy of South Alabama Avenue. Next door to the Lee home, separated by a stone wall, was the house where Truman Capote spent his early childhood being raised by his aunts.

Lee and Capote were friends, and she has acknowledged that she based the character "Dill" after him in the book. Across the street was the home of a mysterious neighbor, who provided the creepy inspiration for the character of Boo Radley. Her father, A.C. Lee, was the model for Atticus.

Surprisingly, when the book was published in 1960, it barely caused a ripple in Monroeville. "People wondered what all the fuss was about," said Clark.

Then Lee won the Pulitzer Prize for Fiction in 1961. The movie followed a year later. Actor Gregory Peck, who played the role of Atticus, joined director Robert Mulligan and set designer Henry Bumstead on a trip to Monroeville to get a feel for the small Southern town.

Now that caused quite a stir.

"Everybody in town," said Clark, "has a story about Gregory Peck."

Clark is now education director of the Monroe County Heritage Museum, located in the old courthouse on the square. Clark's great-grandfather,

Nicholas James Stallworth, was the probate judge who commissioned the courthouse in 1903.

The movie was filmed in Hollywood, but the courthouse was patterned after the one in Lee's hometown.

More than 20,000 visitors — almost three times the population of Monroeville — come here each year in search of Maycomb, the fictional town in the book. They exit the interstate and drive past rural outposts with names like "Burnt Corn" and "Scratch Ankle" to get here.

Clark said lawyers and teachers tend to dominate the names in the guest book. Sometimes, they are content to just sit in the old courtroom, absorbing their surroundings with a quiet reverence. A few years ago, two Oklahoma attorneys had their wedding ceremony here.

The houses where Lee and Capote once lived are no longer there. The Capote house is now a vacant lot with scattered remains of the foundation and stone wall. Mel's Dairy Dream, a nondescript cinder block restaurant, was built where Lee's house once stood.

Clark said visitors don't leave Monroeville disappointed, though.

"Maybe seeing Atticus' courtroom is enough," she said. "And some of them tell us they just go down to Mel's to have an ice cream and think about Harper Lee."

The locals put on performances of "To Kill a Mockingbird" every spring on the courthouse lawn and inside the courtroom. It's one of the toughest tickets in Alabama. Three weeks ago, actors Philip Alford, who played Jem, and Mary Badham, who played Scout, came down from Birmingham to see the May 22 performance.

Lee now lives in New York, but returns to Monroeville every December to visit her sister, Alice Lee, who is in her 90s and still practicing law. She rarely makes public appearances, and Clark said some journalists have referred to her as a recluse. That's not a fair description, Clark said.

"I saw her one Saturday at the post office," Clark said. "And I've seen her at the grocery store."

Clark said the famed author is approachable. "Just don't bring up 'Mockingbird'," she said. "She doesn't talk about it. In my research, the last time I've been able to find a quote from her about 'Mockingbird' was in 1974."

If I had one book to read (besides the Bible) or one movie to see, it would be "To Kill a Mockingbird." And I share this love with millions of others. The book has been printed in 30 languages.

When I think of long-ago summers in the small-town South, I think of Jem, Scout, Calpurnia, Dill, Atticus, Boo and the others.

I've often said, and it's appropriate during this week before Father's Day, Atticus Finch comes close to being the perfect father. If there is a Fatherhood Hall of Fame, he deserves to be inducted.

One of my favorite scenes is when Atticus has just lost his case trying to defend Tom Robinson, a black man, accused of raping a white woman. Jem and Scout (Jean Louise) are sitting in the balcony with members of the black community attending the trial.

The courtroom is silent as he shuts his briefcase at the end of the weary battle. When he turns to leave the room, the people in the balcony rise to show their respect.

All, that is, except for his young daughter. Then the black preacher, Reverend Sykes, turns to her and whispers: "Miss Jean Louise, stand up. Your father's passin'."

In an interview with *Life* magazine in 1961, Lee called the trial "a composite of all trials in the world, some in the South. But the courthouse is this one. My father's a lawyer, so I grew up in this room, and I mostly watched him from here."

When Peck accepted the Academy Award for "Best Actor" for 1962, he was holding A.C. Lee's watch, which Harper Lee reportedly gave him when her father died.

"What made it all work was (Lee) knew the people she was writing about," said Clark. "She wrote about what she knew. That's what every good writer does. She wrote about the layers of a small Southern town in the 1930s. That was her genius."

Stopping for the funeral procession

September 2, 2007

It was one of those summer afternoons when the temperature warms to a broil and your clothes stick to your skin like flypaper.

We were on a country road, doing more fussing about the heat than forgiving it. We wondered out loud how some of the saints who had gone before us survived in the South in the days before air conditioning.

But generations of folks did, and never once blamed their misery on global warming. They were all the better for it, too, even though I'm sure those summers in places like Bainbridge and Tifton had to be brutal.

We rounded a curve and passed a small cemetery. A few folks had started gathering at one of the burial plots. A tent had been erected and some folding chairs had been placed in the shade. No doubt, funeral home fans would be swatting the air once the service started.

Then, a few miles down the road, we saw the funeral procession. About two dozen cars began to file past us in the opposite direction.

So we pulled over, our tires resting in the tall grass and weeds. We waited for each vehicle to pass, every headlight beaming in the bright sunshine.

We caught glimpses of the mourners behind the tinted windows inside the hearse, most of them wearing their Sunday best on a Saturday afternoon.

We did not know whose funeral it was. We did not know if the deceased was a man or woman, young or old, rich or poor, Baptist or Methodist.

I guess we could have gone back later and checked the obituaries from the previous week and tried to match the time and place.

But it didn't really matter who it was or what they did for a living or the color of their skin.

We stopped there beside the mile marker to pay tribute to someone who had lived among us. We paid our respect and showed our reverence.

If you can't honor someone in life, you can at least recognize them in death.

My friend, who was driving, broke the silence in the front seat as he remembered his mother's funeral. She had spent most of her life toiling in the cotton mills. She died almost 30 years ago at age 58.

She was buried on a day in early September, just like today. The procession left the chapel at Hart's Mortuary on Cherry Street, making that final symbolic earthly journey to the patch of ground west of town where she would be laid to rest.

As the hearse made its way through those streets she had traveled so often in her lifetime, the cars around the procession began to retreat like a sea at low tide.

"It meant so much to me," he said. "Those were total strangers, and I remember thinking: 'Thank you. Thank you.' They didn't know my Mama. But she deserved that, at least."

You just don't see that kind of tribute much any more, except maybe in small towns.

I have been guilty of indifference myself. Although I try to pull over, there have been times when I arm myself with the usual excuses. I'm in a hurry. It would be dangerous to stop on a busy four-lane. I didn't know the person. Nobody else is stopping.

I have a friend who is a fourth-generation undertaker. I have often heard him use the phrase: "The world is not going to stop when you die." He uses it to make a different point, but I believe it applies here, too.

We can't find the time — or make the time — in our busy times.

Where did it go? More importantly, how do we get it back?

Little ones

Five weddings and 10 proms

July 16, 2007

Brian Jarrard is living every man's dream.

He is surrounded by girls.

He has one in his arms while keeping a watchful eye on another. He has an attentive ear listening out for Girl No. 3. A fourth is leaning on his left shoulder while the fifth is tugging at his right arm.

They have him outnumbered.

When his first daughter was born, Brian's wife, Julie, gave him a card with a picture of a baby girl's hand.

"Be careful with these tiny fingers," the card read. "I'll have you wrapped around them in no time."

Now Brian looks around.

There are 50 tiny fingers.

He is very wrapped.

Bailey Ann was 5 years old in May. Daughter Callie turned 3 last Christmas Eve.

And, this past Wednesday, Julie gave birth to triplets. All girls.

Welcome to the world, Ellie, Jenni and Maggie.

The Jarrards, who live in Warner Robins, now have five girls age 5 and under. Pink is suddenly the primary tint on the family color wheel.

Obviously, Brian has been doing some thinking about all this. But he's had some help with the adding.

"Five weddings and 10 proms," he said.

He's already heard all the jokes about starting a girls basketball team. Or that he will have to brace for the day when there will be five teenage girls living under the same roof.

Life at the sorority. Cell phone plans with plenty of minutes. Will the man of the house ever get a word in at the supper table? Will the toilet seat always have to stay down?

"We're thinking about having just one wedding day with one big reception," Julie said, laughing.

Brian and Julie met as freshmen on the first day of fall classes at Georgia Southern University in 1992. They were married four years later. Brian graduated from law school at the University of Georgia and has been an attorney with the firm of Jones, Cork & Miller in Macon for the past seven years.

When the Jarrards talked about having a large family, each was working with a different set of numbers.

Julie, who is from Savannah, was thinking more like "two or three" children.

But Brian, who grew up in Dublin, was doublin' the figure. He is the youngest of five boys and has a baby sister, too. So six kids sounded like a nice round number.

Julie found out she was pregnant again after Thanksgiving. "I had a lot more morning sickness than I did with either Bailey or Callie," she said. "So I figured it must be a boy."

In January, Brian took her to the doctor's office for a sonogram. There were three little dots on the screen.

The nurse turned to Brian: "Do you realize your mouth is open?"

Three months later, tests determined the triplets were girls.

"I was thrilled," Brian said. "Girls are great."

What did you expect him to say? After all, he is outnumbered.

"Whoever thought I might be disappointed in not having a boy has never had a daughter," he said. "Girls are perfect."

The triplets arrived Wednesday morning at 8:46, 8:47 and 8:48 a.m. at The Medical Center of Central Georgia. "They each had their own minute," Julie said.

Jennifer (Jenni) was first in line and weighed 4 pounds, 15 ounces. Elizabeth (Ellie) was next and weighed 5 pounds, 6 ounces. Margaret (Maggie) was the last and the largest, checking in at 6 pounds, 4 ounces.

The Jarrard triplets were the fourth multiple births (triplets or higher) at the Medical Center since January. It somehow seemed appropriate they were delivered by Dr. John Barnes, whose wife, Kim, is pregnant with their ninth child.

Brian celebrated his 33rd birthday Friday. And Julie will celebrate her 33rd Saturday. From now on, the Jarrards will be eating a lot of birthday cake during a 10-day span every July.

Of course, there was a chance the babies could have been born last week on 7-7-07. That would have given Brian one less thing to have to remember, since there are now seven members in his family.

"I looked down at my wristband and the three babies' wristbands. I was like Cleopatra with all those bracelets on my arm," said Julie. "Those are the moments when reality sets in."

Not to mention when Brian showed up in the Chevy mini-van with five car seats in the back.

Julie said her husband is a patient and loving man, the ideal father for their daughters. He calls them his "princesses."

"Brian is a good trial lawyer but when he comes home to those girls he just melts," said Julie.

The rise and fall of each breath

October 8, 2006

McRAE — In those hours before dawn, when the air is still and the dew gathers outside her bedroom window, Kaydee Smith places her hand on her daughter's tiny chest.

Her fingers reach to feel the rise and fall of each breath, the soft rhythms of a baby's heart beating in the night.

It has been six and a half months since Kaylee Grace Smith arrived in the world in the smallest of packages. She weighed 1.7 pounds and measured 12 inches.

McRae is not known for its changes in elevation. The hills and slopes begin to flatten as the Golden Isles Parkway drifts east toward the coast.

But Kory and Kaydee Smith have scaled the highest peaks and tumbled into the deepest valleys in their hometown since they learned Kaydee was pregnant with quintuplets a year ago next week.

"We were scared," Kaydee said. "You pray for God to send you a baby, but five at once? I was concerned about carrying five babies at the same time. It wasn't the fear of raising five. It was the fear of getting through the pregnancy."

The Smiths were married in September 2001, on the Saturday following the tragic events of 9/11. They settled into married life and their careers. Kory worked at Robins Air Force Base. Kaydee had a job as a physical therapist in McRae.

They decided to start a family, and Kaydee got pregnant in spring 2004. When she suffered a miscarriage at 13 weeks, they were devastated.

The next October, the Smiths received encouraging, but cautious, news again. The stork was on its way.

A week later, they returned to the doctor's office in Dublin. A nurse friend, Brandi Taylor, suggested that they "take a peek" on the sonogram.

It was crowded.

There was a snapshot of a baby.

And another. And another. And another.

Wait, said Brandi, there was still one more — hiding in the corner.

That turned out to be Kaylee.

The final count? Three girls and two boys.

The odds of having quintuplets? About 1 in 57 million.

Kaydee had taken low doses of a fertility drug for a short time. One thing was for certain. It had worked.

"We were very hesitant to tell anybody because of the miscarriage I had before," Kaydee said. "We wanted to wait until I was further along."

When she went to see her mother, Barbara Powell, never mind that it was the week before Halloween. "She was as white as a ghost," Powell said.

"I need you," Kaydee told her mama. "There are five of them."

Said Powell: "If we get five, we'll love every one."

McRae is no different from other small towns. Secrets often don't stay under lock and key for very long. They shake loose from lips.

"We didn't tell anybody but our family, so I don't know how word got out," Kaydee said. "It wasn't long before it seemed like nine out of every 10 people in McRae knew about it."

The community embraced the Smiths and celebrated the news. In keeping with a tradition on Kory's side of the family, the Smiths began selecting names all beginning with the letter "K."

They were the Special Ks. A "5K" baby shower was planned in February. Kaydee said the outpouring of support was unbelievable.

Kory began selling some of his "big boy toys" to take in a little extra money for the expanding family and to make room inside the Smiths' 1,800-square-foot house. He sold everything from his motorcycle to his bow and arrow.

Said Kaydee: "Anything that wasn't tied down went up for sale on e-Bay."

In the meantime, Kaydee's friends and family spent months trying to "fatten her up" from a tall, thin 125 pounds to around 200 pounds.

You're eating for six, they would remind her. Every two hours, somebody was sticking a milkshake in her face. Or a Big Mac. Or a meatball sandwich from Subway.

Her doctors had hoped she would at least make it through the 28th week of her pregnancy. That would have been near her own birthday on April 16. (She is 27.)

She began having contractions on Feb. 14, Valentine's Day. They rushed to Macon, where doctors were able to get her labor under control. She was sent home three days later with strict orders for bed rest.

Her water broke on March 4. Kaydee would spend the next two and a half weeks in labor. Yes, 17 days, not 17 hours.

Karlee, who was Kaylee's identical twin inside the womb, was born the next day at The Medical Center of Central Georgia. She weighed just 1.5 pounds. She died March 7.

Kooper, Kennadee, Kolton and Kaylee were all born by Caesarean section on March 22. It was the 26th week of Kaydee's pregnancy. (Forty weeks is considered a full-term pregnancy.)

Kooper, who weighed 1 pound 12 ounces, died March 26. Kennadee (1 pound 7 ounces), died three days later, on the same day as Kooper's funeral. Kolton, the heaviest of the quints at 1 pound 15 ounces, died on the final day of March. He and Kennadee were buried on the same day.

It was the darkest week of Kaydee's life. She was physically and emotionally drained.

"After losing four babies, I almost gave up on Kaylee," she said. "I asked God if he was going to take her to please go on and take her then."

As Kaylee struggled to hang on in the hospital's Pediatric ICU, her mother returned to a house with five of everything, from cribs to high chairs. Two of the three bedrooms had been converted to nurseries — a blue room for the boys and pink for the girls, of course.

But, as much as there was of everything, the house was empty.

"I came home with my head down," she said. "I felt so guilty, like I had let everyone down. There was all the pressure to get five babies here. I wouldn't even go to the grocery store. I didn't want to leave the house, to face people."

The family's grief was softened by the miracle they still had in their lives. Every day Kaylee tiptoed toward recovery — a fraction bigger, a fraction stronger.

She became the light of their lives. After 102 days, she finally went home for the first time.

"The happiest day of my life," Kaydee said.

Most of the extra baby gifts they received, from furniture to clothes to infant toys, were donated to needy families. The Smiths met some of the families in hospital waiting rooms and while staying at the Ronald McDonald House in Macon.

Kaylee continues to make progress, although at 6 months, 9 pounds and 22.5 inches, she is about the size of a 3-month-old.

"We don't get out much except to go to the doctor," Kaydee said. "I would love to take her to church, but I can't because of her immune system. We just have to wait. It's like Tom Cruise's baby, Suri. Everyone wants to know where Suri is."

Kaydee's heart is still heavy. She expects it always will be. She has not been back to the cemetery in nearby Helena, where the four infants are buried side by side.

She tried to stop one afternoon last month. She was on her way to her mother's house.

She pulled into the cemetery.

That's as far as she got.

"As I started to get out, there was a strong gust of wind," she said. "I didn't get out of the car."

One day she will.

For now, when her daughter is sleeping, the mother presses her hand against Kaylee to feel her breathing.

There, she finds peace.

The 'pop' star of Pack 422

December 17, 2008

KATHLEEN — Car sales are down. Home sales are down. Parachute sales are down.

But in the Spring Chase neighborhood off Houston Lake Road, popcorn sales are up.

Yep, popcorn purchases have not been affected by this economic ... er, crunch.

Liam Kelley is 7 years old and a fourth-generation Cub Scout. He recently earned his first badge as a Tiger Cub.

He also has become the new "pop" star of Pack 422 in Warner Robins.

On the first day of November, Liam went around his neighborhood selling popcorn as a fundraiser for Scouts. The rest is history.

Liam, which is short for William, has been a Tiger Cub since August. He had never sold anything in his life. He's a cute kid, though, and being adorable is always a good sales tactic.

His parents, Don and Rosann Kelley, had him rehearse his sales pitch and practice his manners before taking him out to ring doorbells.

He blitzed the local neighborhoods. He sold a box to his first-grade teacher. He took orders from almost everybody at his dad's office.

By the time he had finished, Liam had filled 10 order forms and part of another. He sold $5,115 of popcorn. That made him the top salesman for Pack 422, which meets at Christ United Methodist Church in Warner Robins.

He led all sales for the six-county district, made up of Houston, Peach, Macon, Taylor, Crawford and Pulaski.

And he was No. 1 for the entire Central Georgia Council of the Boy Scouts of America, which represents 26 counties and is the largest youth service organization in Middle Georgia.

Liam outsold entire troops and packs in the area. He also helped Pack 422 top the council in total sales with $22,859. (The volunteer sales coordinators for each district, troop and pack are known as — and I'm not making this up — "Popcorn Kernels.")

"As a longtime Scouter in the Central Georgia council, I can honestly tell you I have never seen anything even remotely close to this child's efforts," said district chairman David Johnson. "There is no doubt in my mind we will all have an opportunity to vote for him one day at some level."

Liam isn't quite ready to run for office. Right now, he is focusing on getting all his orders delivered before Christmas.

He had offers to help from local Scout officials, but the Kelley family insisted on delivering everything. Liam spent seven hours handing out orders Sunday, and he's still not finished.

"But we're starting to get our garage back," Don said.

Selling was a lot of work. Liam walked down hundreds of sidewalks and driveways. He knocked on so many doors his knuckles hurt. And at the end of every sales day, he couldn't wait until the next.

It brought back memories for Don, who reminisced about some of his fundraisers during his Scouting days. He once sold tickets that included a coupon for a free Whopper from Burger King. He sold 1,776, which he thought was a nice, patriotic number. So he stopped right there.

For his efforts, Liam was awarded the first-place prize at the Pack 422 meeting Monday night. It was a marshmallow shooter, a toy gun that fires marshmallows.

His parents have warned him that the cat and his 4-year-old sister, Emma, are off limits for target practice. Actually, Emma will be able to defend herself.

Liam sold so much popcorn, he received two marshmallow guns.

A little girl can only fight for so long

May 28, 2010

HENDERSON — The dates are side-by-side on the calendar, like posts on a fence.

The days are separated by 18 hours on the clock and a 9-mile stretch of Highway 41.

Still, the emotions of this Memorial Day weekend are far apart for Alan and Cindy Culpepper.

Proud parents and heavy hearts will be in lockstep.

Tonight, the Culpeppers will watch their oldest child, Drew, graduate with honors from Perry High School. The graduation ceremony will be held at the Miller-Murphy-Howard Building at the Georgia National Fairgrounds.

On Saturday afternoon, they will bury their youngest child, Olivia Grace, in the cemetery behind Henderson Baptist Church.

Her final resting place is near the church playground she loved and the Sunday School room where she learned Bible stories about Noah and Jesus.

Olivia was 7 years old and lived more than half her life in the cruel clutches of leukemia. "Livy" spent almost as many nights in hospital rooms as she did tucked into her own bed at home.

A little girl can only fight for so long.

She died Tuesday, surrounded by her family in the intensive care unit at The Medical Center of Central Georgia in Macon. She had been there for 12 days.

Cindy crawled in the hospital bed with her, and the family played the Disney "wishes" songs she loved.

Olivia closed her eyes and never woke up.

I first met Olivia in the summer of 2008. She and Cindy were staying at the Ronald McDonald House in Decatur after Olivia had a bone marrow transplant at Egleston Children's Hospital.

Olivia was my "wish" child. For eight weeks, I trained every afternoon at the Dance Centre in Macon for a "Dancing With the Stars" benefit at the City

Auditorium. The event helped raise about $66,000 for the local Make-a-Wish chapter.

Olivia's "wish" was a vacation to Disney World. She finally was able to go the first week of April. Trips had been planned on three other occasions, but each time she was too sick to travel.

Her family went with her — Alan, Cindy, Drew and her 14-year-old sister, Elaina. They stayed at "Give Kids The World," a resort where children with life-threatening illnesses can stay while they visit the Magic Kingdom and other attractions.

Olivia had a wonderful time, despite spending two days of her trip in the hospital.

She was diagnosed with acute monocytic leukemia Sept. 11, 2006. It was a sad footnote to an already sad anniversary.

The past four years have had more ups and downs than Disney's Space Mountain roller coaster. Encouraging signs of remission were followed by troubling periods of relapse. Last June, she went to the MD Anderson Cancer Center in Houston for experimental treatments. She participated in a clinical trial and did not return home until December.

"We stayed so long we started talking like we were from Texas," Cindy said. "She got a cord blood transplant from a boy. She thought it was cool to get blood from a boy."

Olivia was in the first grade at Perry Primary School. She missed so much classwork, Cindy wasn't sure her daughter would be promoted to the second grade. But Wednesday, the day after Olivia died, Cindy received word her daughter had passed the CRCT.

Thursday morning, Cindy got a phone call from Rudy Giuliani, the former mayor of New York City and a Republican presidential candidate in 2008.

He called the Culpepper home on Highway 26 to offer his condolences.

Giuliani, a cancer survivor, had met Olivia last month when he was the keynote speaker and she was one of the children being honored at "A Light of Courage" banquet in Houston, sponsored by the Childhood Cancer Family Alliance.

Cindy said those who knew Olivia will never forget her courage.

"She had the heart of a tiger," she said. "She never felt sorry for herself. That was just her. We were amazed at how anyone could have gone through what she did and not feel like a victim."

High notes

The shack where the King was born

August 16, 2009

TUPELO, Miss. — Elvis Presley passed away 32 years ago today, but the King can hardly rest in peace. His fans won't let him. They keep his hips and lips moving.

Many have touched down in Memphis this week, carrying flowers in their hands and hunks of burning love in their hearts.

Traffic is backed up, like memories, along the boulevard. The lines are long at Graceland, the limestone mansion where he lived and died.

"If you want to feel Elvis, then go to Graceland," said Nina Holcomb, who visits several times a year. "There are 23 rooms. You can feel his presence in every one."

Of course, Nina doesn't have to cross west of the Tallahatchie River to get her fill of Elvis. She has several helpings a day, working as a hostess in the tiny two-room house where Presley was born on Jan. 8, 1935.

It is 104 miles from 3734 Elvis Presley Boulevard to 306 Elvis Presley Drive. That's below Memphis, right of Tupelo and only slightly above the poverty line.

Folks come here, too. Maybe not as many, but they still come. If Graceland is the mansion, this must be the manger. And the pilgrimage wouldn't be complete without standing on that Ground Zero patch of dirt where he arrived in the world.

Said Nina: "He went on to become the most important person this side of God."

It takes 90 minutes to walk through Graceland, less than 90 seconds to tour the sharecropper's home. Still, about 75,000 folks a year sweep their soles across the hardwood and linoleum to step on a piece of history.

"I talk to most of them," said Nina. "I've had them come in and kiss the floor. We even had a psychic come through. I've seen them get so emotional they go to pieces. One man had a breakdown. Couldn't even talk.

"When they see this house, which is small and nothing special, it gives them hope. Elvis was someone who was born into poverty who is known in every little remote place in the world."

Elvis' father, Vernon, borrowed $180 to build the house in 1934 with the help of his father and brother. It's a shotgun house, but a bullet wouldn't have to travel far from the front door to reach the back.

A single, 60-watt lightbulb dangles from the ceiling. The windows are small. There is no glitter on the mantel.

Elvis was born in the front room on a winter night. His identical twin, Jessie, was stillborn. The family lived here until Elvis was 3, then bounced around Tupelo (Vernon was sent to prison for check forgery) before moving to Memphis in 1948.

Nina grew up in Tupelo. Her family knew the Presleys. Her father, Ralph Carter, ran a service station.

She met Elvis three times.

She was only 12 when Elvis appeared in his first hometown concert at the Tupelo Fairgrounds in 1956. Her mother didn't approve of the gyrating hips, so her daddy took her. She got to go backstage.

She went again the next year, and she met Elvis a third time when he showed up at the gas station one day.

Now she shares Elvis with others.

"I don't mind answering their questions," she said. "Someone once asked what size underwear he wore. I know he wore a size-11 shoe and size-12 boot. He had a 32-inch waist, so I guess he wore a 32."

Thirty-two.

That's how many years it has been.

The oldest voice in Georgia

January 11, 2009

I learned long ago never to claim something or somebody is the biggest, fastest, first, last, oldest, youngest or prettiest.

Why? Because there's always somebody out there who will try to one-up you with someone bigger, better, older or prettier.

So I'm not going to say Jack Owens is the oldest karaoke singer in Macon, even though he's 91 and a self-professed "old geezer."

(If he was a young boy, he would probably boast he was 91 and a half. But he hasn't been a kid since Woodrow Wilson was in office.)

He even jokes about having a calling card printed with the title: "Oldest Voice in Georgia."

Maybe he is. Maybe not. But if there's somebody out there older who has been booked for three singing engagements the week of Valentine's Day, I want to know about it.

Jack was born in 1917, which makes him only two years younger than the late Frank Sinatra. And he's still doing Sinatra, which is more than Sinatra can say.

Jack is a wonderfully upbeat and positive man who lives at the Cottages on Wesleyan.

A widower, he has a newfound hobby of entertaining great-grandmothers and other assorted seniors at local retirement communities, nursing homes and assisted-living facilities.

When he sings the Broadway tune "Make Someone Happy," he practices what he croons.

He has only lived in Macon for the past eight years, so he doesn't know many of the people who lean across rocking chairs in the lobby or have someone push their wheelchairs closer so they can hear an old Perry Como song in the dining room.

"What is rewarding to me is every time I sing somewhere, I can look out and see them mouthing the words," he said.

He remembers one lady from a local nursing home who sat expressionless in the audience as he reached for his microphone.

"It was like nobody was home," he said.

Suddenly, it was if Tony Bennett was there with her.

I left my heart in San Francisco. High on a hill, it calls to me. To be where little cable cars climb halfway to the stars!

"I had her singing along with me by the second song," he said.

Jack understands why music is the universal language. Music has the ability to reach across the years and connect the dots in extraordinary ways.

He remembers how special it was for his wife, Kay, who died in 2006. He took care of her during her 10-year struggle with Alzheimer's. Even as the years dimmed her memory, her face would light up whenever he would sing to her.

They're playing our song. ...

Jack is retired after 40 years with DuPont. He and Kay moved to Macon in 2001. His daughters, Marcia Caldwell and Kathy Owens-Fox, both live here.

He claims no formal training, just the benefit of teachers who taught him a deep appreciation for music.

He participated in operettas in high school and joined the men's glee club when he was a student at Wheaton College in Illinois. The club toured every spring and gave him his first exposure to the South on a trip through Georgia.

Of course, he never dreamed he would one day be a nonagenarian singing karaoke, belting out the words to "New York, New York" at a Chinese restaurant in Macon, Ga.

But he was eating dinner with friends at the China Gourmet one night and heard local musician Tom Ridgeway playing the piano.

He approached Tom, who is blind, and mustered the courage to ask if he could sing along. For a while, they even became a musical duet every Friday night at the restaurant on Arkwright Road.

When local singer Renee Heath did a musical program at the Cottages at Wesleyan, where Jack lives, they performed a few songs together.

She encouraged him to purchase a karaoke machine and helped him gather some singing material.

Soon, other retirement communities were extending invitations to him to come sing.

Sometimes his legs give out before his voice does, but he loves every last lyric.

On the flip side of Sinatra's "Summer Wind" is "You Make Me Feel So Young."

And, yes, the man who may be the oldest karaoke singer in Macon knows that one, too.

E.Z. and the Sunshine Band

July 26, 2009

WARNER ROBINS — E.Z. Cleghorn has been spreading sunshine all his life.

Those who have come within an earshot of his incredible singing voice or been in the same room with his trillion-watt personality can't help but catch a few rays.

He gives off a light that is contagious.

He wasn't much bigger than a 1-pound box of chocolates when he was born four months premature. It was the day before Valentine's Day in 1986.

His odds of survival weren't much more than the smallest finger on his tiny hands. Doctors were worried his heart would stop beating or that his brain would never develop.

His parents, Debbie and Stanley Cleghorn, picked out clothes to bury him in.

But E.Z. found his place in the sun, although he has never seen a sunrise or a sunset.

He is blind.

His life would change — and everyone else's along with it — when Debbie picked him up from the Georgia Academy for the Blind in Macon one afternoon. She slipped in an Elvis Presley song for the ride home to Warner Robins.

E.Z. was 4 years old and mesmerized by the live version of "American Trilogy." And it wasn't just the words and music.

"What's that?" he asked his mother, listening to the crowd cheering and clapping for the King. Later, he would shake a bottle of aspirin, rattling the pills inside to provide the imaginary applause for his own songs.

Folks told Debbie her child prodigy would either become the next Stevie Wonder or would be selling pencils on the street corner.

Although she would have been satisfied to settle for something in between, it has been much more than that.

When he was a toddler, E.Z. asked his mother take him to the stage after a concert to meet singer Larry Gatlin.

Soon, he was singing with local musicians from bands like Stillwater and Doc Holliday at Smoke's Bar & Grill.

When he was 10 years old, he performed in front of a crowd of 300,000 at the Lincoln Memorial in Washington, D.C., as part of a "Stand for Children" rally for the Children's Defense Fund.

He has belted out the national anthem for area gatherings more times than there are stars and stripes on the flag.

His friends and family have watched him move from one large stage to the next, from Warner Robins High School to the winner of Perry Idol.

They call it E.Z. Listening.

He will attend Mercer University on both a music and academic scholarship this fall.

Trust me, those stages are going to be even larger one day.

With a name like E.Z. — which is way more cool than Ernest Zachary — he would seem to already have his ticket punched. There is no need for some catchy nickname, although he sometimes refers to himself as "Blindie."

I've got a suggestion. Mr. Sunshine.

If you ask him his favorite song, he will skip right past his personal inventory of Elvis, The Beatles, Wet Willie, the Bee Gees and any gospel singer who has ever pulled "Amazing Grace" from the bottom of their throat.

At the top of his play list is "You Are My Sunshine," a song first recorded 70 years ago next month. It is a classic by which almost every mother in America has rocked her children to sleep. It is a song that throughout history has been on almost as many lips as "Happy Birthday."

Its meaning goes much deeper for E.Z. He believes those 157 words and four simple chords are his birthright. They run up and down the frets of his family history.

The first recorded version of "You Are My Sunshine" was on Aug. 22, 1939, by a group known as the Pine Ridge Boys out of Atlanta, who had their own gospel show on WSB radio. The song was released by Bluebird Records, which was owned by RCA.

The Pine Ridge Boys were a duet of guitar pickers named Doug Spivey and Marvin Taylor. (E.Z.'s family tree runs right through the Pines. His grandfather, the late Howard Taylor, and Marvin Taylor were first cousins.)

E.Z. is convinced his cousin Marvin wrote the song. He has done exhaustive research. It is a point of pride.

It's also a source of considerable debate. There are as many people who have claimed to have written "You Are My Sunshine" as there are verses in the song.

Marvin Taylor was born in Eastman and got his musical start in Macon with the legendary Gene Stripling's "Uncle Ned and the Texas Wranglers."

(There were five members in the band, and none of them were from Texas. As the group evolved over the years, it became known as Uncle Ned and the Hayloft Jamboree, which made history on Sept. 27, 1953, when the band went on the air as WMAZ broadcast its initial TV signal.)

Taylor's association with Uncle Ned led him to Atlanta and the studios of WSB, where he was later paired with Spivey. They could be heard on the popular "Cross Road Follies" show.

They recorded several songs in the studio that August day in 1939, including the first-ever version of "You Are My Sunshine."

Where did it come from? Did they pull it out of a hat, and the rest is musical history?

E.Z. said family members on his mother's side have always contended Marvin Taylor wrote the song but never got credit.

In his book, "Pickin' on Peachtree," author Wayne W. Daniel wrote that Spivey once offered an explanation. They had met a young woman from South Carolina in the studios at WGST in Atlanta who gave them the song because it suited their voices.

He said she told them to take it, record it and copyright it.

They followed the first two pieces of advice but failed to copyright it. Within three weeks, Paul Rice and his brother, Hoke, had recorded it, too. He also claimed authorship of the song.

As was the case in the music industry in those days, everything could be bought for the right price.

By early February, Rice had sold rights to the song to Jimmie Davis and Charles Mitchell for $35. Davis and Mitchell are credited with having written the words and music.

Davis was a country singer who used it in his race for governor of Louisiana, where he campaigned riding a horse named "Sunshine." (It is now one of Louisiana's two official state songs. "Give Me Louisiana" by Doralice Fontane is the other.)

For years, Davis claimed to have written the song but later denied it. Bing Crosby and Gene Autry were among the singers to have recorded it over the years.

"My father used to tell us his cousin Marvin wrote the song," said Debbie. "He knew it to be a fact, and he never told lies. Back then, your word was your word."

The Pine Ridge Boys broke up in 1942 after Spivey was drafted, although Marvin continued to write songs. Marvin co-wrote a tune for country singer Marty Robbins called "Oh How I Miss You (Since You Went Away)."

Marvin had a bad eye, so he never served during World War II. But he did work at Robins Air Force Base from 1948-53.

He left Warner Robins after the 1953 tornado and became a minister. In the last years of his life, he ran a restaurant near Thomson.

"I remember we stopped there to eat one time," said Debbie. "My dad thought the world of Marvin."

Marvin died in 1973 and is buried in Macon.

And E.Z., who wants to be a music teacher if his singing career doesn't work out, is looking to give an ancestor his due.

Let the sunshine in.

A sideman gets his due

April 20, 2008

On most days, the meter is running inside Newton Collier's cab.

Sometimes the music is running, too. Maybe something by Otis Redding. Or Al Green.

When Sam and Dave come through the speakers, keeping time to the rhythm of the streets of Macon, it transports Newton back to another place, another moment.

If he listens closely, he can hear himself playing trumpet in the background.

Newton Collier is not one to toot his own horn, but there aren't many cab drivers in America with his kind of musical credentials. Not many had their musical careers unexpectedly launched by the great Sammy Davis Jr.

Or can claim to have introduced guitarist Jimi Hendrix to Macon's own Johnny Jenkins, who became one of Hendrix's musical influences.

No other taxi-driving man has played with the likes of Carla Thomas, Joe Tex, Johnny Taylor, Wayne Cochran, Rufus Thomas, Arthur Conley, Wilson Pickett, Albert King, Percy Welsh and Maceo Parker, who was James Brown's famed saxophone player.

Or can still watch himself on YouTube performing "I Thank You" with Sam and Dave on an archived episode of "The Ed Sullivan Show." (In the video, he is remarkably young and resplendent in his baby blue jacket and black pants.)

Newton's main claim to fame always will be the 10 years he spent with Sam and Dave, one of soul music's most successful duos. He toured the world with them, once doing 280 shows in one year. They were singing "Soul Man" long before there was a Blues Brothers.

Driving a cab is not an occupation that bothers Newton. After all, he enjoys meeting people. It's a way to make a living. He is 63 years old now and "getting to know what arthritis is all about."

If only the music hadn't stopped on an April night 32 years ago this week.

He thinks about that a lot but can't allow his wheels to get stuck in the past. Besides, there is a reason for the smile on his face these days, along with a feather in his cap. Saturday, he will receive the Georgia Music Legend Award at the Barnesville BBQ & Blues Festival. Last year's inaugural award went to Alan Walden of Capricorn Records fame.

For a middle-aged cab driver, it has been quite a ride. Climb into the back seat, and he just might tell his story.

He grew up in what was known as Tindall Field, near Mercer University. The neighborhood is no longer there. The downtown connector, known as Little Richard Penniman Boulevard, came through and wiped out most of it. Mercer's soccer field now sits on what was the old homeplace on Campbell Avenue.

His mother was named Lucile, and his father, Newton Sr., was a cook at the Dempsey Hotel. He also was a musician, although Newton was never quite sure which instrument he played.

Johnny Jenkins and Otis Redding would practice with their band, the Pine-toppers, in a house across the street. When Newton was 9 years old, his mother would not allow him to cross the street, so he sat on the front steps and listened to every note.

He must have been taking notes, too. A woman named Gladys Williams, who had her own orchestra, was his piano teacher. One day, a Rolls-Royce pulled up at her house and she was visited by entertainer Sammy Davis Jr. Newton was there, and Davis let him pick up his trumpet and press it to his lips.

A beautiful sound came out.

He convinced his mother to let him take lessons from Robert Scott, who was band director at Ballard-Hudson High and gave private music lessons at the Booker T. Washington Community Center.

Before long, Newton was in such demand as a teenage horn player that he used to sneak out of the house at night to play in clubs. He would then sneak back to grab a few hours of sleep before school.

He spent years as a studio musician and sideman for some of the great blues and soul singers of the 1950s and '60s.

His first trip to Boston was in the winter of 1965. He traveled with a band in a touring van and had a gig at a lounge with no heat. His lips were nearly frost bitten, but it was his feet that pained him the most.

"I had patent leather shoes, and they don't mix with cold weather," he said. "I had cold feet for a long time."

He hooked up with Sam and Dave the following year and stayed with the group for the next decade. By 1970, he had moved to Boston. Not only had his feet warmed up, but he also met a girl.

On an April night six years later, during a period of racial unrest and riots in Boston, Newton was the victim of a late-night robbery while stopped at a traffic light.

The bullet from a .38 struck and shattered his left jaw and teeth. He had to undergo multiple surgeries, and it ended his music career. Even today, with a plate in his jaw, he struggles to purse his mouth and lips to garner enough pressure to produce a sound.

He returned to Macon and, for a while, owned and operated a record store on Napier Avenue. Today, he keeps his finger on the pulse of the local music scene. He has organized the "Soul Makers" music series. Some claim if the city were to elect a "mayor of music," Newton would win in a landslide.

He is employed by Radio Cab on Houston Road.

The meter is running.

The music is playing.

It stirs the memories.

Redwoods

Tiny is larger than life

April 25, 2010

When she was 16 years old, Tiny Smaha was runner-up in the 1933 Miss Barnesville pageant.

If she had won, she would have gone on to compete in the Miss Georgia pageant that year.

But she never entered another pageant until this year.

She is 93 years old.

"I tell people when I was 16, I wore a bathing suit," she said, laughing. "Now that I'm in my senior years, I have switched to pantsuits."

Tiny has been a resident of Carlyle Place, a continuing care retirement community, since it opened in 2002. After some health problems last year, she moved into the Harrington House Skilled Nursing Center at Carlyle.

Even though she has recovered, she made the decision to stay in the skilled nursing unit, which made her eligible for the pageant.

When the local judges asked Tiny what she would do if she won, she told them: "I will stand at the door at Harrington House and greet people. I will tell them to smile and be happy."

A judge asked one of the other contestants what she would do if she won.

She said she would go home and take a nap.

The other contestant did not win.

Tiny may have missed the Miss Georgia pageant by 77 years, three children, 11 grandchildren and 11 great-grandchildren, but she qualified for the Mrs. Georgia Nursing Home 2010 pageant April 17 in Stone Mountain.

There were 20 other contestants from across the state in the pageant, which is sponsored by the Georgia Health Care Association.

She wasn't nervous. She did not have unrealistic expectations. She figured she might have a better shot at winning Mrs. Congeniality than Mrs. Longevity, especially since one of the other contestants was 104.

I don't know if the judges were prepared to interview a quick wit like Tiny.

Judge: Have you lived in Macon all your life?

Tiny: Not yet.

Judge: How old are you?

Tiny: 93.

Judge: But you don't have any wrinkles.

Tiny: I don't always wear a bra.

(I'm pretty sure she was joking.)

Some of the other contestants wore evening gowns. Tiny had on a modest, powder blue dress, to match her eyes. She showed the judges a scrapbook about her childhood. She is more proud of her family than anything.

When they called her name as the winner of Mrs. Georgia Nursing Home 2010, there were so many tears of joy falling across the stage she practically had to step over the puddles.

If you haven't figured it out already, Tiny Smaha is a hoot. A self-described "people person," the lady believes in the power of laughter.

"It's like a tranquilizer," she said, "with no side effects."

It wouldn't be easy to go through life with a name like Tiny and not have a great sense of humor.

People ask her about it all the time. The name has been with her from the very beginning, although she now jokes she has "outgrown it."

Most assume it's her nickname, but it's not. It even says so on her birth certificate: Tiny Mae Stocks.

She was the youngest of three daughters born to J.W. and Mary Stocks, who lived on a plantation in Lamar County.

One of her sisters weighed 12 pounds at birth. So Tiny, who checked in at only 4 pounds, was definitely the runt of the litter.

Her father took one look in her crib and said: "That's our Tiny." The name was recorded on the pages of the family Bible and followed like a shadow the rest of the way.

She married Phil Smaha, who worked in real estate after they moved to Macon. For years, they ran a dime store on Vineville Avenue called Smaha's Variety Store, which sold everything from shoes to nails.

They raised three children — Joe, Don and Carol Cheshire. Phil Smaha died in 1980. His funeral was held on their 44th wedding anniversary.

For years at Carlyle, she answered to another name besides Tiny. Many of the residents called her the "Soup Lady."

Three times a week, she would make four gallons of either vegetable, chicken or broccoli soup or Brunswick stew. She would make calls from building to building to find out who was sick or needed cheering up.

Since she can no longer cook while living in the skilled nursing center, she gives away handkerchiefs. She ordered another three dozen just last week.

As part of her duties as Mrs. Georgia Nursing Home 2010, she will visit other assisted-living facilities in the state. And that's OK with her, as long as it doesn't interfere with going to lunch with her fellow Red Hat ladies the fourth Thursday of every month.

She was wearing her crown when I went to visit on Friday, but she told me she only put it on for the special occasion. She has no intention of showing it off.

"I'm a person who wants to be known by my deeds," she said.

She may be 93 — and Tiny — but, in so many ways, she is larger than life.

Another year older at the garage

January 20, 2009

Edward "Cap" Cassidy will become a nonagenarian today.

That sounds like a fancy grade of gasoline, but it has nothing to do with oil, just old. You must reach the age of 90 to qualify for nonagenarian status.

Cassidy arrived in the world on Jan. 20, 1920, at his family's home on Pine Street. He has spent the majority of his 90 years some four tree-named blocks away.

Cassidy's Garage, on Mulberry Street, was the city's first gas station when it opened in 1915.

Cassidy has been pumping gas longer than anybody in Macon. He started at his father's garage as a teenager, went off to fly 68 combat missions in the Pacific during World War II, then came home to build a life.

Folks started calling him "Cap" (short for "Captain") when he returned in 1945.

He has been working on Cassidy's Corner ever since.

And he will report for work today, his 90th birthday.

"He told me he was starting to become the town character," said his son, John D. Cassidy. "People are asking him how old he is."

He is old enough to remember when a gallon of gas cost a nickel. He is old enough to remember when heavyweight boxer W.L. "Young" Stribling trained in a room above the original garage. He is old enough to remember the great-grandfathers of customers who still pull up to the curb and ask him to "fill 'er up."

Someone has promised to bring a birthday cake by the garage today, and Cassidy just might have to grab a fork. I suspect there are those who are still trying to fatten him up. After all, he's only 5-foot-7 and 125 pounds dripping wet.

His descendants, Irish to the bone, settled in Macon after fleeing the potato famine in the home country in the mid-19th century.

Five of the Cassidy brothers were among the founding fathers at St. Joseph Catholic Church when it opened its doors in 1903.

Cassidy often jokes that the church, one of the city's most magnificent architectural works, was built by the FBI, which he said stands for Foreign Born Irish.

His father, William Cassidy, opened the garage in 1915, at a time when few Maconites owned cars. He occupied most of the block bounded by Broadway.

The building was once used as a livery stable, where they also shoed mules. As the horses moved out and made room for horsepower, the garage was well-positioned at the confluence of some of the South's major roads.

Nearby U.S. 80 was the nation's first coast-to-coast, all-weather highway. And the business route (Mulberry) of U.S. 41 was once the main artery from the Northern states to Florida.

The other highways — 49, 11, 22 and 129 — all joined lockstep through downtown. In the old days before interstates, it was a prime place to be.

Cassidy and his brother, Billy, had to take over the business when their father died at age 38 in 1930. Their mother, Cecile, kept the books.

John D. describes his father as being as honest as the day is long. He has helped countless people in the community. He has given them jobs. He has bought groceries and loaned money to those who were struggling.

Whenever he has seen a need, he has tried to meet it.

Billy, who worked with him, died in 2002. Last March, Cassidy lost his wife of 65 years. Her name was Clifford. (She was named after her uncle.)

There is something so nostalgic about Cassidy's. You might have expected Norman Rockwell to have placed an easel on the sidewalk and painted it.

Once, after World War II, a soldier's car broke down as he was passing through town. He left the old Kaiser at the garage to be repaired, promising to return in a few weeks to pay for it.

He never showed up. Rather than let it collect rust, "Cassidy's Garage" was painted on the side. It eventually took its place on the roof of the parking deck to serve as an unofficial billboard.

The garage had to be rebuilt after a fire in 1966. But one of the most historic events came 30 years later, when two men showed up one day and said a politician named Jack Kemp was looking for a place to hold a campaign rally. Kemp was running for vice president on the Republican ticket with Bob Dole in 1996.

The Cassidy crew swept the floor, maybe even dusted in the corners a little, and hundreds of folks showed up for the September afternoon rally.

Kemp, a former pro quarterback, tossed the football around for the cameras. The late senator felt quite at home in the garage. After all, he was the son of a truck driver.

There aren't many full-service gas stations left in America. Especially one where a 90-year-old man will pour 87 octane into your tank, wash your windshield and check under the hood.

He will move the metal chair near the open door into the sun for warmth during the winter months, then back inside to seek the cool shade in the summer.

John D. will turn 60 in March and is making plans to retire in a few years.

But not his dad. They laugh about it all the time.

"I told him he's going to have to start grooming somebody to replace me," said John D.

An Ace of all trades

May 9, 2007

The job didn't show up in the classified ads. There was never a "Help Wanted" sign in the window.

The hiring took place nine years ago on a back aisle next to the pipe fixtures at the Ace Hardware store on Forsyth Road.

Bobby Hollis was like a boomerang that morning. He kept coming back. He was building, fixing and tinkering with a number of projects around the house. And he kept discovering he needed to go back to the hardware store for something else.

"You might as well put me on the payroll," he said, enjoying a laugh with store owner George Jackson. "This is the fourth time I've been in here today."

Said Jackson: "How about starting at noon?"

After a few minutes and a few more chuckles, Hollis realized Jackson wasn't kidding.

No, he didn't clock in at 12 that day. But he did start working the next Monday. He's been selling duct tape, door knobs and circuit breakers ever since.

That might not seem unusual except that Hollis has been around longer than that rusty nail at the bottom of the tool box. He is 83 years old and keeps a full-time, 40-hour-a-week work schedule despite battling cancer for the past 18 months.

Hollis is one of those folks who "retired" but was never so "tired" of work that he didn't jump at the opportunity to go back.

"I made up my mind I was going to stay active," he said. "That's what you've got to do. To enjoy life, you've got to live it."

After I asked Hollis to tell me about some of the things he has done along the way, I realized I should have rephrased the question.

Tell me, Mr. Hollis, what haven't you done?

He grew up in Macon, one of six children. His father worked for the Central Georgia Railroad. His mother died when he was 4 years old. He graduated from Lanier High School and has been married to his wife, Carole, since 1955.

I found it most interesting that he and his five brothers all served in World War II and all studied engineering at Georgia Tech. Hollis worked for 45 years as an engineer in the propane business, designing storage systems and supervising their construction all over the world.

In the Army, he was a gunnery instructor. He later ran a summer camp and taught horseback riding, swimming and crafts. (His daughter, Joanna, is an accomplished show rider, horse trainer and instructor. She and her husband now live in Marshall, Texas.)

He is a pilot and accomplished musician. He plays the guitar and mandolin, and he has been a square dance caller and instructor since 1961.

You figure he knows a thing or two about how to fix squeaky wheels and tighten loose door hinges, too.

He's not just a jack of all trades. He's an "Ace" of all trades.

"I have been a teacher in some way, shape or form all my life," he said. "I think that helps me in my job here. I can help people figure out how to do things."

There have been times when Hollis has been accused of talking too much to the customers. Only he doesn't consider that a fault. It's a virtue. It's why people keep coming back.

I know I would much rather discuss the merits of plumb bobbing with a grandfatherly gentleman than to have some young whippersnapper shrug and tell me he doesn't work in that department.

He lives up to the timeless adage: It's not how old you are, it's how you are old.

Bobby Hollis died on Aug. 20, 2007. He was 83. In his memory, a framed photograph was placed in the front of the store. Customers would "borrow" it and take it along in their shopping carts, as if Mr. Bobby were still there helping them.

Handlebars still have a grip on him

February 1, 2009

There is a fancy name for people in their 90s. They're called nonagenarians. I love that word, even if I have to consult my dictionary every time to make sure how to spell it.

They claim 90 is the new 80, but I know some nonagenarians who make 90 look like the new 60. They still go to work, cut their grass, play golf, teach Sunday School and give blood.

Macon's Raymond Hamrick is 94 and — pardon the pun — still clocks in several times each week to repair watches at Andersen's Jeweler's downtown. Ethel Smith, of Eatonton, who died last week and would have been 100 in July, was dressing brides for weddings well into her 90s. The late Hoke Bennett built wooden toys and walked around on stilts in his yard in Musella until he was 95.

Which brings me to Bill Bina Jr., who is 91 going on 9. The man still rides a bicycle that's almost as old as he is. Imagine that. An antique riding an antique.

OK, so he's not as spry as he used to be. The wheels don't turn as fast. Top speed? "About 25 miles an hour," he said. Then he laughed. "That's with the wind at my back."

When you're 91, you learn to slow down and smell the rubber, anyway. He prefers a baseball cap to a helmet, no matter what the law says.

He still grips the handlebars of the racing bike he got when he was 16. It only has one gear and no brakes. The bike is nothing fancy, just functional — except for the brakes, of course.

Bill is a delightful man who wears a smile as if it were part of his uniform. He and his wife, Myrtle, moved to Macon last year to be close to their oldest son, Bill III, who is dean of the Mercer University School of Medicine.

He spent most of his life in the Midwest and a lot of time on a bicycle. If his bike had an odometer, there would be no telling how many trips he has made around the world.

Bill grew up in Chicago, where his father worked for a company that made vinegar. When he was 14, he bought his first bike for $10. He intended to earn the money on his newspaper route, but it was during the Great Depression. When the price was raised from 2 cents to 3 cents an issue, a lot of readers canceled their subscriptions.

There went half my route," he said.

His father once took him to the "six-day bicycle races." The event was part of a popular velodrome bicycle racing circuit that drew thousands of fans across the country and was often referred to as "America's jazz-age sport."

He was so enamored, his father helped him buy the custom-made bike he still rides today. He raced for seven years, including competition at the World's Fair in Chicago in 1934. He rode against such cyclists as national champion Cecil Hursey and Al Vande Velde.

(Vande Velde's grandson, John, was a member of the 1968 and 1972 U.S. Olympic track cycling teams and had a role in the classic cycling movie "Breaking Away." His great-grandson, Christian, finished fifth in last year's Tour de France.)

After Bill's five-year stint as a naval aviator during World War II, he and Myrtle settled in Chicago, where he worked for the Santa Fe Railroad. Their youngest son, Tom, was mentally challenged. In 1968, they moved to Kearney, Neb., and lived and worked for 40 years at the Mosaic-Bethpage home for people with developmental disabilities, where Tom was a resident. Tom died in 2007.

Bill said he hasn't found as many good places to ride in Macon, but he plans to get out more when the weather gets warmer.

He'll be the "old man on the old bike," he said.

Honk if you admire his spirit.

My permanent record

The annual state of myself address

January 30, 2006

Good morning, and welcome to the annual "state of myself" address.

A few of you already know what I'm going to say. President Bush probably does, too, since I'm convinced he has been reading my e-mails.

If the CIA has been tapping my telephone, it now has intelligence on my 12-year-old son. He's sweet-talking girls, and he's not even a teenager yet. As you can see, I have so much to look forward to.

Life, except for the occasional need for ibuprofen, is hunky-dory. I still have a job. My waist size hasn't changed in three years. I can usually remember what happened from Saturday to Saturday, although Fridays are sometimes a little fuzzy.

I swallow so many different vitamins, my bathroom drawer looks like a Scrabble board. The pharmacist knows me by name, which I'm told is a sign of getting old. I'm not taking anything for depression, although I sure could have used something right after the Sugar Bowl.

My wife still loves me, especially when I remember her birthstone is peridot. My two oldest sons are now in college. A financial adviser — if I could afford one — would tell me that's poor family planning.

Dog No. 1 sleeps almost all the time. Dog No. 2 hardly ever sleeps, and needs the equivalent of a dog Valium every time it thunders. Dog No. 3 is finally growing out of her puppy stage. She has stopped stealing shoes from back porches in the neighborhood. But she barks whenever the bread machine goes into the "knead" cycle during the night. I guess our house is well-protected from burglars and bread thieves.

There are quite a few things that amaze me. I still don't understand how I can "Google" my name and have it pop up 2,700 times in 0.19 seconds.

Fried chicken remains my Achilles Meal. I am discovering Sudoku can be addicting. I've been through so many refills on my gel pen, I feel like I'm changing diapers.

I can't remember the last time I took a nap. (I think it was back in 1997.) I have quit shopping in stores and eating in restaurants where they act as if they couldn't care less about my patronage. I still have a Heisman Trophy vote.

My satellite dish picks up more than 130 channels, which makes no sense because I usually have less than an hour a day to watch any of them. I still love gadgets, though. And I wonder if I would be more "hip" if I owned an iPod. (The family poll numbers on that issue are underwhelming.)

Every day, I wonder how I ever survived without a cell phone. Then I remember the story about Henry David Thoreau. He once asked workmen why they were stringing wires through a meadow near Walden Pond. They told him they were installing a new invention called the telegraph, making it possible for people in Maine to communicate with people in Florida. "But what if the people in Maine have nothing to say to the people in Florida?" Thoreau replied.

Think about it.

I don't worry much about identity theft. If someone wants to steal my identity, I will gladly remind them that today is trash day and deadline for Wednesday's column is tomorrow at 4 p.m.

Sure, I worry about the future. Sure, some things are going to have to change. I also believe we have to be careful not to tilt the machine.

Love me. Hate me. Just read me. Please.

The state rests.

The ring that lost its way

July 22, 2009

By the end of this week, I'll be wearing a new wedding ring.

No, nothing has changed in my life, just an adjustment to the third finger on my left hand.

I am still married to the same girl. She's not being traded in. Friday is our 27th anniversary. I am counting on at least 47 more.

I am going to need a new ring, though.

The old one has turned up missing in action. It has been ... er, misplaced.

OK, so I lost it.

I have spent a considerable amount of time these past three weeks in angst. I have been retracing steps and hunkering down with the dust bunnies. After 17 days and several sleepless nights, I finally ordered a new ring.

I know exactly when and where I left the old one, so I can't understand how and why it has vanished. I've checked pockets, drawers, trash baskets and under tables and rugs.

I refuse to blame family members, neighbors, third cousins, Facebook friends or George W. Bush.

I have also refrained from blaming the dogs, although they do have an affinity for eating anything gravity brings down, including paper towels and pizza crust.

Every morning, I wake up with some new inspiration of where my wedding band might be playing.

Sigh.

OK, Mr. Ring, if this is a game of hide-and-seek, I give up. You can come on out.

After spending more than half of my July in 14-carat frustration, I have semi-surrendered.

The folks at Herbert Jewelers in Fort Valley have experience at keeping me out of the doghouse. They have promised a new gold ring in time for my anniversary.

Of course, the cost has gone up since I bought my original ring 324 months ago. And my finger has gotten fatter, so no more pie for me.

Dennis Herbert, whose family's business has been on Main Street since 1945, has offered to take back the new ring if I find the old one.

And I haven't given up.

Seems I have spent my entire adult life on a Missin' Impossible. The "lost" inventory includes car keys, wallets, cell phones, shoes, notebooks, umbrellas and screwdrivers. (Not to mention losing my mind at least twice a day.)

There have been a few narrow escapes with the wedding ring, too. Several years ago, I was helping with a repair project for Christmas in April, now known as Rebuilding Macon. We were working at a house on Grant Avenue in Pleasant Hill. I stuck my wedding band in the pocket of my jeans — along with a handful of nails.

You can figure out the rest. I spent an unpleasant hour on my hands and knees, running my fingers through the soft dirt, grass and ivy as my two oldest sons announced: "Mama's not going to be happy about this!"

I still consider it a miracle that we found it.

This latest disappearance is a mystery to me. I have narrowed the search to one downstairs room. I have offered my kids a cash reward.

After all, this ring has been an extension of my hand. It is well-traveled and broken in. It has gripped my finger in hospital rooms, at funerals, graduations and Little League games. It has been along for the ride as I have written thousands of stories.

And now it's gone.

It's sad when you lose something that has helped you find your way.

Honest Ed: I cannot tell a lie

February 18, 2008

Today is Presidents Day, a day we set aside to recognize the birthdays of two of our greatest presidents — George Washington and Abraham Lincoln.

Lincoln's birthday was actually this past Tuesday. Washington was born Feb. 22. So today we will divide the difference for a convenient reason to give folks a Monday off.

Since both of them were honest men, I'm not sure they would survive in today's political environment. Lincoln, of course, was called "Honest Abe." Washington was known for "I cannot tell a lie." He admitted chopping down a cherry tree, which may explain why we would never invite him to Macon for the Cherry Blossom Festival.

In honor of these two honorable men, I had this crazy idea. I was prepared to take a lie-detector test.

It would be a breeze, I thought. As long as they don't ask me about cheating on that geometry quiz in the 10th grade.

I contacted a retired GBI agent who has been administering polygraph tests for almost 30 years. After receiving a detailed explanation on the complexity and structure of the test, I decided against taking one.

It had nothing to do with my fear of being interrogated in a dark room with a 40-watt light bulb dangling above my head. Nor was I concerned about being implicated for jaywalking on Walnut Street back on Jan. 16.

I wasn't worried about being wired up to a machine that — for all I know — might monitor my blood pressure, biorhythms and somehow crack the code for my locker combination in junior high school.

I guess taking a lie-detector test is like a confessional without the priest.

So today, I plan to come clean. No batteries required.

This one's for you, George and Abe.

I admit that I cried at the end of the movie "Home Alone." I do not always read the owner's manual. I have used more than one mulligan during a round of golf. In the fourth grade, I faked having a sore throat so I wouldn't have to go to school one day.

I never learned how to tie a square knot. I don't floss every day or rotate my tires every 6,000 miles. I have a lower opinion of anyone who wears a baseball cap backward. I have been known to blame dogs and children for things they did not do.

I have gone through the "10 items or less" grocery line with 12 items in my cart. I have voted for myself. I have used Cliffs Notes. I have hung up on telemarketers without feeling guilty. I don't always understand what's supposed to happen when I subtract line 40 from line 38 on the 1040 tax form.

I have falsely accused gravity. I eat an egg for breakfast every morning. I have never watched "American Idol." I love my three children, but I no longer carry pictures of them in my wallet. On lazy days, I take the elevator instead of the stairs. I cannot tolerate being in the same room with fruitcake. I sing in the shower.

I have used "politically incorrect" language. I have dozed in church. Although I know the names of my five nieces and four nephews and many of my 458 uncles, 702 aunts and 2,137 cousins, I cannot remember all their birthdays. I will never be accused of being a big tipper. I have told little white lies to protect people's feelings.

I once watered my lawn on an "odd-numbered" day. I watch Giada De Laurentiis on The Food Network, but not just for her recipes. I did not run that red light. It was yellow. OK, it was in transition between yellow and red. It was orange.

It's brutal being honest.

My million-dollar best friend

July 13, 2007

Dear Jim:

I just wanted you to know how much I have valued your friendship over the past 18 years. You are one of the most thoughtful and intelligent people I know. You are a joy to be around. I guess I should mention your charm and good looks, too.

We'll have to get together for lunch soon. Or play golf. Maybe our families could start vacationing together. I hear Hawaii is nice this time of year.

Please don't think I'm trying to butter you up. It's an honor and a privilege to know you.

Sincerely,

Your new best friend, Gris

P.S. Congratulations on winning $1 million in the lottery.

OK, I didn't really write that letter, even though I believe most of it to be true. I'm sure my buddy Jim Fain suddenly has friends and acquaintances he never knew he had.

Still, I am delighted someone I know and respect won last week's Millionaire Raffle in the Georgia Lottery. When I called Jim on his cell phone to congratulate him, he told me he and his wife, Tina, were in Reno, Nev.

No, they didn't take the money and run. (At least I didn't hear slot machines in the background.)

Jim is a corporate sales manager for Georgia Public Broadcasting (WMUM-FM in Macon) and is attending a marketing conference in Reno.

The Fains, who live in Milledgeville, had one of the four winning tickets in the lottery. Their winning number — 285704 — was announced on what has been called the "luckiest moment of the century" — 7/7/07 at 7 p.m.

Never mind today is Friday the 13th. There's a cloud nine out there in Reno, and Jim is sitting on it.

"This is an unbelievable blessing in a life that has already been blessed," Jim told me.

I first met Jim in 1989 when he was working at the old WAYS-FM radio station. Once, when professional wrestler "The American Dream" Dusty Rhodes was in the building to tape a show for WMAZ-TV, Jim boasted to some co-workers he could whip Rhodes.

"I had curly hair back then," he said, laughing. "They started calling me 'Little Dream.'"

The name stuck. I still call him "Dream." And I imagine the events of the past week probably seem like a dream.

"Surreal," he said.

Jim grew up on Flamingo Drive in south Macon and attended Bruce Elementary. He graduated from Windsor Academy in 1982 and joked that he can now join television personality Nancy Grace and country singer Jason Aldean as well-known Windsor alumni.

He insists coming into a large sum of money won't change him.

"I've never known anything but work," he said. "It's enough money to work for us but not for us to stop working. Our families taught us strong value systems. Growing up, I may not have had everything I wanted, but I had everything I needed."

Jim and Tina were married five days before Sept. 11, 2001, so they never really got to take their honeymoon. They have two children and the stork is due to arrive again in December.

I wasn't surprised when I heard Jim had let several people go ahead of him in line at the Jet Food Store where he bought his winning ticket. He's a nice guy.

He doesn't expect the euphoria to end any time soon.

"I wish this could happen to everybody I know," he said.

I told you he was my new best friend.

Pigment of my imagination

March 20, 2006

If you've been around Macon long enough to take in a few Cherry Blossom festivals, then you realize there are at least 37 acceptable shades of pink.

Pink is the official dress code until sundown on Sunday — unless you're festival founder Carolyn Crayton.

She owns the most extensive pink wardrobe on the planet and has a free pass to wear pink 365 days a year.

Look around. You'll see pink on everything from cars to dogs to trash cans to hats to cornbread. The buttons inspire us to "Think Pink." The blogs and web sites urge us to "Link Pink."

I'm sure there is an official Cherry Blossom pink, but uniformity is not the shade of the day. It's like taking a ride on a color wheel.

There will be as many shades of pink in Macon this week as garden varieties of red at a University of Georgia football game.

Maybe its just a pigment of my imagination, but I've seen everything from soft pink to hot pink to bubble gum pink to Pepto-Bismol pink to Crayola pink.

From the top of Coleman Hill to the shadow of the levee at Central City Park, I've bumped into fuchsia, magenta, dusty pink, punk pink and Arnold Ziffle pink.

A little hue here. Guess hue there. If you were out cherry blossoming early Sunday, deep pink became damp pink. Continuing for the next seven days, there will be a pink high-pressure system showing up on Doppler radar.

If you have somehow ventured into pink territory for the first time this week, let me give you a heads-up.

There is good pink and there is bad pink.

Good pink is when a man is brave enough to wear a pink shirt in public, and finds himself comfortably surrounded by other men also wearing pink shirts.

Bad pink is when a man wears a pink shirt to the truck stop over on Interstate 75, where the preferred color is SAE 10W-Denim.

Good pink is when you eat a stack of pink pancakes in Central City Park on a Saturday morning during the third week of March.

Bad pink is when you get a stack of pink waffles you didn't order at a diner on Pio Nono in the middle of August.

Good pink is the pink line painted down the center of Cherry Street.

Bad pink is when your spouse paints a pink line down the center of your living room.

Good pink is when your mayor ceremoniously cuts the pink ribbon to open the festival, then turns to the crowd and proclaims "It's time to rejoice."

Bad pink is when he gets too caught up in the moment and changes his name to C. Pink Ellis.

Good pink is when you find yourself face to face with a pink poodle at the arts and crafts festival on Mulberry Street.

Bad pink is when find yourself face to face with a pink pit bull down on Seventh Street.

Good pink is when you join the 108 other people standing in line for some cherry ice cream in Third Street Park.

Bad pink is when they run out of cherry, then switch flavors to salmon.

Good pink is when there are very few red marks on your NCAA Basketball Tournament bracket in the office pool.

Bad pink is when the team you picked to win the championship in the office pool shows up in the Sweet 16 wearing new hot pink uniforms.

Good pink is when your boss tells you to take the rest of the day off and go enjoy the festival.

Bad pink is when your boss hands you a pink slip and tells you to go enjoy the festival but not to worry about coming back.

Father-lode of fashion shame

July 29, 2009

SEA ISLAND — I want my children to be proud of me, but there are times when I derive great pleasure in embarrassing them.

It's all part of being a parent. It's harmless fun and can usually be achieved by dressing in an uncool way. The opposite of hip.

Last weekend, I hit the father-lode of fashion shame when we scooted down to the coast for a few days.

Saturday, my wife wanted to get up early to look for seashells. So we checked the tide charts and hit the beach at 6:30 a.m.

When I'm ankle surfing at dawn and haven't had my first cup of coffee, I don't really care how I look.

Stripes with plaids? Sure. Yesterday's socks? No problem. Throw on anything that fits.

I found the ultimate PEW — Parent Embarrassing Wardrobe. Dressed to make ill.

My outfit included a pair of wrinkled seer-sucker shorts. (If I had blue jean shorts, I certainly would have exchanged.)

I also had on my "Life Is Good" T-shirt, the one with a stick man and stick dog that reads: "Dog Days." It's a rather disgusting shade of apricot.

Since I had "pillow" hair, a head covering was necessary. I put on my bright-orange Piggly Wiggly baseball cap, which clashed with the apricot T-shirt. I looked like I just walked out of the produce section.

Last, but not least, I slipped a pair of black Crocs on my feet. They have to be the ugliest — and most comfortable — shoes I own. (My youngest son, Jake, thinks Crocs look silly on anyone over the age of 5.)

After an hour on the beach, I was more interested in seeking breakfast than seeking seashells by the seashore. So I left Delinda in her element and headed back to my sister's house.

As I approached the main road, an older couple turned the corner. They were returning from their morning walk, and I could tell by the way they were dressed that they did not buy their threads at the thrift store. Their clothes were neatly pressed, not a wrinkle in sight.

Two men, both large enough to block the sun, were walking behind them. They had headsets, dark glasses and looked official.

Before I could speak, the man and his wife smiled and said: "Good morning!"

Then I recognized them.

Jimmy and Rosalynn Carter.

The former president, leader of the free world and winner of the Nobel Prize was taking a stroll in his button-down shirt, followed by a pair of Secret Service agents protecting him from terrorists and Sea Island Republicans.

And there I was in my Piggly Wiggly cap, made in China.

Had it not startled me so, I would have reached to offer him a rather sandy handshake. Maybe he would invite me over for grits to talk about national health care.

Of course, the Secret Service would have had to do a background check on me, and I'm sure the red flags would have gone up once they noticed my black Crocs.

So I kept walking, breathless from my chance encounter, suddenly with a strong hankering for peanuts for breakfast. I showered, shaved, combed my hair, brushed my teeth and dressed for success the rest of the day.

You never know who you're going to meet around the next corner.

Do you want hashbrowns with that?

October 15, 2010

It is 7:02 a.m., still 36 minutes before sunrise, and the world is starting to stir.

I am also starting to stir — a large spoon into a batter of waffle mix.

In another three minutes, I will have cooked my first waffle at the Waffle House.

I am wearing navy blue pants, a royal blue shirt, black shoes and a black cap. A few weeks ago, I never could have imagined myself as a "grill operator trainee" at the Waffle House on Zebulon Road.

But I happened to mention in a column about my admiration for those short-order cooks. Suddenly, there I was, cooking eggs before even the rooster got out of bed.

This is how my eventful Thursday morning unfolded:

6:04 a.m. I arrive at Waffle House No. 1061, which opened in 1995 and has the top volume of any of the 11 Waffle Houses in Bibb County. I meet division manager Mark Perry for breakfast, and he issues me an apron and my yellow name badge "Gris." There's no turning back now.

6:59 a.m. Shift change is at 7 a.m., and I meet my co-workers. Mark has called in a few reinforcements because of the increased activity. I join unit manager Joe Glaze, Chuck Smith and Roberta "Bert" Moseley on the front line. Bert is a 31-year veteran of Waffle House and worked four years at Huddle House before that. The salespeople — a fancy Waffle House word for wait-resses — are Shun Hicks, Patty Lacount, Leah Tabor, Sherrie Mosely and Reta Scarbary. The hostess is Erica Hutson.

7:01 a.m. A continuous chorus of "good mornings" begins. Every customer is greeted when they come in the door, and some of regulars are welcomed by first name. When the "coffee clubs" and "think tanks" start arriving, the cooks can start guessing some of their orders when they see them in the parking lot.

7:06 a.m. I celebrate my first waffle! I spray the iron with non-stick cooking oil and set the timer for three minutes. I trim off the "dog ears" around the edges after 90 seconds. I don't know who ordered it, but I hope it was OK. I will serve no waffle before its time.

7:14 a.m. Help! There is an order for five waffles, and I am having a panic attack. I feel like a sportswriter again, when the phones start ringing on Friday nights and the scores come flying in on deadline.

7:19 a.m. I "graduate" from waffles to toast. (Or maybe they demoted me and I just didn't know it.)

7:24 a.m. I feel like a third wheel. These folks are very fast and efficient. "When things are going well, it's like a well-oiled machine," Mark said. I never thought I would have to multi-task between raisin bread, cheese and onions.

7:27 a.m. My twin brother, Joe McDaniel, drops by and orders breakfast. He takes my picture with his camera phone. I thank him for coming, but I can't really talk. I tell him I might get fired.

7:41 a.m. I attempt to learn the Waffle House system of "marking" orders. A condiment is positioned on the plate to indicate how an egg is to be cooked. Or what kind of topping is desired for a waffle. A packet of jelly is placed in one of seven different positions for eggs and one of four for omelets. I ask Joe (Glaze) what happens if the jelly accidentally shifts out of position on the plate. "We're always a quarter of an inch away from another order," he said.

7:55 a.m. It occurs to me that Waffle House is one of the few places where you can watch your food being cooked and dishes being washed right in front of you. Nobody disappears "back in the kitchen." It's all there, in plain view, for 84 eyes in the 42 seats to see. And it never stops. Waffle House is open 24 hours a day, seven days a week, 365 days a year (including holidays.) "If the power ever goes out," said one employee, "they get us a generator."

8:02 a.m. A man laughs and tells me he saw an ambulance parked here last week and thought I might have started cooking early.

8:10 a.m. I am impressed that hash browns can be scattered, smothered, covered, chucked, diced, peppered, capped and topped. (Someone later sends me a message on Facebook: "I'll have mine scattered, covered and confused.")

8:19 a.m. The "Waffle House Song" is punched on the jukebox, and the staff starts singing words like "just come on in" and "you're like family" and "you're always home." I'm convinced they should start a singing group.

8:31 a.m. I have just been informed that a new movie called "Due Date" will be out Nov. 5 and will prominently feature a Waffle House.

8:32 a.m. I look out in the dining room and see several folks reading Thursday's *Telegraph*. God bless 'em.

8:49 a.m. I graduate to eggs. I try to flip one, but only half of it lands in the pan. I think I'll keep my day job.

9:01 a.m. I make a mean buttered toast, but Bert tells me I'm not slicing it correctly. She reaches for a large, sharp knife. "You're not painting a picture," she said. "Cut it like you live." Then she beheads the bread.

9:14 a.m. The jukebox is now playing Johnny Cash's "Ring of Fire." Perhaps this is a friendly reminder not to stand too close to the grill.

9:25 a.m. An order for three scrambled eggs, two pecan waffles and ... Chuck sings "a partridge in a pear tree."

9:37 a.m. I notice a sign on the wall that boasts Waffle House can "make it 844,739 different ways." I'm beginning to believe it.

9:38 a.m. Pancakes aren't on the menu, but waffles can be fixed in a variety of combinations. Joe tells me about one man who came in and ordered a "jalapeno waffle." They fixed him right up.

9:44 a.m. Feeling frisky, I attempt my first omelet, alternating between the two grills. I toss it into the air three times and catch it in the pan. "It's all in the wrist," I brag. My co-workers are impressed. They admire the color and texture. "That's pretty," Bert said. Then, since no one ordered it, she quickly tosses it into the trash can.

10:12 a.m. Charles Giles sits down for breakfast and tells me something on his "bucket list." One night, he wants to go to every Waffle House in Macon and drink a cup of coffee at each one.

10:37 a.m. I start heading down the home stretch. I visit with several people in the dining room. I thank all my co-workers with hugs and handshakes.

10:51 a.m. I clock out early, still savoring the experience. Now it's time to head to the office and try to cook up a 1,154-word column.

The write stuff

Always keep your pen sharpened

August 9, 2009

When I was 7 years old, I knew I wanted to be a writer.

I wanted to press my pencil against the Blue Horse notebook paper and watch the words come out and play.

I wanted to be a writer the same way other little boys wanted to be doctors or fight fires or play for the Green Bay Packers.

In the second grade, I published my own family newspaper. I would write and report on events that happened around the house. I would gossip about my sisters and cover all the backyard football games. (I was the star, of course.)

I wrote the headlines, did the layout and drew my own cartoon strip.

Then I would staple it together and sell it to my mom and dad for 10 cents.

It was my first paying job in the newspaper business.

My mother, bless her, saved every edition. I wouldn't trade anything in the world for them now.

I kept my pen sharpened all the way through grammar school, middle school and high school.

I didn't know if I wanted to write for a newspaper, a magazine or write books.

But I was convinced it was my calling.

I did everything I could to prepare myself. I worked for school newspapers and literary magazines. I attended one of the top journalism schools in the country at the University of Georgia. I was fortunate to receive a summer internship at our sister paper, *The Columbus Enquirer*. I learned more in a newsroom than I ever did in a classroom.

I arrived in Macon, sipped the water and never left. I quit keeping track of the word count long ago. There have been six books and more than 8,000 stories.

I'm not sure where my writing genes came from, except I must have been dipped in an inkwell and it became part of my DNA.

My father was a physician. Like most doctors, his handwriting was so terrible even the pharmacists struggled to decipher it.

My mother has always been the most avid reader I know. As children, we would snuggle on her big four-poster bed, listening to everything from "The Little Lame Prince" to "Puddn'head Wilson."

Nine years ago, I asked my parents to write their life stories. So they penned their autobiographies and became published authors.

There have been many creative influences. I like to believe I've taken something from them all.

In learning my craft, I often imitated and emulated. I would scribble words and file them away with hopes I might one day have the experience and confidence to gracefully retrieve my own.

I would practice turning phrases the same way a baseball player might emulate Ted Williams' swing. Or an aspiring actor might try to square his jaw like Clint Eastwood.

I have been inspired by preachers, dentists, carpenters, saxophone players, backyard gardeners and street poets, too.

Along the way, I have acquired some of the tools of the trade — a coffee pot, a good porch swing and a patient wife who claims my mind never stops working.

I have been fortunate to develop loyal readers. I've worked hard to attract them, even harder to keep them.

Writing is not the kind of craft that can be learned overnight. You have to focus your eyes, train your ears and soften your heart while you develop your voice.

And I'm still very much a work in progress.

Thanks for your patience.

You keep reading; I'll keep writing

June 9, 2008

Maybe one day I'll have time to go back and count all the nouns, verbs and adjectives that have come from the tips of these fingers.

I will try to remember all the folks who introduced themselves on hospital elevators or in the frozen foods aisle at the grocery store. I will try to recall all those names, phone numbers and story ideas jotted on the backs of napkins after civic club meetings and church suppers.

But, for now, the numbers are just round. Thursday will mark my 10th anniversary as local/state columnist. That's roughly 2,000 columns, 1.1 million words, 600 speeches and 83,450 swallows of caffeine-induced inspiration.

I've put enough miles on my car — telling stories from places such as Deep-step and Dog Crossing — to circle the earth 12 times.

Because 10 years is only one-third of my professional life, I really should save the sentimentality for next month, when I will mark my 30th year at *The Telegraph*. After college, I remember telling people I was headed down to Macon to get my journalistic feet wet before searching for some brighter light-bulbs.

Then I met a Macon girl. When I married her, I married Macon. Best thing that ever happened to me.

These past 10 years have been rewarding, both personally and profession-ally. I've written about everything from outhouses to toe floss to lost pythons.

People have shared their stories across kitchen tables and front porches, in pool halls and church pews.

I've laughed and cried with them. I've attended their graduations. I've deliv-ered eulogies at their funerals.

I have found my voice ranging beyond the printed pages. I've been summoned to make commencement addresses. I've been called to preach a few sermons. I recorded an audiobook and started doing commentary for Georgia Public Radio.

No, never a dull moment. I interviewed a munchkin from "The Wizard of Oz" and a lady who claims to have Elvis' big toenail. I wrote about a man who collected 7,900 eight-track tapes and a couple with 94 antique clocks. (It's quite an ordeal when they have to "spring forward" for Daylight Savings Time.)

Journalism school doesn't teach you everything. I now find myself taking dance lessons to prepare for a "Dancing for Wishes" benefit for Make-A-Wish in August. I've bagged groceries, waited on tables and donned silly outfits for charitable causes.

I also got a write-in vote for lieutenant governor, slid down the pole at the fire station and found myself nominated for a Grammy in rather serendipitous fashion. Those are things I can tell my grandchildren one day.

Mark Twain once said to write what you know about. That's the best piece of writing advice ever. I've tried to put a human face on every column. I have tried to teach, not preach. It's my job to engage readers, to serve as a vehicle to connect them.

I have tried to draw from my on-the-job training as a father, son, husband and brother. I'm a fun-loving, tax-paying, grass-cutting, church-going guy who finds himself becoming more emotional as he gets older and hates paying $3.97 a gallon for gasoline.

I still have a great deal of faith in most people. Many of you share those same convictions and life experiences.

In my columns, I have learned to look for the extraordinary in the ordinary. I've learned that words are powerful. They can either build people up or tear people down. It's a choice we all make every day.

During these 10 years, many of you have called, written or flagged me down in the parking lot to thank me for what I do.

In the past, I never really knew how to react.

Now, I do.

Thank you for reading. Thank you for sharing. Thank you for caring.

I'll make a deal with you.

You keep reading 'em. I'll keep writing 'em.

No legible signs of a comeback

September 25, 2009

My mother keeps part of her legacy in a sturdy box.

Inside are love letters her father wrote to her mother during their courtship.

They are tethers to the man she never knew — the daddy who went fishing on the Flint River, caught a death sentence called pneumonia and died before she was born in 1928.

Time has covered his fingerprints on the small envelopes. They carried the return address of Bainbridge Vulcanizing Co., which sold tires. It took a 2-cent stamp to dispatch the letters across the cotton fields and creek beds to my grandmother's home in Brinson.

There was never a need for him to include her address. He could simply write her name in that graceful swirl of vowels and consonants, then attach her hometown and the abbreviation R.F.D.

It was only when she caught the train to Athens and the University of Georgia that he had to be specific: Miller Hall, Room 20.

Thursday was National Punctuation Day, a day when we were to revel in exclamation points, have debates about question marks and pause to celebrate commas.

Forget the war on terror. Let's declare war on dangling participles and weapons of mass conjugation.

I read some of my grandfather's letters early Thursday morning. They were beautifully written, with almost no hairs out of place.

Years ago, my mother gave me an English composition book that belonged to him. He had made notations in the margins, like pages in a family Bible.

Even more admirable than his writing was that he even wrote at all. I'm not sure my grandfather owned a typewriter or could have afforded one.

In this age of text messages and e-mail forwards, letter writing is becoming a lost art. In his day, Twitter was a sound you might hear from a covey of quail. It had nothing to do with rolling his thumbs across a tiny cell phone keyboard in 140 characters or less.

My grandfather didn't tweet. He quilled.

The man possessed incredible penmanship, which is vanishing like invisible ink. I wonder how long it took to craft those letters, balancing words on the page under the flow of a fountain pen.

My mother remembers being taught the "Palmer Method of Penmanship," using rhythmic motions of the arm and hand to form letters. She learned to push and pull characters through the dotted lines with her pen, like a needle and thread.

At the top of the blackboards in her classrooms were permanent diagrams of how each letter of the alphabet was shaped. Those chalky blackboards are changing, too, replaced with dry-erase boards.

Today, many school systems are placing less of an emphasis on cursive writing. If we ever do become a paperless society, I wonder if we'll be a nation of typists instead of writers.

I will never win any penmanship awards. Neither will at least two of my three sons. (I'm not revealing which two, but they know who they are.)

Maybe it's genetic. My father was a physician and had handwriting that could only be interpreted by pharmacists. I print almost everything, rarely using cursive except to sign my name.

Penmanship is either losing its way or already has.

Sadly, I'm not seeing any legible signs of a comeback.

Grammy of my dreams

November 12, 2006

I can automatically take myself out of contention for a number of awards.

I will never win the Heisman Trophy. I have voted on it every year since 1994, but I will never win it. I'm too old, too slow and have no eligibility left. The only passing statistics I can claim come from driving my car on the interstate.

Likewise, I will never be a candidate for the Nobel Prize in physics. I am scientifically challenged. If it has anything to do with arithmetic, count me out — no pun intended.

I don't consider myself Grammy material either. I associate the Grammys with folks like Frank Sinatra, Bette Midler and Ray Charles. I do, however, have an octave range of 14 notes in the shower, and I'm quite proud of that.

Still, I'm quite shocked to announce — in fact, my hands are trembling as I type this — that I have been nominated for a Grammy Award.

Actually, it has nothing to do with musical talent or ability to carry a tune.

I have been nominated in the "Spoken Word" category for the audio book I released in the spring called "Gris & That." It's a collection of 16 columns I recorded with the encouragement and support of Joey Stuckey and his wife, Jennifer, of Senate Records and Shadow Sound Studio in Macon.

It was Joey who submitted my name a few months ago. He has been a voting member of the National Academy of Recording Arts and Sciences since 1999.

When Jennifer told me about the nomination, I couldn't believe my ears. I had always dreamed about maybe one day winning a Pulitzer Prize. But a Grammy?

Although it was exciting, I tried not to get too carried away. I told a few friends and colleagues. It was announced at my church during a Wednesday night supper.

(OK, I confess. I did insert the words "Grammy nominee" into my bio. I'm allowed to have a little fun.)

I figured a "nobody" like me wouldn't get much notice on a national level. The category has been around since 1959, and past winners include such big names as Charles Kuralt, Hillary Clinton, Maya Angelou, Orson Welles, Edward R. Murrow and Carl Sandburg.

But Jennifer called back two weeks ago. The audio book made the cut! Out of more than 1,000 entries in that category, it survived when the list was trimmed to 103.

"Your name is on the ballot — two down from Garrison Keillor!" she screamed.

OK, stay calm I told myself as I hyperventilated into a paper sack.

I looked through the names of some of the heavyweights on the list — Bob Newhart, Jimmy Carter, Carl Reiner, Mike Wallace, Tim Russert, Anderson Cooper, Amy Tan and Frank McCourt.

The "Spoken Word" category includes a wide range of genres. There is everything from audio books to radio commentary, drama, comedy and even speeches. (Martin Luther King Jr. won posthumously in 1971 for one of his speeches.)

"You're in some pretty amazing company," Joey said.

Still, I am trying to keep everything in perspective. The ballots were due this past Wednesday. I'm sure countless Grammy voters looked at "Gris & That" and scratched their heads in unison.

Ed Who? Gris What?

If I do, by some miracle, make the final ballot in December, I will at least get to attend the Grammy Awards in Los Angeles in February.

I think I'll hold off on buying a tuxedo, but it's a nice thought.

OK, I didn't make the final ballot, so I didn't get to buy that tux and go to L.A. The winner of the "Spoken Word" category was President Jimmy Carter. This upset me because he had already been leader of the free world and had won a Nobel Peace Prize. Why did he need a Grammy, too? He probably stashed it away in a closet down in Plains.

Life's share of foot soldiers

April 19, 2010

Sunday was National Columnists Day. If you want to wish me a belated one, now is your chance.

I appreciate all the cards you did not send me. At least you have an excuse. Hallmark doesn't make them. And the mail isn't delivered Sunday.

April 18 is also a day newspaper columnists must share with International Jugglers Day. (There are times when I'm not sure there is much of a difference.)

National Columnists Day was started 15 years ago by former *Kansas City Star* columnist Bill Tammeus and Dave Lieber, of the *Fort Worth Star-Telegram*.

It is not a pat-yourself-on-the-back kind of day. The National Society of Newspaper Columnists encourages its members to "write a column about how great it is to be a columnist."

April 18 is the day we observe because it is the anniversary of the death of Ernie Pyle, considered the patron saint of the profession.

Pyle, the famous World War II correspondent, was one of America's first embedded journalists. He wrote about common folks, the ordinary Joes on the front lines.

A master storyteller, Ernie took his readers where few others dared to stick their pen and paper. On a portable Corona typewriter, he filed stories from foxholes in France, desert outposts in North Africa and below the decks of aircraft carriers in the South Pacific.

His friend, author John Steinbeck, once told *Time* magazine: "There are really two wars, and they haven't much to do with each other. There is the war of maps and logistics, of campaigns, of ballistics, armies, divisions and regiments. ... Then there is the war of the homesick, weary, funny, violent, common men who wash their socks in their helmets, complain about the food, whistle at the Arab girls, or any girls for that matter, and bring themselves through as dirty a business as the world has ever seen and do it with humor and dignity and courage — and that is Ernie Pyle's war."

In April 1944, while awaiting the invasion of Normandy, Pyle was awarded the Pulitzer Prize for distinguished correspondence. A year later, April 18, 1945, he was killed by a Japanese sniper on a tiny island in the Pacific.

Yes, he died with his boots on. He died doing what he loved the most — reporting from the battlefield.

I have never been to war. I have never had to compose a story from the bunkers. I did spend a week in Junior ROTC camp at Fort Benning and wrote about my experiences as an intern for *The Columbus Enquirer*.

Now, when my editors ask me to put bullets in my stories, they are talking about typographical marks. And I'm convinced when Winston Churchill said, "Nothing in life is so exhilarating than to be shot at without result," he could have been referring to the rush of being on deadline.

I have never suffered any major injuries in my journalistic pursuits, unless you count paper cuts, headaches, ankle sprains, falling out of my chair trying to answer the phone (not the most graceful way to impress folks) and hitting a deer coming back from an assignment in Valdosta.

Still, I am honored to have been able to share the stories of those who have served, made sacrifices and defended our freedoms.

I have admired their purple hearts and watched their tears splash the words on the page. I have listened as they told about how war either strengthened their resolve or broke their spirit.

As a homefront columnist, I realize you don't have to be a soldier to fight a war. I have written about people waging their own personal battles against illness and injustice. I have watched them fight their way back and dig themselves out.

Life has its share of foot soldiers, too. Newspaper columnists have an obligation to tell their stories. It's our duty. We are embedded journalists. At least we should be.

Thanks, Ernie.

From broken heart to heart for service

July 11, 2010

I always knew I wanted to be a writer. As a child, I wrote stories, poems and even published my own family newspaper. I sold it to my mom and dad for 10 cents. It was my first paying job in journalism.

When I went to college, I still had aspirations to become a writer. But I also wanted to be a fraternity boy. Parties. Dates with pretty sorority girls. Nothing, it seemed, was more important to me than those fashionable Greek letters.

I went through rush, but the fraternity I wanted to join did not offer me a bid. I was black-balled.

It's not easy to deal with that kind of rejection when you're 18 years old and still trying to find your way in the world. I was crushed.

A few months later, I was walking down a hallway in the dormitory. I don't know why I was on this particular hall on the third floor. My room was on the seventh floor.

I passed an open door and heard someone call my name. It was a guy from one of my classes. I did not know him well, but he recognized me and invited me in to visit. When I sat down, I noticed some Greek letters on his bulletin board. I was not familiar with the fraternity, so I asked him about it.

He told me he belonged to a service fraternity. There was also a social aspect to this fraternity — the guys liked to party and have a good time — but the major emphasis was on service projects on campus and in the community.

He asked if I would like to attend a meeting. No rush. No bids. No obligation. Just show up.

Within a few months, I had pledged. I made lifelong friends — brothers — and still stay in touch with many of them. But, more than anything else, that fraternity instilled in me a heart for service I carry with me to this day.

So, one of the biggest disappointments of my life paved the way for one of my greatest joys.

Was it a coincidence that I walked down that hall that day? I don't believe in coincidences. A friend says they are simply those moments when God chooses to remain anonymous.

I carried that heart for service with me when I graduated and began working at *The Telegraph*. Once I got settled in Macon, I became a volunteer with Big Brothers/Big Sisters. For the next four years, I mentored a young man from a single-parent home. I believe I made a difference in his life, and I still keep in touch with him and his family.

Not long after I began volunteering with Big Brothers, a cute little Mercer University cheerleader was hired as a social worker.

In two weeks, we will celebrate our 28th wedding anniversary. We have built a beautiful life together and co-authored three wonderful sons.

So, of course, I still think about that "road not taken" all the time. How different my life would be!

In the 12 years I have written a column for this newspaper, I have been able to combine two of my greatest passions — telling stories and helping people.

They have shared their lives with me across kitchen tables and wide front porches, in parking lots, pool halls and church pews. I have laughed with them. I have cried with them. I have attended their graduations. I have delivered eulogies at their funerals.

And, all the time, I have tried to step up and reach out. I have served on boards and planning committees. In the name of charity, I have bagged groceries, taken ballroom dancing lessons, dressed up as Elvis, waited on tables, served as a bus tour guide, got "locked up," played in golf marathons, sold brooms door-to-door and read Dr. Seuss to so many schoolchildren every page in "The Cat in the Hat" is dog-earred.

But it has been much more than hammers and dancing shoes and giving up a Saturday morning to judge chili cook-offs.

I have tried to use the power of a newspaper column that reaches thousands of people as a vehicle to connect the folks who need help with folks who can — and want — to help them.

On Friday night, I was honored and humbled to receive the 2010 Will Rogers Humanitarian Award at the National Society of Newspaper Columnists convention in Bloomington, Ind.

And, yes, I have reflected and wondered where I might be and what I might have been doing this weekend if that college kid of long ago had been delivered those Greek letters he thought he wanted.

I certainly don't think I would have been at Indiana University, accepting an award named after one of America's most beloved heroes, Will Rogers. I wouldn't have been wiping away a few tears, while holding a replica of the same statue of Rogers on display at the U.S. Capitol in Washington.

What's that line from the old Garth Brooks song? Some of God's greatest gifts are unanswered prayers.

I would like to dedicate this award to the people of Macon and Middle Georgia, the readers of this newspaper who inspire me. You are my role models. You are my heroes. I count you among my greatest blessings.

You see, I told the folks in Indiana that where I live and work, a humanitarian is not just a word used to describe someone who does good deeds. It is a way of life.